Riding
with Rilke

Riding
with Rilke

REFLECTIONS ON MOTORCYCLES AND BOOKS

TED BISHOP

W. W. NORTON & COMPANY
NEW YORK LONDON

For information about permission to reproduce selections from this book,
write to Permissions, W. W. Norton & Company, Inc., 500 Fifth Avenue,
New York, NY 10110

Manufacturing by Courier Westford
Production manager: Anna Oler

Library of Congress Cataloging-in-Publication Data

Bishop, Edward.
Riding with Rilke : reflections on motorcycles and books /
Ted Bishop. — 1st American ed.
p. cm.
Includes bibliographical references.
ISBN-13: 978-0-393-06261-8 (hardcover)
ISBN-10: 0-393-06261-9 (hardcover)
1. Motorcycle touring—United States. 2. Motorcycle touring—Canada.
3. Bishop, Edward—Travel—United States. 4. Bishop, Edward—Trvel—Canada.
5. United States—Description and travel. 6. Canada—Description and travel. I. Title.
GV1059.52.B57 2006
796.7097—dc22   2006018910

ISBN 978-0-393-33074-8 pbk.

W. W. Norton & Company, Inc.
500 Fifth Avenue, New York, N.Y. 10110
www.wwnorton.com

W. W. Norton & Company Ltd.
Castle House, 75/76 Wells Street, London W1T 3QT

1 2 3 4 5 6 7 8 9 0

for *Hsing*

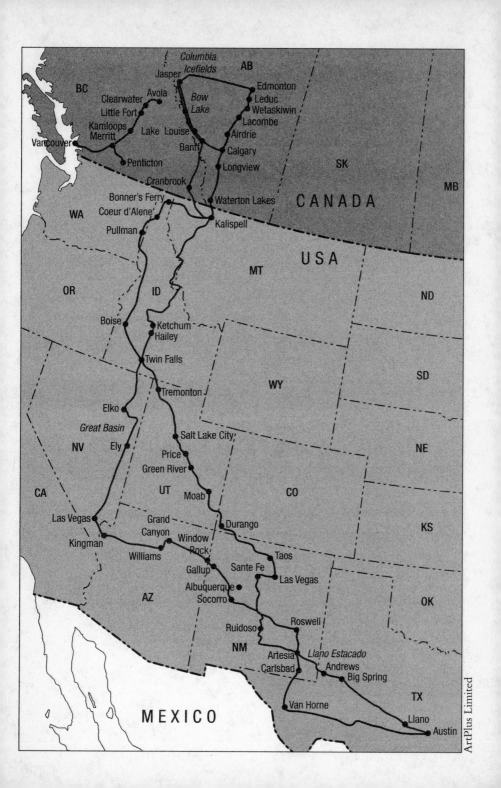

TO THE READER

When you cross from Canada into the United States you move into a realm where the temperatures almost triple and the distances shrink by a third (depending where you are on the scale): you shift from metric to imperial measurements, kilometers to miles, Celsius to Fahrenheit. To be consistent with the road signs and temperature readouts I encountered, I have usually used metric measurements while in Canada and imperial ones while in the United States. The problem is that Canada phased in metric measurements in the early 1980s and many Canadians, especially those of us of a certain age, think in both systems. Certain measurements have no resonance: six feet under or six feet tall means nothing as 1.89 or even 2 meters, and doing 160 kilometers an hour will never be the same benchmark, or rite of passage, as 100 miles an hour. Even my Ducati became confused at one point, but I trust the context will make things clear for the reader.

CONTENTS

Prologue: The Crash   *1*

PART ONE   GEARING UP

1   Why a Duc?   8

2   Longview   17

3   Archival Jolt   28

4   Rhythm   40

5   Romance of the West   54

6   Taos Tangle   64

7   *The Virginian* and West Texas 'Dillos   76

PART TWO   HAVE LAPTOP, WILL TRAVEL

8   ReCovering *Ulysses*   96

9   Archives and Honky-Tonks   115

10   Readers, Riders, and Shooters   123

11   Continental Courier   140

12   Ducati Spirit, Roman Circus   150

PART THREE RIDING HOME

13 Off the Shelf   166

14 Bad Chain   185

15 Hunting Kokopelli   196

16 Route 66   205

17 The Idaho Kid   217

18 Scene of the Crime   226

Epilogue: Riding with Rilke   *239*

Acknowledgments   *258*

PROLOGUE

The Crash

I'm riding the crest of the last morphine shot, lying here in the trauma ward. Yesterday they let me eat ice chips and helped me sit up in my "clamshell," my new plastic body cast. "Don't be impatient," they tell me. "Tomorrow you get your last tube out." It's been only ten days since I laid the bike down. "You're making rapid progress."

THE RAIN HIT as I swung west from Lake Okanagan up toward the mountains, and I hunched behind the windshield. I needed to make rapid progress. Hard droplets, already banging like frozen corn on my helmet, could turn to snow at the top of the pass. The engine settled into the climb, with that relaxed *ticka-ticka-ticka* old BMWs have. It's not a sound that makes you want to race; more seductive, it tempts you to quit your job and ride to South America. It makes going for groceries a romantic adventure. That's why you seldom see Beemer riders without their saddlebags, even going to

1

the corner store—might just buy that milk and keep on heading south.

The summit proved gusty, and the bike twitched in the crosswind. That's the trouble with windshields: in exchange for a cozy pocket of warm air you get a jib sail. The motorcycle belonged to my girl-friend, Hsing, who was taking her turn in the car behind with all the camping equipment. Hsing had christened the bike Matilda, which didn't begin to do justice to her personality. I would have voted for Lola. Whenever I approached 130 kilometers an hour, Matilda began to waggle from side to side. Hsing liked it, this saucy little shimmy. "It's like the samba," she said.

I had to admit it seemed benign. Not like old British bikes. My friend Robert once had an old Norton that used to go into speed wobbles, those strange tremors that occur somehow when the vari-ables of engine vibration, road surface, and the position of the planets all come into cosmic disharmony. Dreaded by all motorcyclists, the speed wobble can never be predicted; all you can do is pull in the clutch and ride it out. One day on a straight Kansas highway Robert suddenly found himself speeding down the center line flipping from side to side, sparks spraying up from one footpeg then the other as he held his terrified boots up beside the gas tank, watching helplessly as the oncoming cars veered off to avoid him. He knew he was dead. It was just a matter of moments.

Yet somehow he managed to stop the bike. He waited till his own shaking had subsided, and rode on. At the time, I envied him. I had no romantic tales of hair's-breadth escapes. I was a cautious rider and knew I would be one of those who rides for thirty years without a scratch. I put the thought behind me as I came over the ridge and the road opened to the plains below, wide turns coasting down into the valley, then tighter loops through the B.C. ranchland into Merritt. I could already taste the coffee in that espresso bar on Main Street.

NORTH OF KAMLOOPS the sky cleared and the road opened up. It was afternoon now, and all those motor homes had scurried off to get an early campsite. The towns rolled by—Little Fort, Clearwater, and on toward Avola. The sun warmed the pavement, and the road wound through narrow valleys no crosswind could reach. A perfect afternoon.

I hummed inside the helmet, sounding even to myself like an off-key kazoo, but happy. I could heel over into corners marked 60 kilometers an hour going over 100 and Matilda loved it. Where cars have to follow the line, bikes can use the whole width of the lane, shaping the road to their own design. Sometimes I would near the 130 mark and feel the dreaded wobble, but I would back off and it never became serious.

A good road has rhythm, and riding Highway 5 through British Columbia was like skiing a giant-slalom course; the bike dropped easily into one bend after another. The sun warmed the tarmac, and the trees gave off the hot pine smell that reminded me of the piñon in the high passes of New Mexico. A clear summer day on a winding road in the mountains: this was one of those rides motor-cyclists live for.

I was traveling a little faster than the tourists, but traffic was light and I passed them easily. Then I came up behind a big semi trailer. His tail lights were at my eye level and bits of grit kept flicking off his mud flaps. I wanted some open road in front of me instead of this wall of aluminum. A quick check and I pulled out. I felt a spasm of unease—I had not realized this was a double trailer. I would need a lot of road to get by.

The buzz in the footpegs told me I was over 120. The shoulder-high wheels beside me were making me a little tense. The vibration switched to the handlebars, letting me know we were up to 125, and then I felt the first tremor in the frame. Nearing 130. I kept accelerating gently. I was only halfway up the truck. Still no one coming in my lane, but I had a long way to go.

The tremor grew to a wobble. Nothing serious, but I knew I couldn't go any faster. I glanced at the speedo: 130 exactly. I eased off just a bit and held steady. Then, as I neared the wheels of the front trailer, I could see a van rounding the bend toward me. What could I do—go on or drop back? I couldn't brake hard now in this wobble. The front of the truck was close. Better to keep going. Hope the van would slow up . . .

I can't seem to get this next moment clear. I try to force the memory, to run back the mental videotapes frame by frame, but it's as if my mind keeps slipping off to one side or the other as I get nearer the crash: like when you bring two magnets of the same polarity together and they dart this way and that, refusing to touch. I can feel it there, on the tip of memory, just out of reach.

I was beside the driver's door of the semi now, almost home but wobbling hard. And then the blast from the truck's front wheels caught my windshield. The wobble turned to a violent judder. The bars began to thrash from side to side. I had no fear, only the quick thought, "Maybe this is going down." I never felt the fall. My helmet clunked once on the asphalt, and I was out.

HSING, WHO SAW IT ALL from inside the car, told me what happened. "It was awful," she said. "I could see you wiggling, and then flopping this way and that like something was shaking you, and all of a sudden it smashed you over." Strange. I only remember the road rising slowly to meet me, and then a giant hand suddenly slapping me on the back.

"The bike hit the pavement and spun around. You were facing back toward me, down on the road, still on the bike. You skidded into the gravel and the cylinder head dug in, throwing up a big cloud of dust. Then you slid off the edge of the road backward, you and Matilda still together, probably still going 100. You flew through the air, and that's when you and the bike came apart. You tumbled like a rag doll, and the bike landed about a yard from your head.

"I stopped the car and ran down into the ditch, shouting your name. There wasn't any response. Your visor was open and I could see your eyes staring straight out, glassy and unfocused. Your color was horrible, your face an ugly pasty-white. I'm sure for a few moments you didn't have a pulse. I kept calling your name and you didn't respond at all. I really thought you were dead."

I thought I had had a dream—a dream of a motorcycle accident—and I had just woken up, and I was lying on something soft and cool. Then I realized it had really happened, I was lying in a ditch, and there was a dull ache in my back.

Someone was saying, "Can you feel your fingers? Can you wiggle your toes?"

It turned out to be Hsing. I felt disconnected. My peripheral vision seemed to have shut down and as I lay there hands moved in and out of my field of view. Voices seemed at once near and far off. I was conscious of light, of coolness, of the comparative softness of the ditch, yet I couldn't really place my body.

"I'm cold," I heard myself say, so I guess I was, and somebody brought a blanket. They draped it gently, yet it made everything hurt.

It felt like the lead shields they lay over you at the dentist's office before they scuttle out of the room and zap the X-rays. I could hardly breathe at first; the blanket seemed to be crushing my chest right through to my back. I took shallow gasps, and gradually the pain receded, warmth moved in. I could hear them talking again. A voice said it would be twenty minutes or so until the ambulance got there. That's a long time, I thought, and I could feel the cold creeping out of the ground and into my spine.

I wanted to shift, and said, "My back hurts a bit," and someone said, "You're lying on a stump. We don't want to move you. You should stay where you are."

I said, "Sure, of course." I didn't really mind. I must be in shock, I thought, because I don't really mind anything. After a time I could hear the far-off wail of an ambulance and thought, Great. That one's for me.

PART ONE

Gearing Up

ONE

Why a Duc?

I t wasn't a mid-life crisis: it was mid-life money. I had inherited some cash and was desperately afraid I would do something sensible with it, like put it on my mortgage or into mutual funds. So I bought a Ducati Monster. I had the fall term off and planned to go to the Harry Ransom Center in Austin, Texas, the improbable location of the best archive in the world of British modernist writers such as James Joyce, Virginia Woolf, George Bernard Shaw, and T. E. Lawrence. Then I got a travel grant from the Ransom Center. They didn't say how I had to travel. September would be perfect for a ride.

My friends looked at the short wheelbase and hard, sloping seat of the Monster, and said, "You're taking *that* to Texas?" Why not? I would take it one short stretch at a time. If you thought about the whole project, you'd never start. I bundled up my research notes, bubble-wrapped my laptop, and phoned UPS. I'd be traveling light.

I looked forward to escaping my academic persona, trading tweed for leather, transforming myself into a lone rider heading down the highway.

THE RIDER HEADED OUT *at dawn. A fine mist was rising from the empty highway.* That's how it was supposed to be. The truth is I finally got out of Edmonton and onto the crowded freeway at noon after fiddling endlessly with my borrowed saddlebags. There was just enough room for them to fit between the taillights and the heel of my boot, and just enough space between the tip of the exhaust pipe and the plastic plate on the bottom of the bags to keep them from melting. This first day was to be a shakedown day anyway.

"Just ride as long as it's still fun," Pasquale had said as he showed me how to fit the saddlebags. He was a man of many rides and many bikes (he kept a Ducati, a Moto Guzzi, a Laverda, and a BMW in his garage, and stored another old BMW in Italy). As he made me an espresso he said again, "Ride as long as it's fun. Don't try to make that extra 100 kilometers at the end of the day like you would in a car." Good advice, and I needed it. My friends in the BMW club felt the day was ruined if they had not done 500 kilometers before breakfast. I was grateful for this permission to do it my way. I had spread my big Alberta Motor Association map of the western states and provinces on the floor the night before and felt slightly ill. Big as it was it still didn't reach past New Mexico and I had to unfold half the Texas map to find Austin. This was the last time I would allow myself to look at the trip as a whole until it was finished. I'd made the 350-kilometer trips to Banff or Jasper several times. I had a sabbatical and no schedule. I would just make a series of 350-kilometer rides until I wound up in Texas.

I rode to Calgary and hung around Sport Cycle while Brian, the owner, adjusted my carburetor jets for the high passes I would meet in Colorado and New Mexico. I've always suspected that shop owners make you wait longer than necessary just so you'll look at the gear for sale. I picked up a stylish Italian helmet, guaranteed the quietest on the market, also lighter because it had carbon fiber in it. I put it on. It fit my loaf-of-bread-shaped head better than my old one. That would make a big difference over a long journey. Comfort equals safety. A happy rider is an alert rider. Also it was dazzling: yellow with flash graphics. That bright yellow would increase my visibility to other motorists. As a responsible rider I felt I had to have it.

Then I looked at a carbon-fiber windscreen. I had seen one like it in England. Kind of ugly—short and stubby, like the end of a coal shovel. Kind of cool too, though; it fit the character of the bike. And the guy in London had said it made a big difference to turbulence on the highway, and gave some protection from the rain. This would be important on a long ride. I had to have it. And in the rain I would need overboots. I was using black leather gaucho boots I had bought in Spain more because of a Bob Dylan song than because they were good for motorcycling. (In fact they came with slick leather soles and the first time I wore them I nearly dumped the bike at a stoplight.) I had siliconed them and put rubber soles on them, but clearly I needed these rubber overboots that came in their own drawstring bag and fit right in the top pocket of your panniers. I had to have them.

I knew what was happening but I couldn't stop myself. Brian was the master of the soft sell. That was evident on the day I bought the Ducati in the first place.

THE NEW DUCATI MONSTER had finally reached the showroom in October. A card on the tank said:

ZIPPERS SCRATCH.

PLEASE DO NOT SIT ON THE MOTORCYCLES UNLESS YOU ARE
NAKED.

I stood and looked at it. "It's okay," said a voice behind me. Brian. "Go ahead."

"Oh, thanks. Thanks." I got on reverently, making sure my belt buckle didn't touch the tank. It fit exactly. I got off.

"What about this Moto Guzzi over here, how much is it going for?" I asked. There were no deals. Brian didn't do deals. He had a used Guzzi out back though. We went and looked. It was big and ugly, and like many Guzzis, because they are so reliable, completely neglected. Beside it was another Ducati Monster, a new one with a dented tank.

"What happened?"

"The owner dropped it turning into his garage. He decided it wasn't for him so we bought it back from him."

"Oh. Does it run?"

"Sure. It runs fine. We just have to redo the tank, the peg, and there where it's scraped on the muffler."

"So, could you start it up? I'd like to hear what it sounds like."

"Sure."

It started with a touch. Brian revved it a couple of times and then let go of the throttle. It idled perfectly. That rasp I remembered from my brother's old Ducati 250. We stood listening to the bike idle for a while.

"It's okay," I said. "You can turn it off now." He switched it off. "Sounds pretty good," I said. "Thanks."

"They sound even better with after-market pipes," he said. "Come and hear Patti's." We walked through the store to the curb out front and he started up his wife's bike. Same rasp, only louder, deeper. Yes, this was what I remembered. My brother had had a less-than-legal megaphone on his bike.

"That's nice," I said. "Pretty loud."

"Yes," he said, "but still legal. You should hear the racing exhaust on my bike."

"Could I?"

"Sure," he said, "it's in the back." We went back into the shop. Brian's red 851 was next to the Monster. He turned it on and waited; we listened to the high-pitched whine of the fuel-injection system priming itself. Then he pushed the starter. The roar filled the shop and when he twisted the throttle the roar rose to a banshee wail. He grinned at me; I grinned nervously back. I felt like I was standing on the launchpad at Cape Canaveral. He shut off the bike. My heart was thudding.

"Thanks. Wow."

"Yeah. Same basic engine as the Monster though," he said. "Same sound when you free it up. Of course these carbon-fiber pipes are expensive. Not the sort of thing most people put on right away."

We had turned and found ourselves facing the Monster again. From the undinged side it looked perfect. The sun warmed the bronze-colored frame, made the gold inserts in the front brake discs sparkle, and picked up the fine lines in the gold sleeves on the inverted front forks. The tank was a deep black, not flat and shiny, a finish you could see down into, and on top, behind the inset gold gas cap, was a line of fine gold script that said, "Made in Italy."

"So, I don't suppose you'd let me ride it," I said, "just up and down the alley?"

"Sure," said Brian. "I'll get the key."

That was easy.

I started it up. Clutch clatter, exhaust, and a half a dozen other little mechanical sounds. The grips were thin and hard, the brake light and positive, like the brake on my mountain bike. I backed cautiously down the driveway. I'd read about Monsters, about how you could do wheelies without even thinking about it, about how the steering was so quick you could find yourself heeled over in an instant.

I rocked back and forth a couple of times, finding the catch point of the clutch. Easy. I gave it some throttle and started off. Effortless. The pegs were far back, but I found them and settled on the bike. Even more comfortable than in the showroom. I turned at the end of the alley and came back, getting only as high as second gear. Everything just worked. I turned again. I pulled up and turned it off. It felt like . . . mine.

"It's okay," I said, not meeting Brian's eyes because my heart was leaping around in my rib cage like a salmon on a spawning ladder. "So, uh, what's it going for? Since it's used and all."

"Oh, it's not for sale."

What??

"Not till the spring anyway," he went on. "We're going to rejet the carbs and put different pipes on it. Use it to show off some of our accessories in the March show."

NoooIneeditnowIneeditnow.

"I see."

"The one in the showroom is still for sale. Though there's one guy who's pretty serious about it. He said he was going to come down when he gets off work at five today."

Oh yeah, the old "interested party" routine. I know this. I'm not going to bite.

"Well that's okay. I'm not really in the market anyway."

The "I'm not really in the market" gambit.

"Sure. There's not much riding season left anyway." *Refusing to be drawn.*

"So do you discount your bikes now that it's October?" *A casual probe.*

"No. The dollar has dropped against the lira and the next shipment will be 15 percent higher. That Monster in the showroom is the last one I could get at last season's price."

Oh sure: the "last season's price" maneuver.

"Well, there's a Honda VFR about the same price up in Edmonton, and they've dropped it a thousand." *The classic "it's cheaper down the block" riposte.*

"Hondas are good bikes," he said evenly.

Damn. The underhanded "if you're content to ride with the rabble" cut.

"They've got an excellent warranty," I countered weakly.

"Excellent," he parried, giving nothing.

"Tuning's much easier than on a Ducati," I said. *A wobbly thrust, and we both knew it.*

"Though when tuned by someone who knows," he said carefully, "the Desmodromic heads are just as reliable."

DESMODROMIC!

A palpable hit—Desmodromic, the valve control system unique to Ducati; the pride of Italy; the envy of motorcycle cognoscenti everywhere.

(They even make T-shirts with Desmodromic valves on them.) Who wants a motorcycle made by people who make lawn mowers?

"I've seen Desmos run for thousands of clicks . . ." he was saying.

Desmo, Desmo, the very word was like a charm. My heart ached and a drowsy numbness pained my sense; I could feel my fingers reaching for my checkbook.

"Yes, well. Gotta go," I mumbled.

My friend Dave had been standing by silently through all of this. I flopped into the passenger side of the car. "Drive," I said. "Get me out of here."

I babbled all the way to the city limits; then I calmed down a little. "So, like, how was I back there? Do you think he could tell I was interested?"

"I think he could tell," said Dave, who is no help in these matters.

"Whadjathinkofthebike?" I said calmly.

"Great bike. Looked good."

"Shit. Okay. Look. If we drive fast we'll be home at ten to six. I'll phone and make him a cash offer. He'll have to come down. Right? He doesn't want to have that thing sitting in his showroom all winter, does he?"

"No . . . Of course he mentioned that other buyer . . ."

"Oh Jesus yes!"

". . . though it's probably just a line."

"But what if it's not? *WHAT IF IT'S NOT??* Maybe I should phone from a gas station at Red Deer . . ."

"Don't worry. It's Saturday. The guy couldn't close the deal anyway—the banks aren't open."

"That's true that's true okay fine. Fine. I'll phone when I get home."

I got home; I phoned.

"Hello, uh, could I speak to, uh, Brian, please."

"Hi, Ted."

He was waiting.

So I got the Monster for full retail.

But that's okay. I would have paid more.

"YOUR BIKE'S DONE," Brian called from the back. He came out and looked at the pile of stuff on the counter. "Want me to put on that windscreen while Patti writes up the helmet?"

TWO

Longview

Exultant, that New Road and New Gear euphoria coursing through me, I headed west into the sun, out the Bragg Creek road, and then down on Highway 22 to Turner Valley. I had cleared the boundaries of my past life. I was On the Road again. On to Longview. Everything was happening in capital letters. I passed through Black Diamond, ignoring the old hotel there because it was a Saturday night and Brian had said the bar was noisy. I didn't need that. Besides, I liked the idea of spending my first night at a place called Longview.

Longview turned out to be nothing, just a few buildings on either side of the highway. I checked in to the overpriced strip motel. "If you hurry," said the woman at the desk, "you can get to the Four Winds Restaurant before it closes." This at ten to eight on a Saturday night. So I unloaded the saddlebags, dropped them in the cold white room and strode down to the Chinese restaurant. I took a seat at one of the Formica tables. A beefy rancher sat across the room from me, devouring a steak while half-scowling. This is going to be horrible, I thought, feeling quite sorry for myself. Then an Asian girl with a lovely smile brought the menu. She smiled at everyone: she smiled at the two old women who hobbled in; she smiled at the cook as he barked out the order; she smiled at the beefy rancher, who turned out to be Bob and who wouldn't have another cup of coffee but would have a piece of pie; and she laughed delightedly when I told her I wanted a clubhouse sandwich with tea, Chinese green tea. The smile and the hot tea warmed me. Longview was wonderful after all, and as I strolled back up the deserted street I could see the rolling prairie stretching out under the stars on either side. I was glad I had come. It was a good jumping-off point. I knew from the map that for 103 kilometers there would be nothing, not even another hamlet on the road. Just the high plains, and off to my right the mountains. A long view.

Back at the motel, my back cramped and twisted after trying to get my mystery novel into the feeble glow of the bolted-down bedside lamp, I lapsed into a long view of my career. I was dragging my heels on my work with Virginia Woolf's *Jacob's Room*. I had loved the book as an undergraduate: it's about a young man who goes to Cambridge and then travels alone across Europe to Greece, where he is disillusioned by the Parthenon and seduced by an older woman. What's not to like? Of course Jacob is killed in the First World War, but I never thought about that. It was the travels that I liked. I remembered the scene on the train on the way to Olympia where he thinks "how tremendously pleasant it is to be alone; out of England; on one's own; cut off from the whole thing."

Jacob's Room is important in Woolf's career because, even though it's her third novel, it is the first "real" Virginia Woolf novel—experimental, jagged, written in short chunks with space breaks on the page where a transition would be in her earlier novels. It marked a break with tradition and a personal break for freedom: her first two novels had been published by Gerald Duckworth, the half-brother who had molested her. Now Virginia and her husband, Leonard, had their own printing press, and with this novel they expanded beyond hand-setting type in their basement to working with a commercial printer. With *Jacob's Room* the Hogarth Press moved from being an obsessive hobby to becoming a genuine publishing house. The novel was published in that magical year of modernism, 1922, which also saw the publication of James Joyce's *Ulysses* and T. S. Eliot's *The Waste Land*. In fact they were all rubbing shoulders—"Tom" Eliot came to dinner one night, Virginia wrote in her diary, and he read his new poem: "He sang it & chanted it rhythmed it. . . . The Waste Land, it is called." And *Ulysses* came round to their house in Bloomsbury in the prim hands of Joyce's English patron, Harriet Shaw Weaver, who offered it to the Woolfs for publication at the Hogarth Press. Virginia hated it and said it was too large for them to print.

In a classic case of one thing leading to another, I had written a little article on *Jacob's Room* and the way it changed in the course of its creation. Now I was involved in copying out the entire hand-written manuscript, complete with strikeouts, squiggles, and margi-nalia, for a university press in New York; and, for a British press, producing a scholarly edition of the published work, with introduc-tion, footnotes, and one of those lists of the textual variants at the end that nobody ever reads. The work was worthy, the presses estimable, yet my work seemed a long way from the pleasure I had once felt slipping the little Penguin paperback of *Jacob's Room* into the pocket of my leather jacket and going off to read between classes on a stone bench in the Arts building. I knew that had nothing to do with anything, least of all scholarship, yet I couldn't shake it.

Also I had looked at some of the Hogarth Press books in the Special Collections of our university library—the little *Two Stories*, bound in wallpaper, with the crooked text block and poorly inked type. I loved the feel of them. And always when the thick oak door closed behind me in Special Collections I felt at peace. The railway-station din of the library foyer ceased and the humidity took over. A caress. The University of Alberta takes better care of the vellum and parchment—goat and sheepskin—of medieval manuscripts than it does of human skin.

In winter the humidity in my office could drop to 15 percent; the fresh air intake was cut to a trickle on weekends, and every November I would get a nosebleed just from walking in on a Monday morning before the stale dry air of the past two days had been expelled through the exhaust ducts. But in the archive the humidity stayed a constant 35 percent, a paradise of moderation. A spa. Your whole body felt happy as your pinched pores opened up again. You would feel it first in your nose and the back of your throat, those tender membranes. If you came every day for a week, even the tough skin on the back of your hands would loosen up. In Austin it was the reverse: the heat and humidity outside that basted your body with sweat and turned your armpits into rotting swamps was sucked away. Temperature and humidity in perfect equilibrium.

This constant temperate zone was part of what made the archive seem timeless, a single season, and it was constant in another way. Where the main library was, as one librarian put it, like a great beast, exhaling books in the fall, inhaling them in the spring when exams were finished, the archive took only short breaths, allowing books out from the stacks to the reading room, taking them back at the end of the day. A library was never actually all there. Though I knew cataloguing was always going on, the archive felt complete.

Returning to the Special Collections at my own university always felt like going home. It was years before I realized that the blond oak of the shelves was taking me home—it had the same hue and grain as the wood in the library of my parents' house. The room was nothing grand—the blueprints designated it as the small spare bedroom on the main floor—but on two walls my parents had put in floor-to-ceiling bookshelves made of light oak. In the longer wall they had built into the bookshelves a niche with a narrow daybed. At one end was a reading lamp, fixed to the wall high enough so that you could sit up and lean against the end wall of the niche to read. The narrow shelves above held my grandmother's Shakespeare plays, individually bound in morocco leather (which, I always felt, made them too good to actually read). Long drawers below the bed held my father's collection of maps, creased and refolded ("The first thing you do when you get a map is refold it so that the part you need is facing out"), always ready to be taken out and pored over. During the day you could look out over the road into the poplar trees in the ravine, and at night the lamp gave the wood paneling of the niche a tawny glow, made a warm cave in the darkness. The door to the library was in the corner and the bookshelves jutted out into the room so that nobody coming in knew at first whether you were there or not. You felt twice-removed from the outside world, secure to dream.

HIGHWAY 22 ROLLS AND CURVES through sage-covered prairie, flirting with the Rockies on your right side, and as the bike warms and the morning coffee hits the bloodstream it's impossible not to ride a little too fast.

The bags were solid, the carburetors were happy, and the windscreen made 130 a perfect cruising speed. Then pools of mist began to collect in the dips. Longview turned to No-view. A proper fog rolled in. I wiped my visor . . . put it up . . . pulled it back down . . . left it open a crack—now I knew why all those British bike magazines had ads for gloves with little wiper blades on the thumb.

Big-horned cattle were grazing loose in the ditch. I would honk and wave and they would raise their heads and look at me soberly, but as the fog got denser my cheerful greetings turned to drawn-out fog warnings. I could see the news clipping: *Austin Epic Ends as Bike Bashes Steer. The motorcycle collided with a cow in the mist and both ignited upon impact. "The whole place smelled like a barbecue," said the constable crisply.* No, this was not the way to go. I slowed, glad that there was no one behind me. Another advantage of traveling deserted roads, I thought, remembering multi-car pileups in the fog on Highway 401 outside Toronto. My pledge for the trip was to avoid freeways and chain restaurants. I would stick to the small roads and eat in mom-and-pop cafés.

At lunchtime I reached Waterton, the famous lake posed between the Rockies and the prairies: face west and you think you're in the Alps, face east and you can see all the way to Winnipeg. Unless you're wrapped in low, cold clouds. Here I was some 600 kilometers south of Edmonton, still wearing my electric vest, thermal jacket liner, silk underwear, Gortex pants, polypro glove liners, thick socks. I felt like a kid in a snowsuit, with my arms puffed out from my body and my Gortex pants going *swish-swish* as I walked through the town. Not your Marlon Brando *Wild One* entrance. Resort towns in the off-season feel even more deserted than ghost towns, the remaining residents like caretakers in a graveyard. Dry leaves scuttled across the road. In the town center the empty T-shirt and souvenir stores were even gloomier. Then I had a cappuccino and a big hunk of pie. I felt great. Waterton wasn't so bad. Cold and misty, but hey so is Scotland. Mood, I decided once again, is a direct function of blood-sugar and caffeine levels. I hopped back on the bike and motored up to the hotel to take some pictures. There an old Brit came up to me in the parking lot.

"Aye, that's a nice bike," he said. "She reminds me of a Vincent."

I glowed. The Vincent is the classic V-twin, the most coveted motorcycle in the world. What a fabulous place Waterton was, with perfect strangers coming up to you and offering intelligent compliments on your prized possession.

The man told me about the Nortons and Ariels he used to race. "But that was a long time ago, those bikes were crude compared to what they have now. What kind of frame is this?" We discussed the Ducati's light-alloy trellis frame (it looks like a crisscross ladder that comes down each side of the bike and suspends the engine between the two sections), different from the heavy frames on British bikes that run like a spine down the center. We chatted happily in the cold wind while the man's wife and another couple waited in the car nearby.

"A pleasure," he said, shaking my hand. "Have a good, safe trip."

"The pleasure is mine," I said, and it was. I was finding out that one of the best things about a motorcycle trip is that people you would never meet otherwise will come up and talk to you. "Won't you be lonely?" some of my non-biker friends had asked before I left. "I doubt it," I had said, and on the ride down I never was.

AT THE BORDER I pulled up to the pylons and took off my helmet right away. ("It makes you look more human," Brian had advised me at the bike shop). I got the file folder with my documents out of the saddlebag. I could have carried them in my jacket, but I wanted to have a file folder to look as professional as possible when I asked for the business visa.

"What kind of Business is this anyway?" rasped the border guard when I told him I was a professor.

"Research. I'm looking at original manuscripts at the university in Austin, Texas." I showed him my invitation. "I'm on sabbatical," I added helpfully.

"Humph," he said, shuffling some documents. "How come they didn't have this in the summertime so they wouldn't have to give you a sabbatical to do it?"

You sound like my lawyer brother.

"Well, it's very hot in Austin in the summer so they advise visiting scholars to come in the fall."

"I see." *Thump. Thump.* He stamped the papers. I took them and moved aside to make room for a German couple.

"Say," said the guard. "Did you say these are secret manuscripts you're looking at?"

Right, this is *The X-Files*.

"No sir, original manuscripts. First drafts by writers, that they won't photocopy or send out."

"I see."

I hate crossing borders. I always feel guilty and I know that out here in the middle of nowhere the guards have the power to make life miserable for a while if they really want to. Besides, it wasn't far from here that I had been thrown out of the States in my teens for being a ski bum ("Yer takin' jobs from our valley boys," the Montana sheriff had said) and this is the area where those unofficial militias were running through the underbrush with AK-47s preparing to overthrow the government. It's hard not to be a bit paranoid. I was certain that border guard was a colonel in the underground.

When I pulled into Montana's Glacier National Park at the beginning of the 50-mile-long Going-to-the-Sun Highway I did get the sun: the clouds lifted, the temperature rose to 70 degrees Fahrenheit, and at the information center I packed my warm gear away in the panniers. Maybe I should have brought a tank bag, I thought as I stuffed in the gear. A tank bag sits on top of the gas tank, stores things you want to get at frequently, and has a clear plastic envelope on top where you can keep your map. On the Ducati, though, because you sit down behind the tank, you can never tilt your head low enough to see the map while you are riding; also, because the Ducati has a short wheelbase, a tank bag feels claustrophobic; also, a tank bag spoils the lovely line of the tank and frame. Why buy a sport bike and then make it look like an overloaded shopping cart? I left the bag with Pasquale. Later, in the heat of west Texas when my sagging saddlebags roasted their plastic bottoms onto the end of my shiny new exhaust pipes, I would wonder if a tank bag might have been a good idea after all.

The winding road was too crowded for fast riding. Hordes of German tourists leaned out of restored 1930s touring coaches. I didn't mind. One of the great joys of motorcycling is riding slowly, taking in the landscape all around you. I pulled into a viewpoint and read the pamphlets I had picked up. (I used to scorn the tourist info until a travel-journalist friend chastised me. "Grab everything," she said. "You'll always find at least one thing you can use.") I learned that the western section of the Going-to-the-Sun Highway had been built in 1910, but that work on the steep and dangerous main section did not begin until 1921. Though the pay was good—$1.15 an hour for excavating, down to 50 cents for unskilled work—they had trouble keeping crews on the job, what with having to climb anywhere from 1,000 to 3,000 feet a day, working in rain and sleet, waking up in tents collapsed by snow, and meeting black bears and grizzlies at the cookhouse. Three men died—two from falling, and one from a rock falling on him. Finally in July 1933, with a ceremonial lunch of chili and a passing of the peace pipe among leaders of the Blackfoot, Kootenai, and Flathead tribes (long-standing enemies), the pass was declared open. I snapped a couple of pictures and burbled on, letting the bike's compression hold me, *poom-poom-poom* all the way down to the valley floor. At the bottom as I crossed the Flathead River I saw a girl in a bathing suit on a gravel bar in the middle of the stream. Amazing. Just that morning I had been freezing, even with my electric vest.

In Kalispell I made one circuit of the main street, and then pulled up in front of the old Kalispell Hotel, built in 1911 at the archetypal address, 100 Main. I changed into a clean shirt and a white cotton jacket, and the woman at the desk said, "There, *now* you don't look like a bike gangster."

Still, you wouldn't ride a bike if you didn't want to cultivate a bit of an outlaw status. I was working on my Entrance, one of the most important aspects of being a biker. You come into town and cruise slowly down Main Street—*rump, rump, rump, cough-REVVvvv-rump-rump* (obviously a high-powered machine, dangerous if not for your expert control)—and at the end of the street do a slow U-turn and come back to the café. You back the bike up against the curb, taking long enough that you know all eyes are upon you, take off your helmet, put your sunglasses back on, and walk toward the door. You use the Strut: shoulders back, head high, just a hint of pelvic thrust.

You step inside the door and, chin still high, moving only your head, survey the room (even if it only has four tables). Then you take off your dark glasses and hook them in the left-breast pocket of your leather jacket the way fighter pilots do in the movies. Don't look. This is crucial. If you have to fumble for the pocket, you've blown it and you might as well get back on the bike and leave.

Okay, by this point the men are cowed, the women trembling, and the girls behind the counter moaning softly. One flutters over with the menu and you look her in the eye and say, "Coffee. Black," and then something insinuating like, "And give me a wedge of your . . . cherry pie." (I hate black coffee, but whoever said, "Jed! There's a stranger in town and he drinks his latte with a double shot!"?)

Anyway, I'm still working on it, and there are usually some creamers on the next table that you can snag on the way back from the washroom.

THREE

Archival Jolt

From Kalispell my route to Texas could have taken me straight south, but I had jogged west, up through the mountains of western Montana, across the Idaho panhandle, dropping south from Coeur d'Alene on Highway 95 toward Pullman. For me, Washington means Seattle, Starbucks, Mount Rainier, and big wet trees. Southeastern Washington is another country. I had seen nothing like it except in southern Spain, between Seville and the Sierra Nevada: huge gentle hills covered with wheat or black loam, where occasionally a little puff of dust would appear—a tractor working far off, a Tonka toy in the immense landscape.

When I stopped for lunch at Worley, Idaho, the waitress told me if I wanted some good riding, I should cut off Highway 95 at the sign marked LOVATT VALLEY ROAD, and take the little road to Tekoa. Soon I was winding through the fields on fine blacktop. The grain grew to the edge of the road like on a country lane, and there was no traffic at all. The corners of these back roads are never marked for speed, so you can find yourself in a nasty off-camber, decreasing-radius bend with bumps at the apex that set your wheel hopping to the outside. To the locals it'll be "that tricky one up by old Sam's place," and if you don't know old Sam or his place, well then you shouldn't be going so fast. Fact is, probably shouldn't be here at all.

"Why ain't you over on the Interstate?" they will ask you as they pick you and the bike out of old Sam's cornfield. Or maybe you'll make it through the bend and come face-to-face with old Sam himself—driving a big thresher machine that takes up fifteen-sixteenths of the road. You see a giant paddlewheel coming toward you and hope like hell the edge of the road isn't crumbly. Best were the long sweepers you could see carving through the grain and up the next hill and you knew you could swing through easily at 75 miles an hour or more. Near the end I found my guide, a local in a red Dodge pickup truck who led me at 65 through a bunch of bends marked SLOW, and slowed to 25 for some that were not marked at all. I was happy to follow. I had learned a long time ago that on the back roads the fastest car would never be an out-of-state Porsche; it would be a dusty Ford Tempo with a bumper sticker from the hometown radio station. Horsepower was no match for local knowledge.

The pickup turned off just before we reached Pullman, at a little town in Washington State called Palouse. On the outskirts two signs on a single post jutted out, pointing the same way up a pretty dirt road:

GUNCLUB →

CEMETERY →

I was going to stop and take a picture, but thought no, the symbols in real life are just too corny. Besides, though the border guard had me thinking about Americans and their love of guns, what I had been feeling as I rode down through Bonners Ferry, Sandpoint, and Coeur d'Alene was how like Canada it all was. These towns were directly below Cranbrook in British Columbia, and the rivers and the Native names linked them: Kutenai or Kootenay in Canada, Kootenai in the States. The pull really is north-south and the United States is really a lot like Canada, I thought generously. Later I would adjust my thinking.

At this point, hungry and running low on gas, what struck me was how long it took to get anywhere in the States with these long miles. The kilometers clicked by with satisfying regularity in Canada; the miles seemed to go on for, well, miles, elongating as in dreams. I had grown up with miles, had been used to the neat correspondence between the speed limit and an hour—60 miles per hour, 60 minutes in an hour, so the speed limit was a mile a minute. It was odd how the texture of time and space could be altered by measurement; in my teens the distance from Jasper to the Columbia Icefields was 60 miles, as a grownup it was 100 kilometers. I couldn't imagine going back to the languorous miles of my youth. Yet here the miles and speeds to cover them were both foreign and familiar, and I remembered learning to think in metric—110 kilometers an hour was a shade under 70 miles an hour and meant you probably wouldn't get a ticket; 120 was 75 and meant you had better watch for speed traps; 130 was just over 80 and earned you a hefty fine if you were caught.

My musings ended as I braked hard for a truck slowing for the lights at the edge of town. At the end of the day when I was tired I tended to drift off, ride on autopilot. I pulled into the first gas station, a Conoco. I liked to gas up at the end of the day so that the bike was ready to go in the morning; also, stopping at the edge of town allowed me to ask for directions and to adjust from road to city mode. I would be traveling at 30 miles an hour rather than 80, but the dangers would be much greater; I would have to be looking for street signs and watching out for other vehicles at the same time.

I WAS HERE to look at the Leonard and Virginia Woolf library, which had somehow wound up not in New York, not in London, but at Washington State University. Scholars wondered how a place so out of the way, so unsophisticated (the students of WSU call themselves Wazoos) could have acquired the Leonard and Virginia Woolf library, and stayed away in droves. It's like the real estate agents say: "Location, Location, Location." And WSU is nowhere—you have to fly to Seattle, take a shuttle over the Cascade Mountains to Spokane, and then a bus down to Pullman. So nobody does. And yet I was glad. Partly this was just rooting for the underdog ("Go Wazoos! Block that punt! Get that library!"), and partly sentiment. Before the advent of the printing press, if a scholar wanted to read a book he (and generally it was a he) had to travel to wherever one of the few copies of that book was held, usually in a monastery library (convents didn't have libraries).

The gypsy scholar survives today, but instead of trekking overland or sailing across the Mediterranean to the great library at Alexandria (the biggest in the world before, legend has it, Julius Caesar torched the place), she or he will catch a cheap flight to the British Library, or to the big libraries on the eastern seaboard of the United States: the New York Public Library, the Beinecke at Yale, the Rosenbach in Philadelphia. It helps to have everything under one roof; you can settle in and work instead of chasing around (though even with a major writer like Woolf you might find the manuscript in New York, a typescript in London with a bit in Sussex, and the page proofs back in the United States, and then when you decide you need to check something about the publication history you realize you have to go back to England and take the train from London out to Reading to the Hogarth Press archive). Yet historically such centralization has not been so good. Tyrants have found it as easy to destroy books as scholars have to consult them; much of what has endured has come from private collections that escaped notice while the prominent institutions were being burned or looted. For future scholars interested in tracing the history of writing, any clay tablets they consult will now come not from Baghdad but from some little collection in the Middle Eastern equivalent of Pullman.

BACK ON A CAMPUS again I felt like an outlaw, not a professor, clumping around in my bug-stained boots and black leather jacket. They looked me up and down in the library when I asked for the archives, and once I was there two people were very quick to ask, icily, "May I help you?"

It was great.

Outlaw bikers call themselves One-Percenters because it is only this small fragment of motorcyclists that is criminal (at least that was the claim of the American Motorcycle Association in the 1950s). Yet in the media and in our imaginations they are the 99-percenters. Nobody would have made *Easy Rider* about two lawyers on BMWs crossing the country. Even if their saddlebags were full of coke. Now of course it is the lawyers and accountants who dress up in black jackets from the Harley boutique and, every Sunday, ride their immaculate hogs out to a truck stop on the edge of town. It's easy to mock this, but the image exerts a powerful force. Friends told me of their neighbor, a professional woman in her late forties who had started to ride. Short and softspoken, she is not an immediately commanding presence. One Sunday during a ride she and her husband stopped at McDonald's. She was in full leathers and thought nothing of it until, with her burger and fries in hand, she had to get through the long food lineup to get to the ketchup station. She took a step forward and even before she could say "Excuse me," the lineup parted like the Red Sea. "It was wonderful," she said, "They thought I was a Biker!" Whether you're riding a cruiser or a dirt bike or a big touring rig, in the eyes of the world you're a bit of a hooligan or you wouldn't be out there. We reject it, we deny it, we explain at length that there is a difference between a Rider and a Biker, but we secretly relish it. We like the idea that we're mad, bad, and dangerous to know.

IN THE ARCHIVES they were courteous—I had sent a letter some weeks before stating my intent to look at the Woolf material—and asked, "What exactly are you looking for?" Good question. "I've come to see the Virginia Woolf library," I said, or some such plausible answer. The truth was I had come looking for the Archival Jolt.

Fifteen years ago, I had been working in the British Library's Manuscript Room, sifting through the Virginia Woolf manuscripts. The hoary clerks, with tufts of hair coming out of their ears and noses, had with bad grace been bringing me what I needed. The windows were open, and we could hear traffic noise from across the parking lot: an unobtrusive drone that glided in on the warm June air and drew you gently toward sleep. You weren't even aware at what point you stopped reading, when critical reflection turned to daydreaming, when your eyes slipped out of focus and let the print blur, and your measured breathing took on that hoarse quality just shy of a snore.

My eyes fell shut. They just dropped down like the metal shutters on a Paris shop at the end of the day. Bam. I forced them open. I felt like I was doing bicep curls with my eyelids. I got them up, licked my middle finger, and swabbed saliva on my eyelids, the old cross-country driver's trick. It gives you about ten seconds, better than nothing, and helps break the rhythm of heaviness. I slumped forward, elbows on the table, thumb and forefinger on either side of my face, my thumbs at my cheekbones pushing down, my forefingers at the edge of my eyebrows pushing up, stretching the skin, using the pain to keep my eyes open. Was this really reading? I wondered.

I opened up the next manila envelope and slid out a single sheet. It was handwritten and my eyes winced after the sojourn in typescript. Still, it was only a single page and it was well spaced. I would be out of here soon. I found myself reading a letter I had read in print dozens of times before. Anybody who works on Woolf practically knows it by heart, it's reprinted so often. It begins:

Dearest, I want to tell you that you have given me complete happiness. No one could have done more than you have done. Please believe that. But I know that I shall never get over this: and I am wasting your life. It is this madness . . .

I felt a physical shock. I was holding Virginia Woolf's suicide note. I lost any bodily sense, felt I was spinning into a vortex, a connection that collapsed the intervening decades. This note wasn't a record of an event—this was the event itself. This writing. And it was not for me. I had walked in on something unbearably personal. It probably took less than thirty seconds to read the letter, and in that interval I had been blasted back to March 1941 and staggered up to the present, time roaring in my ears, and no one had noticed. The other readers in the room were still nodding away.

I placed it on the reading stand, wiped my fingers, which turned out to be cold and dry, and turned the sheet over. There Leonard had written in green ink the date: "11/5/41." This detail set off an unexpected aftershock. I realized I seldom thought of him, of how he had had to wait twenty-one days before the body was found. Three long weeks, answering questions from *The Times,* taking calls from friends. Then a group of teenagers, throwing rocks at a log in the river, found it was not a log at all and dragged what was once Virginia Woolf ashore.

The coroner misquoted the suicide note, and so did the newspapers. Leonard had to issue corrections, and at the cremation, which he went to alone, they played the wrong music. He went home that night and played the "Cavatina" from Beethoven's String Quartet in B-flat, op. 130 to himself on the gramophone. A few days later, he carefully dated the note I had in front of me. I remembered none of the scholarly discussion about the dating. I only saw the pain and the attempt to bring order by dating and noting the circumstances of the letter.

I decided to call it a day. I put the letter back in the manila envelope, wound the string around the roundel at the top, and took everything back to the desk. I retrieved my bookbag and umbrella from the coat-check kiosk and walked out into the brilliant sunshine. I had no interest in biographical readings of Woolf, so the note was of no use to me. Or so I thought. What I didn't know was that I had just become an archive junkie.

Later I read the work of anthropologist Paul Stoller, who argues that we must include the tactile, the auditory, the gustatory, and not just the visual, in our scholarship. He quotes Walter Benjamin on "corporeal knowing," a useful concept; I now see that the suicide note added nothing to my textual knowledge, but it added enormously to my corporeal knowledge, a knowledge difficult to quantify or describe, but not for that reason to be dismissed or ignored. It did make me aware of Leonard's place in all this. I had become the recipient of the note. Part of the reason we work in archives is, I'm convinced, for the archival jolt, a portal to knowledge and, in itself, an assurance that we have connected with something real.

IN PULLMAN I got a much more mundane jolt: there was no Woolf library. Though special-collections libraries were for me serene oases, they are in fact contested terrains, for they straddle the border between libraries and archives. Initially the Woolf books had been housed together, but archivists and librarians order things differently. When a new curator, a librarian, took over, he shelved the Woolf books separately, according to their subject call number, dispersing the collection. That was his job; yet for an archivist the job would have been to keep the documents together, to treat them as a text in themselves, even if possible to keep them in the same order that they had been shelved in the Woolfs' house.

The word "archive" derives from the Greek *arkheion:* the residence of the superior magistrates—the *archons,* those who command. The documents or laws were filed in the homes of the magistrates, who had the power to interpret the documents. The concept of the archive as the repository of law, watched over by those invested with the power of the law, is still with us, disavowed but inescapable. Back when I was a postdoctoral fellow I had worked in the Berg archive at the New York Public Library, under the infamous curator Lola Szladits. A junior librarian staffing the desk at lunchtime asked me on my way out, "Have you felt the lash yet?" I had not, but I was there because a friend had been ejected from the archive when Szladits discovered he was a mere graduate student. He said, "She shouted at me, 'I won't have *my* material used for *cheap theses*!' And that was that. I left the next day. You might as well do the edition. She'll never let me back in." I had always suspected that the most fulsome thanks in a book's acknowledgments were directed to the most difficult archivists.

In any case, what I wanted in Pullman no longer existed. They had four thousand books and it would have taken days to assemble them. Some from Virginia Woolf's father had drawings in them; Leonard wrote in the margins, Virginia did not. The way a book looked could tell you much about how it was used, whether it was a favorite reference or just a keepsake. I had not come to read individual texts, and I already had a list of the books in their library so I knew what they had acquired. What I wanted was to gain some sense of what had been read. Most of us when we go into other people's homes will surreptitiously check out the bookshelves and the music collections, forming our impression of the owners' character from what they read and listen to. Most of us know that others do this and so the books in the public spaces will be arranged to particular effect, different from the working books. A personal library is not just a repository, it is a display, a performance. Leonard's files for the Hogarth Press displayed a military precision. Virginia's notebooks let the end of one novel run into the notes for the next and might include a book review starting from the back and written upside down on the blank leaves (she wrote on only one side of the page), so that at a certain point the two texts met, topsy-turvy and going in opposite directions. How would she have arranged the library?

I looked at some of WSU's special treasures, such as the first American edition of Woolf's *Mrs. Dalloway,* complete with dust jacket, and made some notes, just to be doing something, and then consulted some of the memoirs about Woolf for my own private research interest: the convergence of motorcycles and modernism. The first motorcycle had been invented in 1885, when James Joyce and Virginia Woolf were both three years old. In the 1920s, when their work came of age, the motorcycle too discovered a form that would define it for the century. Often emerging from the factories that had produced armaments, motorcycles became part of the motoring mainstream.

In 1927, with the profits from *To the Lighthouse,* the Woolfs acquired a car. Virginia's lover, Vita Sackville-West, recorded Virginia's driving attempts in Richmond Park:

> Leonard [Woolf] and I watched her start. The motor made little pounces and stopped dead. At one moment it ran backwards. At last she sailed off, and Leonard and I and Pinker went for a walk at 5 miles an hour. Every five minutes Leonard would say, "I suppose Virginia will be all right . . ."

Virginia herself wrote to her friend Ethel Sands, "I have driven from the Embankment to Marble Arch and only knocked one boy very gently off his bicycle." Woolf never did manage to learn to drive a car, but she apparently considered becoming a biker. After meeting Virginia, Frances Marshall (who was to become a member of the Bloomsbury Group) wrote:

> I was bowled over by her irresistible cracked charm. . . . She is going to be the newest motor-bicycle addict, for she says Leonard won't let her drive the car and a motor bike is just what she wants.

I tried to picture Woolf thundering across the Sussex Downs or roaring up Oxford Street on a motorcycle. *Mrs. Dalloway* would certainly be different if the character had gone to get flowers on her Royal Enfield. I couldn't imagine it. I doubted Woolf would have lived as long as she did had she taken up motorcycling, and we never would have had those last great novels.

FOUR

Rhythm

When I left Kalispell the chain was snatching a bit, making the bike jerky at low speeds, but I set it in Pullman and as I pulled out of the parking lot in the morning . . . smooooth. When I tighten the chain, I feel like a real mechanic. After all, I'm using *two* wrenches. Clearly, *Ted and the Art of Motorcycle Maintenance* would be a short book. I don't tune the carburetors. For a Ducati, you need a two-year training course and proficiency in Italian even to find the carburetors. And to set the valves, you need special tools and special shims that come handcrafted from Bologna and cost twice as much as those for any other motorcycle. (Shims are the bits of metal that go under the valve stems to change how far they open and close; I've never seen one, but I'm assured they exist and when they appear on my work order, they are extravagantly expensive.) I'm told that for old BMWs, you can, in a pinch, make the shims out of beer cans. My biker friends wonder why I, the least Mr. Fix-It of mortals, would buy such a complex bike. They miss the logic of it: even if the bike were simple to work on, I would still have to take it to a mechanic. With the Ducati, no one can be expected to work on it, and you can complain about those perverse Italians who make it impossible to do your own maintenance, suggesting, without saying so, that you would otherwise be stripping and rebuilding the engine every morning before breakfast for the fun of it.

I began discovering my rhythm for the ride: in the first half-hour or so, I tended to drive around the speed limit. Then when the bike was warmed up and I was through fiddling with my jacket and gloves, the air coming in the arms and back vents and not down my neck, I would start to blast—a steady 80 miles an hour with occasional bursts up to 100 miles an hour to clear the carbs and get the adrenaline going. I would usually have the road to myself and would ride hard, focused on the road, ignoring the scenery. In the dozy mid-afternoons, I would just cruise, obey the speed limit, and look at the view. Maybe even stop at a secluded picnic site and take a seventeen-minute power snooze. Late afternoon was often the best riding; after being on the bike all day you are relaxed and efficient, but not yet tired and sloppy. Before dinnertime I would find a motel, and I tightened my motorcycle chain every evening after checking in, taking care of the bike before taking a shower, like the old cowboys who made sure the horses were looked to before they fed themselves.

I crossed from Washington back into Idaho, following Highway 95 through the Nez Perce Indian Reservation and down the Payette River, carving through the narrow pine-treed valley, dipping the bike from side to side in an easy motion. I had always felt comfortable on the Duc; now I was beginning to feel I belonged on it, and though

I still wasn't ready to do wheelies in the parking lot, I was beginning to use a little of the bike's power. When I passed slower vehicles I usually stayed in sixth gear; the engine is strong enough that a lazy roll of the wrist, down and up, takes you from 60 to 80 and back again as you arc gracefully in and out of the pass lane. Sometimes, though, I would get stuck behind a double semi. If it was more than a few seconds, I would drop down to fifth. More than a minute and I would drop down to fourth and squirm back on the seat. Any longer and I would pop it into third. The engine would be revving hard now, eager to go, and so was I, hunched lower over the bars, waiting for a shot of clear road. *Pow!* I would nail the throttle and hang on as hard as I could. The engine screamed, the footrests tingled, and I would hit fourth. *Pow!* Another surge and the engine dropped to a low bellow, now right in the middle of its torque curve, soaring, this was what Ducatis were born for, and we were doing 100 as we reached the front of the truck. I would shift up into fifth and swing back in, and when I checked my mirrors the truck would be just two blurred headlights far behind. I would sit up, slow to 80, pop my eyes back into their sockets, and mutter, "Be still my beating heart." After a couple of miles I would remember I still had a sixth gear and slip it in.

For anyone used to four wheels instead of two, even accustomed to driving fast cars, there's nothing like the absolute quickness of a motorcycle. It was a rush, no question, and I felt some sympathy for those irresponsible young men who would go canyon racing at night in California. But if the road is crowded and you have to do those rocket-sled passes fifteen times in a row, it gets to be tiresome. I was in no real rush and learned to just sit well back, or better yet, pull into a "scenic outlook" and let the line go by. I was coming to appreciate another one of Pasquale's aphorisms: "You can go as fast as you like on a motorcycle—but never hurry on a motorcycle."

THE DUCATI OBSESSION began for me when my younger brother Lloyd bought a 250 cc Mach 1 from his friend Vince who had raced it. "He set it up for the track," Lloyd said proudly. "He even took off the kickstarter to save weight." The little Ducati certainly looked cool, with the white swoosh on the bright red tank, and the narrow black seat with the snaps along the bottom.

"So how does it start?"

"You bump-start it."

"What's that?"

"You put it in gear, hold in the clutch, and push it. When you get running you hop on it sidesaddle and let the clutch out at the same time, then hop off and keep running. It'll catch, and then you pull the clutch back in and rev the throttle."

"You have to do this every time you start it?"

"Yeah, it's great, just like a real racing bike, and they gave me this straight-through megaphone. It reduces back pressure. It's not street legal but they'll never do anything here in the mountains."

"Well, it'll keep the bears away."

A strange thing, when you think of it, this love of Ducatis flourishing in the mountains of Western Canada. Every day Vince, determined to make my brother worthy of his new purchase, took him up the 40 kilometers of winding road to Maligne Lake, or the tighter road just back of the town to Pyramid Lake. Just 8 kilometers, but switchbacks so tight and steep that you could almost scrape your kneecaps if you had the nerve. Vince had bought a Bultaco Metralla, another 250 cc single, even lighter than the Ducati. Every morning

Lloyd and Vince would set out. You could hear them from across the lake, the basso *thump-thump-thump* of the Ducati with its megaphone, not loud but so deep you expected a giant to come round the corner. Blending with the bass came the higher pitch of the two-stroke Bultaco, echoing back across the still lake from Signal Mountain, and we wondered if the fire warden up there in his tower could hear them, and see the two bright specks, shiny black and silver-red, flashing in and out of the trees, as they wound on the far side of the valley up the Pyramid road. We wondered if he would phone the RCMP, but he never did.

Amazingly, nobody died, nobody crashed. There were always bear about halfway up the Maligne road and lots of deer on the Pyramid road, but they scampered deep into the forest when they heard the roar approaching, and so every morning Lloyd would follow Vince deeper and deeper into the corners, soaking the lessons into his frame. He discovered that heavy-braking RVs had made the road in the downhill corners fold up the way a hall rug does when you slide on it. The chatter bumps made the front wheel of the little Ducati hop sideways in an alarming manner, and Lloyd learned that you had to get off the brake and just wait for the tire to bite.

"You've got to try it," he said to me one day. I said okay.

"Remember," he said, "clutch in as you run, hop on, pop the clutch, hop off, keep running, and pull the clutch in and rev the throttle." It looked easy. Lloyd now could do it quicker than most riders could kickstart their bikes. A couple of quick strides, hop on, hop off, and then he would sling a leg over and go.

I pushed the bike out to the dusty road. It was a lot heavier than it looked. I clunked the shifter down into gear, pulled in the clutch lever (stiffer than I expected), and started to run—the slow-motion running of a dream, arms stretched out, straining against the weight of the bike. I ran a few steps, hopped on, and popped the clutch. The bike stopped dead. I nearly went over the tank, and the bike wobbled before I managed to get my feet back on the ground and hold it upright. This was harder than it looked.

Back I went, digging my toes into the dirt, kicking in slow motion again. "Keep going, keep going!" Lloyd called from his deck chair on the patio, "Keep running as you rev it!" Now the bike was really heavy, as I pushed it in gear, and it was making a sputtering sound but wasn't catching. I ran on, the Ducati and I sputtering more and more slowly till we stopped in the shade of the big tree at the end of our neighbor's driveway. Damn. The dust from the road gently billowed past me and stuck to my sweat-streaked forehead. I sucked in great gasps of air, smelling the hot pine and high-octane gas. I turned the bike around, staggering slightly, my arms like rubber. The little Ducati weighed a ton.

"Don't slow down this time!" called Lloyd helpfully.

I didn't even want to ride anymore. I just wanted to go for a swim and have a beer in the shade, but I was determined to be determined. I clenched the bars and locked my elbows. Off we went again, the bike and I, up the road in our slow glissade. I hopped, popped, the engine caught, and I was lurching down the lane like a crippled drunk. But the engine was running. I slung a leg over the little seat and I was off.

I hadn't ridden much—around the block on a Honda 90, around the neighborhood on a 650 Norton Atlas that belonged to a friend's older brother. The first felt like a randy bicycle, the second like an elephant. This Ducati was different. It fit. I slid back on the narrow seat and my knees slotted into the depressions in the tank.

The bars brought me forward but not too low, and as we picked up speed the boom of the exhaust moved pleasantly behind me. I won't say I "became one with the bike." My shifts were harsh and my braking jerky, yet the bike seemed accommodating, willing, waiting unobtrusively for me to call on it. As I leaned into the corners, all that was left in view was the little speedometer; the bike seemed to have no mass and yet be enormously solid. Where the Norton settled comfortably into a corner but seemed to want to be hoisted out of it at the end, the Duc easily righted itself and leaned into the next. It seemed to be moving before I asked it to, anticipating the corners. Soon I was just riding, not thinking about riding. I got to town, turned around and came back, a little braver now. I passed through Jasper Park Lodge, enjoying the looks of the tourists, and then, cutting through a long bend by Lake Annette, glanced down at the speedometer and found I was going 70 miles an hour. Hey, I was a rider.

Later I read a British road test of the Ducati that said the Veglia speedometer was wildly optimistic: it registered an indicated top speed of 106 miles an hour, but the best they could squeeze out of the bike, measuring with their own equipment, was 83 miles an hour. They were disapproving. I didn't care. What counted was spirit, not mathematical precision. I gave the bike back to Lloyd and didn't ride again for years but the memory lay dormant, forgotten until I eased the clutch out on the Monster in the alley behind Brian's shop.

ON THE OUTSKIRTS of Boise, Idaho, I pulled into the Red Lion Inn. The courteous clerk gave me a room far at the back of the sprawling complex, around six corners and across as many parking lots, where my bike couldn't be seen and scare away the quality folk. I dropped my gear and decided to walk into town for dinner.

"I can give you a ride," said the pretty blonde in the Red Lion polo shirt when I asked at the front desk for a map.

"Are you sure?" Of course bikers are cool, but I had no idea it would be this easy.

"No problem, glad to do it. I'll meet you out front." Wow! She's just getting off work and she wants me. Wrong. I strolled out front and she pulled up in a thirty-passenger courtesy bus.

"I have to go in to pick up these elderly ladies I dropped off earlier." Oh, great. So now I was lumped with the geriatric contingent.

"Of course I'll walk home. It's just handy to have a ride in so I can get my bearings," I said, squaring my shoulders and trying to look intrepid.

"Sure," she said, "but if you get tired just call."

I would have walked five miles on chopped glass first.

I noted that "Boise" does not rhyme with "noisy"; the s sounds like an s, not a z—Boy-sea. I also noticed the overall accent changing, a southwestern drawl creeping in. I no longer merged verbally with the natives. They pronounced the name of my country "Kyan-uhduh." I found a place called the Beanery where they served enormous club sandwiches with side orders of mashed potatoes covered in mushroom-burgundy gravy. I decided to have dessert too, a dark wedge of pecan pie. It was a cold day and I needed to replenish the calories. I added a dark ale from a local brewery to my order. I noticed that I was getting a biker gut.

A friendly bar, a few good cafés, and a decent bookstore are the requisites of civilization, and Boise had them. In the morning I bought Tracks, Robin Davidson's story of how she made a lone journey with camels across the Australian outback. I picked it in part because it was thin and fit perfectly into the inside pocket of my jacket. It had the right heft as well as the right style. Different modes of travel demand different books. On an airplane I seem to need more action, something like a Martin Cruz Smith thriller. On a motorcycle, at the end of the day I want something with the quiet, intense focus of Carol Shields. I had *The Stone Diaries* in my saddle-bags, but it was too lumpy for restaurant reading. One summer in Europe I carted around *Don Quixote,* bored and suspecting that the famous windmill scene gets all the attention because it is only thirty pages in and everyone gives up after that. But I became enchanted with Cervantes and his writing of the book more than with the Don and his adventures, or rather they merged, and the novel's leisurely journey calmed my own. Sometimes when I'm traveling I begin to feel like a gigantic open nerve on the verge of overload, and that if I see/smell/touch/taste/hear one more thing I'll explode and all my sensory impressions will be splattered across the landscape. It helps to write (which is why you always see travelers hunched in a scribbling frenzy over their journals or blazing away at the keyboards in Internet cafés), but the right book creates a space, orders the cosmos for you, and you look up from it ready again to take in more.

I hated to leave Boise because I was dreading the interstate. I did 175 miles at 87 miles an hour nonstop. Horrible. The engine roars, the wheels go round and round, and the landscape never changes. The freeway is constructed in sections like some giant road-race set, and every two seconds you get a jolt from where the sections meet. You can't remember what it feels like to lean into a corner. Your wrists hurt, your spine starts to ache, and you feel as if you're sitting on a paint shaker, rattling your teeth and going nowhere. Twist the throttle and the noise gets louder, but there's no sense of increased speed. Ugly children make faces out of the back of minivans. There are no towns. You see nothing alive. The I-84 takes you through Mountain Home, which is one of those fraudulently named places like Greenland that aimed to attract settlers. If honesty had prevailed, Mountain Home would have been called Flat-Brown-Boring-Scrubland Home. There wasn't a mountain in sight, and I jolted by on the freeway without stopping.

As you come over the bridge into Twin Falls, the land suddenly yawns and another world appears. You look down to a cool green-blue river, and the unexpected color explodes against your retinas like the flavor center of a Jolly Rancher candy. You see a bright lawn with a little bungalow in the middle, then the eye adjusts and the green lawn proves to be a golf course, and the bungalow a distant massive clubhouse. The scale is vast. As I parked at the visitors' center on the far side of the bridge, I wondered why I had heard of the Snake River Canyon, and then there it was: a tombstone-like monument to Evel Knievel's failed attempt to jump the canyon with a rocket-powered "Skycycle" on September 8, 1974. I asked the senior volunteers in the center about Knievel. They remembered him well.

"Oh no, he never made it—he didn't even git in the water," snapped the little woman behind the desk. "He landed on the bank and his sickle went in the river. His chute opened right as he was going up the ramp."

She took me outside and pointed up beyond the bridge to where the outline of the dirt ramp still stands.

"Did he ever try to do it again?"

"No. Fact is, I don't think he was really trying to do it the first time. The land on the other side belongs to the Bureau of Land

Management or is privately owned, and that Evel he never got permission from anybody for a landing. He knew it was all a hoax.

"His son wanted to try it, for the twentieth anniversary, but a lot of folks around here remember the first time and they didn't want it. This kind of . . . of phenomenon, of *farce* you may call it, doesn't attract the kind of people we want. Last time it was wild. People sleepin' on front lawns, usin' them to, to go to the bathroom, an' they burned a Cadillac car, *and* they wrecked a sem-eye, ripped the doors off the back to get at the beer. Oh, it was awful. Then Evel he went away from here with a lot of unpaid debts. So when his son couldn't get the backing and raise the insurance money we were all glad. But you should see Shoshone Falls. It's right on your way if you're going out back to the old Highway 30 to Burley."

I thanked her, and because she had been so kind I did go to Shoshone Falls. They are unremarkable, but the park with thick green grass was extraordinary, and I laid out my jacket and had a fifteen-minute power snooze. As I came to, gazing up through the leaves of the big trees in this oasis, I wondered what this canyon does to the consciousness of the people who live nearby knowing there is this huge gash in the earth, a Jules Verne lost world. A canyon so deep and strange that even Evel wouldn't dream of really trying to jump it.

I STOPPED FOR GAS just inside the Utah border at Snowville (population two hundred) as the sun was going behind the mountains. After I had paid for my gas, a guy with a flatbed truck full of squashed automobiles came over. "Long way from home," he said, looking at my license plate. I had finally come far enough that people would say that. He told me that he rode a Harley but had ridden

Ducatis and other bikes when he was stationed in Europe. And he told me, "Utah is the best-kept motorcycle secret in America. Everybody goes through on the salt flats. They never see those twisty roads up in the mountains. Suits me just fine."

He was bunking in his rig tonight ("Unless I get lucky. Which I probably won't"), but said that the café/bar at the corner was a good place. All it takes is the exchange of a few friendly words and a place looks different, but I had decided to push on another hour to Tremonton. I wished I had stayed put. The only choice was a motel on the interstate attached to a Denny's. A lifesize wooden statue of a cowpoke called Mitch stood in the lobby, and Mitch smelled of stale sweat and old cigarette smoke. The room had more cigarette burns than TV channels. It was the sort of place where you walk to the shower naked in your motorcycle boots not because you're kinky but because Who-Knows-What lurks in that inch-deep russet-orange acrylic shag. Stephen King must have a story somewhere about a malefic interstate shag carpet from hell that wraps its greasy tendrils around the toes of comely coeds and drags them screaming into its devouring embrace. I flossed forlornly and watched one of the religious channels, trying to tell myself that this was so bad it was great. The Quintessential Interstate Lodging Experience, I told myself. It didn't work. I burped softly; the Denny's fish and chips tasted just as bad the second time. I turned out the light, wondering why the knob felt both greasy and sticky. I decided not to pursue it.

THE NEXT DAY'S RIDE rinsed away the memory's slimy residue. For my money, the best motorcycle road in the universe is Highway 31 in central Utah from Fairview to Huntington, southwest of Price. It's so small that it doesn't appear on my western states map. It's designated as a Scenic Byway, which means it doesn't go anywhere; it cuts across from 89 to 10, both already just gray roads on the big map. This is what you want. The little roads that no one will find in advance. If you take out your map, find Salt Lake, go south to Provo, then jog east and south off the interstate, just a little, to Thistle on Highway 6, twenty-seven miles south on 89 you'll find Fairview. Draw a squiggly diagonal over to Huntington. That's it.

It was three in the afternoon in Fairview, and I was depressed and tired, stabbing at a piece of crappy pie delivered by a surly waitress who took so long I thought they must have been putting the apples and raisins in one by one. I wasted forty-five minutes on a snack. I would never make Moab tonight now, and I hadn't had any really interesting road all day, just miles of semi-suburban connectors running past clean, prosperous Mormon homes. Park City, Springville, Mapleton—they all seemed like sets for *Father Knows Best*. I was grumpy as hell. Why I hadn't just taken the direct route to Price I didn't know. Yes, I did. It was my "mandate." My pledge to myself to seek out the smallest roads possible, to avoid the direct route, to eat in mom-and-pop diners. Yeah, well I was eating in one now and it sucked. No wonder McDonald's was taking over the world. I slurped some of my lukewarm coffee with nondairy-petrochemical-byproduct-whitener. I paid the bill and walked out. The waitress didn't say "Come again."

Five minutes later none of it mattered. I found myself going a little faster, a little faster, a little faster. . . . My memory of the country is a blur—bright creek, slender pines—grabbed in laser-glimpses between corners. I tried to ride fast and stay off the brake, fast and smooth, using the Duc's linear power. I kept it in third—there it pulls hard all the way from 30 to 75 miles an hour, and when you back off it's like throwing out an anchor. This is why riders love big twins. Then I blew by a slow camper, snapped down my visor, and dived into a bend at 80—and found *everythingoingintoslowmo*. Instead of feeling fast it felt as if I could get up, do a tap dance on the tank, smoke a Havana cigar, get back down, and finish the corner with time for a snack. Glorious. Better than drugs.

I was getting set to gobble up the next line of plodders when I saw the roof lights on the Jeep in front—the county sheriff. Damn. I throttled back and shut it down. By the time he turned off I had lost it, finding myself a bit ragged in the next corner. But I didn't care. I waited, found the groove again, and stayed in it all the way down until the winding gorge dumped me, like a swimmer off a water slide, out into the flat gray desert of Castle Valley, and the main road on to Green River and Moab.

FIVE

Romance of the West

I reached Green River, Utah, at about five. The river may be green
but the landscape sure is not. Again, one of those names that
conjures up verdant images that dissolve like mirages once you reach
them. Still, unlike Mountain Home this one wasn't completely
fraudulent, and just south of here in a harsh red mountain range the
Hole in the Wall Gang relaxed between bank robberies, and after
sipping water out of desert creeks the cool depths of the Green River
must have seemed paradisal. Jesse James, Butch Cassidy, and other
second-tier outlaws had slept in this valley. I chose the Sleepy Hollow
Motel. I liked the look of it, brick with neat white doors and little
cedars in front of the air-conditioning outlets. The Budget Inn across
the street was probably cheaper, but with its plain white siding it
looked cheaper, and more institutional. The Sleepy Hollow was the
kind of place where my parents might have stayed. I had not planned
this, but I found myself looking for these little 1950s motels, maybe

twenty units in an L, with a flat-topped wing coming off the office that you pull in under, out of the rain or the sun, in front of the big window that lets the clerk see you and you him. And the clerk would be the owner. The Sleepy Hollow was right next to the city park, a flat expanse of grass ringed with trees, with a U.S. Air Force rocket ship up front by the road. I would have preferred a swing set, but parks change more slowly than the rest of a city. Rockets too defined the fifties. When I walked back from the Tamarisk Restaurant across the bridge, I was proud to see that my motel had lit the NO of its VACANCY sign, while the Budget Inn was still pleading for customers.

I slept well, woke early, and got a coffee from the Chow Hound Drive-In, another throwback to the 1950s. I thought about how my mother always used to like being on the road by herself, having family behind and friends ahead, but knowing that nobody could reach her or know exactly where she was for a few days. I found a picture of her at sixteen in gauntleted gloves and dark glasses, sitting on a motorcycle. The bike belongs to a friend; I don't think she ever drove it. Yet sometimes, riding on a deserted highway, I imagine I feel her presence. If I think about it too much, the idea starts to spook me, but the sensation always comes gently, unbidden, and it pleased me to imagine her riding that bike somewhere behind me, or in the other lane, just out of my vision. Or ahead, too distant to see but out there, leading the way.

WHERE GREEN RIVER IS NOSTALGIC, Moab is frenetically up to date. A mountain-bike town where everyone is young, tanned, gorgeous and moneyed, obsessed with bikes, bodies, and the next day's ride. Did I resent them because I too used to have conversations that began, "Wow, you're running a 13-28 cluster with only a 32 granny gear in front?!" At McStiff's, where the beautiful server greeted the locals with that little trill in her voice (how do they do that?), I ordered a local microbrewery beer and a burger. I got a smile, but no trill. Back at the motel I called Hsing, but she was out and she doesn't believe in answering machines so I couldn't leave a message. I had told her not to expect calls very often, but it had never occurred to me that she wouldn't be there to take a call when I felt like making one. Some of the shine was going off this lone rider business.

Outside in the parking lot I had seen a heavily loaded Honda Transalp, one of the dual-purpose (dirt and pavement) bikes that are so popular in Europe where their upright seating position and long suspension travel make them great for cobblestone streets. I strolled out to look at it, and the owner came out. He was Dutch, making a tour of the United States before he went back to medical school. How was the bike? He loved it. He asked about my Ducati. I loved it. I admitted though that there were times when I wished I could take it down some of the unpaved side roads I saw on my map, and I wondered what the Ducati Elefant would be like.

"Horrible!" he said.

"You've driven one?"

"Worse. I owned one. Like you, I thought it would be the perfect bike, a combination of the wonderful Ducati engine in a more relaxed frame. Somehow, I don't know, I just did not like it, and one night going to my fiancée's house I took a corner I'd been through on my other bikes—I have had nine—many times before and the bike just did not turn. I went through a hedge, across a ditch, and fell in the field beyond. I was not hurt but I never trusted the bike after that. But let me say this. I think it is not a bad bike. It was a bad bike for me. Sometimes you get the wrong bike. And that's it. It does not matter how well you ride. You do not fit, and it will not get better."

"So what did you do?"

"I sold it. I lost 5,000 guilders but now I have a bike I trust."

I was glad to hear this, I said, not glad that he had lost 5,000 guilders but because it was good to have an experienced rider confirm what I had felt. I told him how I had bought a beautiful blue BMW K75S, a bike renowned for its smoothness and all-round abilities; it was good in town, good on the highway, and with shaft-drive and liquid cooling it would last forever. I read all the tests and except for one cranky British one that said the bike was ridiculous, every one lauded it, though when I went back afterward I could see that the praise was always cool. They were holding back something. Anyway, I loved the look, wanted the craftsmanship, and yet the minute I rode out of the dealership I knew it was a mistake. It was partly the height—I teetered at stoplights. Partly the stretch to the handlebars— maybe an inch too long, which can make the difference between making a bike seem as big as a house and having it disappear under you. I wanted to adore it, but I only admired. When you find yourself making lists of virtues, you know it isn't love. So that first long winter I had two bikes in the garage, and the guy who bought my BMW got a fabulous deal. I took a bath, but I didn't care. Money is the worst reason to stay in a relationship.

NEXT MORNING I visited the famous Monument Valley outside Moab—Hollywood films from *Stagecoach* to *Thelma and Louise* have stamped these spires on every North American's image of the West. Then I cut southeast into the Four Corners region, so called because it is the one place in the United States where four states touch at once: Utah, Colorado, New Mexico, and Arizona. The landscape and its history mock the administrative designations, for this was the area of the Anasazi, the indigenous "Ancient Ones" who lived in what is now the southwest United States for seven hundred years and then mysteriously disappeared in the thirteenth century. As Chaucer was documenting a short local pilgrimage in *The Canterbury Tales,* the Anasazi were moving outward on their vast quests, spokes on a now rimless wheel, passing into oblivion. No one knows if they were driven out by famine or by enemies. At Mesa Verde outside Mancos, Colorado, I took the guided trip with forty-nine others to Balcony House, one of the dwellings built into the cliff wall of the mesa that sloped up some 1,000 feet from the plain. The trails had gone from abandoned to trampled in one generation. We clambered up and down ladders and poked our heads into rooms, and thought about what a beautiful view the Anasazi had. But these were bunkers, not condos, occupied for only the last hundred years of the centuries the Anasazi had lived here. Water and food had to be carried up, and in grinding the corn the women ground down their kneecaps, and ground particles of rock into their flour that ground down the teeth of everyone eating the bread. We all thanked the guide and repaired to the Mesa Verde cafeteria for genuine Navajo snacks.

As I stood in the lineup, a man in his sixties began talking to me as if we were picking up a momentarily interrupted conversation: "Yep we're full-time RV'ers now. I quit last November. We've been all over since then. Where're you from?"

"Edmonton, Alberta."

"Hey! We were just up there."

"Well, dear," said his wife, "that was Montreal."

"Yeah I know, but—you know—Canada . . ." I explained that Alberta was just above Montana, but he gave me a vague "uh-huh." Though the coasts are clear, the geography of the middle remains patchy for most. "My last day, after punching out," he continued, "I came home—the motor home was packed and ready to go—and I put my alarm clock under one front wheel and my lunch pail under the other, and had the wife take a picture of me running over 'em both." A wonderful image. But I was troubled by the images rattling round in my brain of Anasazi bodies grinding themselves into dust. And now we were grinding their remnants to dust. Mesa Verde too was an archive and it brought home the central paradox: preservation and access were yoked to violence and destruction.

THE BIKE TOOK ME down through Mancos, past Hesperus, and into Durango. Durango! This was thrilling—I felt like I was entering the Old West now. I hummed Bob Dylan's "Romance in Durango" ("Soon the horse will take us to Durango . . ." something something) and remembered the masked Durango Kid from movies when I was a kid going off on my own to the Saturday matinee at the Garneau theater. I liked the sound of the name. Duh-*rang*-go. Like a bullet ricocheting off a rock. (I read later that the Durango Kid was played by Charles Starrett, a Dartmouth graduate who initially disliked westerns, but found them a gold mine: he made sixty-five Durango Kid films between 1940 and 1952. His trademark flowing scarf was something a wardrobe man grabbed in haste, ripping it from a nightgown Rita Hayworth had used in a film. I'm not sure what my ten-year-old self would have thought of this.) I squared my shoulders and strode into the Strater Hotel, all red brick and white cornices, three storeys high, the best place in town in 1887. It had slid into disrepair but was now restored, catering to the gentry once again.

A slightly seedy-looking guy was standing hesitantly at the oak counter. "Do you have a single room?" he asked.

"Certainly," said the clerk in her little striped blouse and period skirt, "I have one at $145 and one at $120."

"Oh," the guy crumpled. "I'll, uh, I'll think about it."

"Certainly, sir," said the clerk pertly, knowing he was going to be sleeping in his pickup truck tonight. With my black jacket and matted helmet hair, I looked worse than the other guy, but I was ready. Two single rooms left at 6:30 P.M. on a Tuesday night: they know they're not going to fill them.

"I want a room and I don't want to pay over $60," I said, cutting her cheapest rate in two.

"Oh! Well. I'd have to ask my supervisor." She turned to a woman doing the books at a desk behind the counter.

"I couldn't go below $68," the woman snarled without looking up.

"Done!" I said, slapping my MasterCard on the counter with what was probably unseemly triumph. Hsing was always after me to bargain, and it had taken me four states to figure out that mid-week, off-season, if you make like you're going to walk away, the price will sometimes drop to half. The clerk sniffed as I carried my dusty saddlebags up the restored staircase. I showered and cleaned my boots and strolled out onto Main Street, throwing her a smile as I passed through the lobby. Her eyes skittered away. I felt like Brando.

After dinner I went looking for a Laundromat. I travel with just road jeans and shirt, street pants and shirt, plus five pairs of socks and underwear, so by the time the underwear runs out the road jeans are stiff with bugs. I passed a cappuccino bar where two guys were playing jazz guitar, so I put the clothes into the machine and came back. There were three stools at the counter; I put my knapsack on the end one and went up to get my macchiato. When I came back a girl was sitting on the next stool, smiling—expectantly? I moved the stool slightly away and just glanced at her with a nod in my discreet Canadian way, showing that I wasn't intruding on her space. I looked at the musicians, then down at my coffee.

"Hi," she said, her smiling face close to mine, "where ya from?" She was about eighteen and slender, with blonde-brown hair and remarkably fine skin, and small breasts that caught the light fabric of her tunic as she shifted toward me on the stool.

She had the waif-hippie look and from her skin, at the nape of her neck where the tunic slid down toward her shoulder, came a hint of . . . patchouli oil or some other sixties scent.

"What?"

"Where ya from?"

"Oh, yes, from. Um, Canada. Alberta actually. Edmonton."

She smiled.

"Do you know Edmonton?"

"Never heard of it," she smiled.

It turned out she was a musician, a violinist, and had just been jamming with the guitarists. I asked her what kind of music she played.

"Gypsy music. It's wild, I'm getting really far, I just do my own thing—African drummers, you know, it gets crazy—it's hard for me to play the way these guys do. In fact Tom told me after that I should work on my minor-seventh scale. Scales!" She frowned then laughed, "and I sing."

She looked at me intensely (green eyes, large and luminous—drugs? tinted contacts? what was she saying?).

"Do *you* play anything?"

Yes, yes, oh god yes anything you want.

"No, not really. A little guitar, like . . ." *was that her knee touching mine under the counter?* "like everybody does," I gasped.

Holy mackerel, how was I going to handle this? I mean who knows what kind of person she is. What about diseases? And besides I'm in a committed relationship. Steady.

"Do you live in Durango?" I asked.

"Sort of. I go away when it gets cold. Last year to Oregon, that wasn't so great. The year before to the South Pacific—Hawaii— that was *wonnnnderfull*." She riffed on the word. "This year I want to go to Central America, but I just found out the immunization shots cost $300. *Three hundred dollars!* That's like . . . wow . . . I don't know . . . I was going to hitch to the border and take trains and buses, but now . . ."

Hitch? *Hitch??* I thought I'd gotten used to these time warps. There were two VW vans out front with the side doors open, people and dogs lazing out onto the sidewalk. Fine. But hitch? Nobody did that anymore. An attractive woman, alone? You can't do that these days.

She was still talking, "Being a musician is great because you really connect with people. People want to get into you, to find out what makes you tick."

"Hmmmm."

Was she crazy? A victim of systematic abuse who now hated her lovely body and offered it to strangers in return for rides?

And what did she want with me? This strange violin-playing psycho gypsy with the incandescent eyes. Maybe she lured strangers into the back of her van and chopped them into bits and fed them to her dog called Freedom.

"What's your name?" she asked.

I told her and she told me hers—Lenore, or something. She slid off the stool.

"I've got to go," she said, "got to get some sleep." She paused and yawned beautifully. "It's been nice talking to you, Ted. Have a good trip." Her fingertips touched me between the shoulder blades as she passed by, then she was gone.

"It's probably done by now," said the guy behind the counter.

"Huh?"

"Your laundry—you asked me about the Laundromat. It's proba- bly done."

"Right." As I carried my clean laundry back through the hotel lobby, the young clerk wasn't on anymore but that was okay. I didn't feel like Brando anymore.

SIX

Taos Tangle

I coffeed up at the Durango Coffee Company just across from the Strater Hotel, letting their Italian roast root out all those morning fuzzies the toothbrush hadn't got. At Pagosa Springs I cut south, onto the little gray line on the map, a winding road leading up over the 10,000-foot Cumbres Pass, perfect for a high-speed blast. But I felt dozy, with nothing to prove, and plonked along at 50 miles an hour, reminded of how pleasant it can be to not take it to the limit, to ride at the speed limit on an empty curving road. My instincts were right this day: I came over a hill straight into the radar of a state trooper. And smiled as I passed legally by.

Once I crossed into New Mexico all the names on my map turned Spanish—Tierra Amarilla, Tres Piedras, Arroyo Hondo. In Taos I pulled into El Rincon, a B&B with a blobby faux-adobe exterior. Where the Strater Hotel in Durango had heavy Victorian fabrics, this room had hard tiles and bright yellow walls. The special at all the small restaurants from here on south would be the enchilada platter, not Salisbury steak. I took my notebook next door to the Caffe Tazza, ordered a coffee, and started to make notes on the day's ride. There should be a word for enforced eavesdropping, for conversations you don't sidle up to but have thrust upon you. A couple at the next table were talking, or rather the man was talking, a weaselly character, balding up from the forehead, in a brown leather jacket, waving long fingers to punctuate his monologue. He was a poet, his name was Ron, and he was telling his friend, loudly enough that the whole café had to hear, how he had gotten the jacket from his alcoholic fiddler buddy who was a *way* better cartoonist than any in *The New Yorker*.

"I've noticed that about alcoholics," the woman murmured, "they don't hang on to stuff." Another feral-looking guy joined them, and the conversation turned loudly to karma and personal energy, in earnest up-cadenced sentences.

"I know this guy? And he can't wear wristwatches? Even toasters don't work when he's around?"

"Energy. Man, I've got it too. I put out streetlights all the time?"

For all the New Age trappings, the scenario was old: verbal arm-wrestling to impress the girl. I wondered if there was enough daylight left to ride up to the D. H. Lawrence ranch. "Oh sure," they told me at El Rincon. "It's only five miles."

WHAT THEY DIDN'T TELL ME is that it's five miles of steep, bumpy gravel. The Ducati gets A++ in the canyons, but as a dirt bike it rates only a B–. The big rear tire that grips on tarmac glissades on loose gravel, and skitters over the chatter bumps made by cattle trucks braking for corners. The shocks, made for responsive cornering on pavement, resent clomping through deep potholes. After a couple of miles my wrist bones were being ground to powder.

I tried to remember my one off-pavement lesson. My friend Dave and I had been riding up from Calgary, taking back roads to avoid the freeway, when we hit a long stretch of road construction with gravel the size of baseballs. This was nothing to Dave, who had spent his teen years on a Husqvarna dirt bike charging down cut lines near the family cabin at Devil's Lake. My only experience with off-roading had been a short driveway.

"You'll be fine. Just remember three things. One, put all your weight on the pegs. Don't stand up, but lift your bum a couple of inches. That lowers the center of gravity from seat height to the level of your feet. Two, hold the bars loosely. The front wheel will wobble, but if you let it move a bit it will be okay. Try to hold it tight and you'll slide out for sure. Third, look at the horizon. Look down and you go down."

"Are you sure that will work?"

"Absolutely," he said. "Hey, and if it doesn't, at least you crash looking at the horizon. Anyway, we won't be going very fast. I used to come off all the time on my Husqvarna. It's just like falling on a mountain bike. And your Ducati is light—we can easily pick it up."

But it'll be scratched. "Okay, sure, no problem."

The technique worked, and it worked here on Mount Lobo as well. The bike squirmed like a three-year-old at a shopping mall, but it never got out of control. My quads started to quiver, so I sat down and just pressed through the footpegs, and then finally relaxed into the bike, as much as I could, confident that in spite of the wobbling it wasn't going to play any tricks on me. I even braved a quick wave at the cattle truck that passed me going down.

At the top I creaked off the bike and found myself alone at the log ranch house feeling the sharp bite in the air that comes when you get above 8,000 feet. I had the place to myself. The house served as a writers' retreat, and signs reminded you that this was a private residence. They didn't want people peering in the windows. I was glad that the ranch, now owned by the University of New Mexico, was still a place for writers.

The Lawrences had come here in 1922 at the behest of the very rich and much-married Mabel Sterne/Dodge/Luhan. (This much I already knew; later in Austin I would wander from my appointed research into the manuscripts of Lawrence's Taos writings, and the background of his New Mexico visit.) With an income of US$14,000 a year—when a U.S. Senator made half that amount—and a passionate will, Mabel was used to getting what she wanted. What she wanted with Lawrence was to "seduce his spirit," to get him to take "*my* experience, *my* material, *my* Taos, and formulate it all into a magnificent creation"—though she had not yet actually met the writer. Enraptured by his travel book *The Sea and Sardinia,* she wrote him a long scroll of a letter, enclosing a necklace for his wife, Frieda, and Indian herbs to conjure him. Lawrence, replying from Sicily, was intrigued but cautious, worried that Taos might house "a colony of rather dreadful sub-arty people." Yet, he concluded, seeming to make up his mind firmly just in the writing of the letter, "I like the *word*. It's a bit like Taormina." Lawrence agreed to come, though he got cold feet and came the long way round, from Sicily to Ceylon to Australia. Finally he reached Taos, and Mabel got more, and less, than she bargained for.

I strolled over to the homesteader's cabin where Frieda and Lawrence had lived. Mabel initially dismissed Frieda as "the mother of orgasm . . . no more" and saw herself as the superior muse. But the boisterous, abrasive, and aristocratic Frieda—cousin of the Baron von Richthofen—proved as strong-willed as Mabel (who did observe Frieda had "a mouth like a gunman"). Relations among them all deteriorated and before long Lawrence, weary of Mabel's passionate conversation, was communicating only by note. They left in the spring of 1923 and came back a year later. Mabel, recognizing this time that they all needed some distance from each other, gave Lawrence and Frieda the ranch. The distance was welcome but brought its own complications. Frieda and Lawrence, wary of any obligation to Mabel, gave her in return the manuscript of *Sons and Lovers*. Just so that Mabel could not be mistaken about the value of the gift, Frieda wrote to her that the manuscript was worth more than US$50,000—much more than the US$1,200 Mabel had originally paid for the ranch.

It turned out that the manuscript valuation was merely the opinion of Swinburne Hale, a poet who had come to Taos to be with family following a nervous breakdown. He later went mad. Lawrence himself put the value of the manuscript at between $3,000 and $4,000—and even this was probably high: in 1937, seven years after his death, the manuscript of *The Rainbow* went for $3,500. In any case, the point was not lost on Mabel who noted in her memoir that the gift had "a sting." She later gave the manuscript to her psychoanalyst A. A. Brill (a student and translator of Freud). For Lawrence, the whole unpleasant wrangle alerted him to the value of his manuscripts and he now began to consider their monetary, as well as aesthetic, value. He wrote to his publisher, Thomas Seltzer, asking him to put all his manuscripts in a safety-deposit box. It intrigued me that the *Sons and Lovers* manuscript, which scholars would revere as a sacred document and pore over for portents of the great art that emerged from it (as I had been doing with Woolf's *Jacob's Room* manuscript), was for the writer the equivalent of a wad of currency, a stack of bills to fling at a presumptuous patron to discharge a debt.

On this second visit they also brought Lady Dorothy Brett, the only one of Lawrence's friends to take up his offer to form a utopian society in Taos. Lawrence and Frieda lived in the three-room home-steader's cabin and Brett bunked in a tiny one-room shed.

Brett was an unlikely candidate for ranch life. As a child she had taken dancing lessons under the eye of Queen Victoria, and later studied art at the Slade School in London. She was a friend of Virginia Woolf's and George Bernard Shaw's, and she had just had an affair with the widower of Katherine Mansfield, John Middleton Murry (whom she would meet on her motorcycle down in the country). She was almost totally deaf and went everywhere with an ear trumpet she called Toby. Mabel hated her. With her prominent front teeth, Brett looked like a "paralyzed rabbit" and she was always underfoot, with her "brass dipper swallowing up Lorenzo's talk to me." Frieda, for her part, looked on in scorn as Brett typed up Lawrence's manuscripts in the mornings and helped him move rocks in the afternoons. She began by tolerating and ended by shouting at Brett, reproaching her for *not* having an affair with Lawrence. Frieda could abide sex but not this creeping spinster devotion. Lawrence, inevitably, wearied of her and wrote a story about an aristocratic English virgin who is repeatedly raped by her Mexican guide. At one point Lawrence even accused Brett of stealing his manuscripts and selling them (she hadn't). An odd figure in full cowgirl garb, a stiletto in her boot and an ear trumpet in hand, she nonetheless conceived a real devotion to the West, separate from her feelings for Lawrence.

She bought a house in Taos and spent more than fifty years there, staying active into her nineties before dying in 1977.

THE CABIN WAS LOCKED, so I sat in the wooden chair on the porch and then walked across the yard to the giant pine tree that Lawrence likened to a "guardian angel." I lay down on the bench to look up through the branches, to get the perspective Georgia O'Keeffe used for her famous painting *The Lawrence Tree*. I was half-hoping for a sense of connection with Lawrence, a writer who had always annoyed me and impressed me in equal parts. In *The Plumed Serpent*, Lawrence complains that Mexico is "Either hard heat or hard chill"; there's "No lovely fusion, no communion. No beautiful mingling of sun and mist, no softness in the air. Never." He derided what I embraced. For me the trouble with Britain (or our own West Coast) is that there's nothing *but* fusion. Wet wood rotting into wet ground, water dripping off wet leaves so that even when it has stopped raining it has never really stopped. What I long for are clear, pure, hard seasons. Harsh rains that crash down and then sweep on, edges defined with a knife blade. Bright light on snow, a slab of deep blue sky. Not stark but beautiful: beautiful because stark. I read Lawrence because he made me see. I wanted to fight with him on every page.

The ranch made me think of him differently. Lawrence spent a total of eleven months in Taos over three years. This was not Banff or Yaddo, New York—no luxurious writing retreat. It would have been hard work repairing the chimney, building a porch, chasing Susan the cow. I liked his compulsion to go into the kitchen and do the dishes at other people's houses. Less attractive were the rages in which he hit Frieda and beat the dog, terrifying it so much that it wouldn't come back to the cabin. Still, he would sit under the tree every morning and write at a little table. It must have been brisk; at 8,600 feet, even in June there would sometimes be ice on the water bucket when they woke up.

He wrote most feelingly of New Mexico when he was no longer there. He visited a Hopi reservation to see a snake dance and found it just dirty and depressing. Yet when he was in Italy, looking back, New Mexico had become a magical land. In his wonderful three-page essay (I like Lawrence short, *ristretto;* he has less room to rant) "A Little Moonshine with Lemon," he has been drinking wine, remembering the moonshine he would drink on cold nights at the ranch, and the memory is more intoxicating than either:

> I wonder if I am here, or if I am just going to bed at the ranch. Perhaps looking in Montgomery Ward's catalogue for some-thing for Christmas, and drinking moonshine and hot water. . . . Go out and look if the chickens are shut up warm: if the horses are in sight: if Susan, the black cow, has gone to her nest among the trees, for the night. . . . In a cold like this, the stars snap like distant coyotes . . . the nearly full moon blazes wolf-like, as here it never blazes; risen like a were-wolf over the mountains.

Even the Montgomery Ward catalogue seems exotic now that he is in Italy. The polarities are reversed for Lawrence: Italy seems young, the United States old; it is the ranch, not the Italian town, that is full of ghosts, and the moon in Taos, not the European moon, that blazes like a "were-wolf." He puns on moonshine—at first it's the light of the moon, then it's the real moonshine (the United States is in the grip of Prohibition). In Italy he is drinking vermouth, and the essay ends with him wondering what would happen if he called Giovanni, the waiter, and asked for *"Un poco di chiar' di luna, con cannella e limone,"* literally "moonlight with cinnamon and lemon." He knows his experience doesn't translate, yet it doesn't matter: he has transported us to the ranch, made a voyage out of not being there.

I climbed, short of breath, to the white shrine built by Frieda after Lawrence's death. At the ranch Lawrence had received fan mail and had thrown most of it unread into the fire, but he kept the envelopes to spit into. His tuberculosis was getting worse, though he refused to acknowledge it, insisting that it was bronchial trouble, not his lungs. He died in Venice in 1930. Four years later Frieda had his body exhumed, cremated, and asked Angelo Ravagli, her Italian lover and eventually her third husband, to bring the ashes to the ranch. There they mixed the remains in with the cement for the altar—to foil a plot by Brett and Mabel to scatter the ashes across the desert. But whose ashes? There are stories that the original ashes were left at a train station or at a friend's house or lost en route. Ravagli said later in life that he was worried about getting them through customs and so just brought an empty urn and filled it up in New York. Nobody knows exactly where Lawrence's remains reside. I liked the idea of this post-mortal diffusion, and though Brett thought the shrine looked like "a station toilet," I didn't mind it (I've always admired a well-wrought outhouse). But reading the effusive entries in the visitors' book (every third line testifying to "passion"), I felt even more estranged from the cult of Lawrence, and turned to leave the shrine.

From the top of the white staircase the landscape unfurls through wispy piñon forest, across the purple sage, all the way to the Colorado mountains. The air felt pure, as high mountains always do, yet scented—hot earth, pines, strange smells I didn't recognize— somehow both voluptuous and attenuated. For a moment I felt I was soaring. It was probably just the altitude and low blood sugar. I didn't feel any closer to Lawrence, who seemed irrelevant now, but I knew I would not forget the ranch. Back on the Ducati I juggled adjectives as I bounced down the road. I couldn't nail the feeling; it was like trying to grab smoke.

The judder of a cattle guard brought me back to the ride. I had to watch it, this writing in my helmet. Late in the afternoon I would often write while I rode. Effortless prose that would snarl as soon as I tried to put it on the page. This wriding/riting was dangerous. The editor of *Cycle Canada* told me he often missed exits on Toronto's Gardiner Expressway because he was trying to finish a paragraph. I had a more dangerous problem—my internal writer turned off the depth perception and I wouldn't notice that vehicles in front of me were slowing or had stopped. Another cattle guard clanged under me. Looser rails in that one. The engine was revving hard in second gear, forgotten while my mind drifted. "Sorry," I said to the bike, and shifted up. I had better stop thinking about riding and ride. And get some dinner.

I ATE AT A CHEAP RESTAURANT off the central square, the enchilada platter, and then wandered into the La Fonda Hotel to see the paintings by D. H. Lawrence in the Greek owner's office. Derided as disgusting and obscene, the paintings had been banned in London in 1929 and only escaped burning on the condition that Lawrence never exhibit them again. The desk clerk who let me in was a rough-looking character with an oxygen hose in his nose and a tank on wheels beside him; he still looked tough and talked as if the tank weren't there, running through the spiel he'd given a thousand times. I wondered how many times more he would get to give it before the tubes couldn't keep him going. He took my $5 and closed the door, leaving me to burgle the office if I wanted. I'm sure nobody did; they wouldn't have known where to start. The junk in the office was as fascinating as the pictures—six pairs of identical tasseled shoes against the wall, a framed photo of a huge-breasted woman inscribed to the owner, piles of papers everywhere. The next day I couldn't remember the pictures; what stuck in my mind was the row of tasseled shoes and the guy with the oxygen hose in his nose.

On the way back to my room I passed Caffe Tazza again. A sign out front said, POETRY OPEN STAGE. Why not? I stepped inside. All the tables in the small room were full and a few people were standing. That was good. I leaned against the wall near the door, so I could slip out if things got bad. The mood was Beat rather than Hip; nobody smelled of patchouli oil (in fact a couple of them smelled just plain bad—wet wool and stale sweat), and one guy chanted, shouted, sang his howl against the EnviroEnemies who are turning us all into *"Chemicaaaaallllllssss!"* Ginsberg would have been proud. Next up was Ron, the leather-jacketed poet from this afternoon. When his name was called he left the room and then came slouching in from the street wearing shades and sucking on a cigarette and carrying a little cassette recorder playing Thelonious Monk. This might have been cool, except that the efficient MC, thinking his poet had gone home, had already started making announcements about next week's reading. So Ron had to stop, turn off the recorder, and go back outside. His friends cried, "No he's here, he's here!" The MC stopped, and Ron slouched in again with the same Thelonious Monk riff playing. He shouldered his way through the group of three in the inner doorway, snapped off the cassette, whipped off his glasses (briefly snagging one ear), and looked up from his crumpled exercise book. *"Why do I love you!?"* he shouted.

Who cares!? I wanted to shout back, but I was a well-bred Canadian and this was not my town. Knowing this could only get worse, I slid out into the night. I understood now what Lawrence had feared in Taos.

SEVEN

The Virginian and West Texas 'Dillos

It's a quick ride over the pass from Taos to Las Vegas, on the eastern slope of the Sangre de Cristo range. Las Vegas is a quiet little town, the opposite of its gaudy namesake 600-odd miles due west in Nevada, and I had come here because it was the only place between Edmonton and Austin where I had a contact. My guide was Patti Milligan, a friend of a friend in Alberta, working at the Armand Hammer College outside of town.

"It's part of the United World Colleges, which sounds religious but isn't," she told me. "The founder was inspired by a NATO Defense College meeting back in the 1960s. He felt that the way to bring about world peace was to bring people together, but young people together rather than generals. The first one was in Wales, the second in Singapore, and the third was the Lester B. Pearson UWC of the Pacific, in 1974. There are now ten of these colleges around the world." I remembered wanting to go to Pearson, attracted by the

76

kayaking and hiking and scuba diving, but my grades weren't good enough to apply.

"Outdoor activities are part of it," said Patti, "but the main thing is the cultural diversity. We have 200 students here, and in any given term at least 150 of them are from outside the United States. But come, I want to show you the town."

Las Vegas goes way back. Pueblo Indians settled there in the 1100s and 1200s before being forced out. Coronado cruised through in 1541 looking for gold, and in the nineteenth century more and more Spanish came to settle in the meadows—*las vegas*—at the base of the mountains. (I had thought *las vegas* was Spanish for "slot machine," but no.) In 1835, twenty-nine men got together to apply for a land grant from the Mexican government, and set up a plaza with buildings around it. They had made a good choice: the town was on the Santa Fe trail, and it grew quickly, becoming a hub for trade out onto the plains of eastern New Mexico and into west Texas. But as more rail lines crossed the territory, the prosperity of Las Vegas declined. They got a head start on the Depression, losing four of their six banks in the 1920s and sliding further in the 1930s. It had never really recovered, which was why so much of the old town was still intact.

"It looks like a movie set," I said.

"It was. In 1913 a filmmaker named Romaine Fielding used the hotel as a base while he directed a bunch of westerns. A couple of years later Tom Mix shot a bunch of movies in and around Las Vegas too." We were standing by the bandstand in the central plaza, a delicate structure surrounded by trees and a picket fence, a genteel replacement for the windmill that originally stood here and did double duty as a gallows.

"That's the Plaza Hotel over there," said Patti. "Where everyone goes for their grads. The Romero family—they were the high rollers in the town—built it in 1882." The year James Joyce and Virginia Woolf were born. Las Vegas would have seemed like another planet from upper-middle-class Dublin or London. "The Romeros wanted it to be the finest hotel in the territory, but this was still the Wild West. Doc Holliday stayed here, and Pat Garrett brought Billy the Kid through the plaza to stay in the Las Vegas jail, which I'll show you in a minute, but first I want to take you to my favorite place, the Victory Bar." We turned our backs on the posh hotel and walked toward a plain white building with an ugly aluminum air-conditioner pod hanging over the front window. Inside it felt more like a diner than a bar, with a short counter and a couple of booths at the back, and a deer head on the wall with a straw party hat on one antler.

Patti introduced me to Rose, a slender woman in a rose suit and big square 1970s glasses. In a big recliner chair at the end of the bar, propped up with a pillow and covered with a thick quilt, sat her mother, a tiny wraith with what looked like a dead muskrat on her head. Patty told me how Rose, a schoolteacher, was the youngest girl in the family and thus expected never to marry and always take care of her mother. Even though her mother was over ninety, every day she insisted on being brought down to the bar. "This was my refuge when things got claustrophobic at the campus. You meet all types here. It's quiet now, but there is a ballroom in the back and when Rose's father owned the Victory it used to be a center for dances.

"Let's walk down the street to Estella's Café. You'll love this building—it'll remind you of Italy."

"Italy?"

"Yeah, there was this vogue for Italian-style buildings. See?" We stopped out front. "They've got those tall, skinny windows on the second floor, with hooded arches over them. Completely different from the Mexican architecture. And this one across the street, it's not as ornate but you can still see the cornices over the windows—it was a jail at one point. They shot the jail sequence in *Easy Rider* here."

Patti explained that we were in west Las Vegas, the Chicano side. "Coming to Las Vegas really changed my perception of the U.S. We tend to think of it as homogeneous, the big melting pot, but there are all these pockets of people who don't fit the mold. When someone speaks of 'wetbacks' it makes you think of people who have just crossed over the Rio Grande, but in fact this is one of the oldest immigrant cultures in the U.S. A little island of Latino culture that has been here for five hundred years. It's still resented, though: there's a strong redneck element in New Mexico. Still, no worse than you find in Alberta. A guy with one tooth who worked for an undertaker tried to pick up a male friend of mine at Rose's bar. The general attitude was 'Let 'em be.' You can learn as much about cultural diversity there as at the college."

Over a Budweiser (no designer breweries here), I said it sounded as though she was going to miss the Victory Bar when she had to go back home. "You know what I'll miss most?" she said. "The smell of chilies in October. After the harvest they roast them in big barrel roasters over the flames and sell them by the sack. The whole town smells wonderful."

WE CROSSED THE SQUARE to Los Artesanos, the bookstore owned by Joe and Diana, the couple who had been her "foster family" when she first came to Armand Hammer College as an undergraduate.

They were now in their early seventies, and though they had been out here nearly half a century they still spoke with New York accents and radiated a Manhattan energy.

They specialized in books about the Southwest, and so I asked about *The Virginian* by Owen Wister. I'd heard about it from my rancher cousin Janet. She lives by herself in a two-room log cabin in central British Columbia and goes out every morning riding herd with a deer rifle in a scabbard by her side. She chops wood to keep the stove burning all night so she doesn't freeze to death, and when she gets into "a bit of a scrape," like having a horse fall on her, she grits her teeth and carries on. She's very beautiful, with long blond hair and a wide smile, and big Bob, the log-house builder over in the next valley, has been courting her for years. She married young to a sweet guy who proved to be an abusive alcoholic and she reckons (she actually says "reckons") that she's better off on her own. She has a mythic stature in the family, and though we call her Calamity Jan we figure she can do just about anything. She reads a lot in the winter, and she had read *The Virginian* nine times. I admitted I thought it was just a movie and could only remember the line "When you call me that, *smile!*" She smiled and told me I better take some time out from that Joyce stuff and read it.

It turned out Diana collected Owen Wister's work. "I like Owen Wister," she said. "He grew up in the East, was educated at Harvard, and then came West, and he threw himself into it completely. What I like about him is he wasn't a snob." Joe checked a card and brought up a copy of *The Virginian*. "We only have a first edition," he said apologetically, "and it's expensive." On the front cover, embossed in red on the tan cloth, was a six-gun in a holster with a rope snaking around it; the letters of the title and author's name were red and edged in gold, and on the spine was a spur with a red strap. Pasted to the inside cover (the "fixed endpaper," I would learn later) was a square of white paper that had obviously been cut from a typed letter, with the signature below in black ink, "Owen Wister." So the book wasn't signed but it included an autograph. I wondered if I could afford it. It had a nice heft and I liked the fact that the edges were worn. It had obviously been read many times. I finally asked how much. Joe looked at me hard through his thick glasses: "$65."

Sixty-five dollars? I thought all first editions cost thousands. "I'll take it," I said. It was too thick to fit in my motorcycle jacket and too frail to jam into a saddlebag, so I had Joe address it to me care of the Ransom Center in Austin. To put the price in context he showed me a catalogue entry for an inscribed edition that was going for $6,500. I learned that Wister's first encounter with the West had come two years after he graduated from Harvard and was sent to a Wyoming ranch to recover from a nervous breakdown. Wister knew the book wasn't perfect, but he knew the effect he was after. He wrote to his English professor, Barrett Wendell, "Yes. Construction is practically nil. Yes. Style bothersome at times. I don't think I mind about the construction. It's meant for a picture rather than a plot, and meant to wander some as the hero & all his kind wander." It worked. The book had been a huge success, reprinted fifteen times in the first eight months, and eventually selling more than a million and a half copies. I wondered if the most compelling myths of a place were constructed by those from outside. President Roosevelt, to whom the book was dedicated, loved it. The blurb, a packed three-paragraph essay, made me want to read the book, though I couldn't see why a copy that sounded just like mine ("lightly soiled, nicked at head; rear hinge loosened") was worth a hundred times more just because it was dedicated to his old professor and came with a letter. Like the tenderfoot narrator of *The Virginian,* I had much to learn.

Joe talked as he wrapped the book, tales of false proxies, water rights, and shifty subdividing Texans. "Santa Fe's ruined," he said flatly. "It's been discovered by Hollywood. A real estate friend of mine told me there were twenty-eight houses on the market between two and four million. Unbelievable! This happens to places. We know some people who were up in Utah, they had a house in the hills but only a half-acre of land. Then Hollywood discovered the area, built weekend places all around them, it was noisy, and, *and* they expected the locals to take care of their places when they weren't there. The real problem is water. You put in more people and soon you haven't got enough water. But you don't want to hear all this." I did; I felt like I was in a western.

"Come and look at the back," said Patti. She led me back down five steps to a snug little apartment with deep wine-colored Navaho rugs on the floor and books lining the high walls. I instantly wanted to live there. "I did," said Patti. "This was my place when they were my family." Patti told me Joe and Diana were getting tired, and starting to think of selling the bookstore.

"Buy it!" I hissed. "If you don't I will."

"I know. I should, but the whole place would need to be reorganized." Joe was typing my address onto the stock card for *The Virginian.* Diana, Patti told me, was a writer and she wanted to buy a computer so she wouldn't have to endlessly retype her drafts. Joe wouldn't allow it. He worked for the school board and had to set up their computer system (he used to be an engineer and "liked fiddling with machines"), but had so many headaches he swore when he quit that he would never touch another computer. He bought six

Underwood typewriters from the school board for $5 each, and spent about $30 each refurbishing them. That's what they were using in the store. "All our records are by hand," he told me proudly. I couldn't imagine doing without the blitzkrieg efficiency of machine searches, but I'd never gotten over my love for card catalogues, the smell of wood and paper, and the feel of the worn cards. I told him I was honored to be in there.

I strode out into the street knowing I had my first First Edition. The plaza had a new brightness and I was walking with a bounce. This was the garage-sale high I'd seen in Hsing, the thrill of the spontaneous purchase. It was exciting, and it seemed important, and it didn't seem like spending money; no, it was more like making an investment.

"I'll buy the drinks," I said as we angled across to the Victory Bar.

As I LEFT LAS VEGAS it smelled like rain. From the outskirts I could see the mountains and the dark purple clouds behind them. The road signs warned DANGEROUS CROSSWINDS and I could already feel gusts. I looked at the table-topped mesa in front of me. "Starvation Peak," Patti had told me, so called because some settlers took refuge from Indian raiders up there; the Indians waited patiently at the bottom and the settlers starved to death. The light and the story made it seem ominous, and off to my right swirling white clouds began boiling out of the purple mass, rolling over the mountain range like waves caught in slow motion, all their swirls defined. Very Georgia O'Keeffe, beautiful and threatening. The road began to curve in that direction, taking me straight into it.

"Maybe it's not actually raining there," I thought hopefully, just as a bright quicksilver line creased the purple mass dead ahead. Lightning. *Am I grounded on a bike?*

"Pull off when it starts to rain," the instructor had said at Safety School. "The road is slipperiest in the first fifteen minutes because the oil on the pavement floats on the water. After it gets washed off, the motorcycle will be stable on the wet asphalt. Be careful, though. If too much water collects in the grooves of the lane you may hydroplane." At that point Hsing and I were still struggling to pilot our bikes around the pylons without killing anyone. Later that month on our first road trip together the rain hit conveniently close to a Tim Hortons. We had some hot tea and changed into our rain suits—me in red, white, and blue, Hsing dazzling in Day-Glo yellow and reflective stripes. "I feel like we've changed into Super Heroes," I said. "I feel like a fire hydrant," said Hsing. I had to admit, as we waddled out to our bikes, that we were about as sleek as one of Tim's apple fritters.

It's bad enough suiting up over dry clothes in a restroom; it's something else at the side of the road when your boots and jacket are wet and your jeans are soaked. "Park under an overpass," the instructor had said, but there was no overpass here. I stopped at the top of a rise, as far into the park lane as I could. I tugged on the nylon pants, then struggled with the jacket that was flapping like an unfurled sail. I didn't want to take off my helmet because the rain was coming hard now and I couldn't turn enough to find the armholes. Finally I got them and turned to the rubber overboots. They looked like big black condoms and they snagged on the toe and on the heel. I hopped around hunched over like Kokopelli—the ancient Indian flute player who was in all the souvenir stores—doing the Dance of the Rain Booties and trying not to stagger into the traffic. I had been cold but now I was in a lather, stewing inside my unbreathable nylon. Finally I pulled on bright yellow dishwashing gloves over my leather gloves

("They're cheap, you can buy them anywhere, and they're highly visible. Just be sure to get extra-large," the instructor had said). The problem was my dishwasher-glove fingers stuck out an inch beyond my hand, so every time I shifted or braked I would have to flap the finger ends out over the lever. Doubling my reaction time. "No sudden movements," the instructor had said. No fear of that. With my big rubber booties I felt as though I had clown's feet. I shifted carefully into first gear, shoulder checked as best I could against the choking Velcro strip of the rain jacket, and wobbled back onto the highway.

I made it just as the hail slashed down. The week before they had had a storm so bad they had to close the highway and shovel the pellets off. Thirty miles to Santa Fe. Ten minutes before, it had seemed like nothing; now I wondered if I'd make it. The hail rattled on my visor and stung like buckshot on my knees (I've never experienced buckshot but I'm sure it would be like this). The grooves in the road began to fill with water, so I rode the crest between them, trying to remember about hydroplaning and wondering whether this was the right thing to do.

I drove a steady 60 miles an hour and the big trucks inched by 5 miles an hour faster, throwing up more spray and taking forever to get past. Cars that I had roared by earlier caught up with me and stared at me as they passed. I started to get chilled. I squinted through my fogged visor at my odometer. On a motorcycle you're outside the frame, and on a sunny day you feel free. But when it rains you're trapped inside your helmet with no defroster and no windshield wiper. Eventually your vision focuses between the raindrops and you adjust the air coming in under the visor, but you're still peering through a porthole. In *Easy Rider* it never rains.

Still 20 miles to go. Twenty minutes. Should I pull off? There weren't any gas stations or any towns. Even if I did find some road-side diner, the time it would take me to struggle out of the rain suit would take me halfway to Santa Fe. I wasn't getting wet, aside from my own rubberized sweat. Still, I looked for a place to pull off and I dreamed of the steaming hot soup the admiring waitress would bring.

I learned long ago that the only way I could accomplish anything was to tell myself I could quit if I want to—that I could quit hiking and set up camp halfway up the pass; that I could quit high school and go work on a tramp steamer; that I could mow half the lawn and do the other half next week. In short, that I didn't have to go the distance. All that inspirational stuff about focusing on your goal and never wavering from it just made me want to open a beer and apply for unemployment insurance. But once I'd decided I could quit, things didn't seem so bad. Then if anyone should say, "Wow, what you're doing is difficult," or even moderately interesting, I would square my shoulders and think, "Pff, a mere bagatelle." It's true I wasn't certain what a bagatelle was (though I suspected there wasn't an actual bag involved), but the books I was reading at the time always linked "mere" with "bagatelle" and it was always some beau-tiful object or difficult exploit that the hero treated as if it were nothing.

Anyway, a Dodge Neon honked at me and I nearly fell off the bike, but the five young people inside smiled and I realized they were giving me encouragement. I squared my shoulders and nodded to them as hard as I could without making the bike wobble. Then a minivan with a family honked and waved, and then a pickup gave me a cheery *beep-beep,* and I felt warmer. It was only 15 miles to Santa

Fe and this wasn't too bad at all. Then a young guy in a scuffed VW
Jetta with a bike rack on the top and "Oakley" and "No Fear" stick-
ers on the back window came by and flashed his lights and gave me
a big wave. I took my yellow-gloved hand off the handlebars and
gave him a jaunty thumbs-up sign. Lightning and hail? A mere
bagatelle.

I REACHED SANTA FE, got gas and directions at an adobe Texaco, and
slopped into the visitors' center. My wet booties, red white and blue
action-hero rain suit, and yellow dishwashing gloves had the clerks
scurrying to help me and they quickly had me out of there and into
a room at the Budget Inn. The rain stopped as soon as I had unloaded
the bike (the rain god is a trickster who loves to torment motorcyclists), and I walked up to the plaza to look at silver and turquoise
earrings for Hsing. I like earrings because they're easy—they're either
short or long, but otherwise they all look alike. The buildings all
looked alike too. Everything was adobe: the gas stations, the motels,
the McDonald's. Taos was the boutique, Santa Fe the theme park.
Yet here too there was the smell of burning pine, the piñon, heavy
on the damp air. It hung over the genuine and the false adobe,
capturing a spirit of the Southwest that couldn't be packaged out
of existence.

At the cappuccino bar the next morning I listened to the guy
behind the coffee machine telling a customer that the air pressure
had dropped so radically that the water would not come through.
This meant it was going to rain, he said. Three times he dumped the
coffee and started again. I figured he had just tamped the espresso
too tight in the strainer and was too pretentious to admit it. A
few pounds of barometric pressure are not going to faze a mighty

Rancilio. Still, he could be right. The newspaper said, "Cloudy with showers in the afternoon."

"That's just a cover," said the woman who obviously owned the place. "That way, if there's ten hours of rain they can say they predicted it." The coffee was fabulous, but the people just barely polite. They had that special resentment-born-of-dependency that sours the air in tourist towns. I missed Las Vegas.

I WANTED TO VISIT the Anasazi ruins at Bandolier, just outside Santa Fe, but I was at that point in the trip where you start weighing options: "If I do this, then I can't do that, and I'll have to motor straight through . . ." I had a couple of big maps, "Western Provinces and States," and "Central Provinces and States," and even one monster that just said USA in big block letters on the front. I consulted them when I needed to make decisions about the general direction I was headed, but mainly I left them in the saddlebags. I would ride all day and have gone only 2 inches on the big map. I had faxed Austin from Durango and cheerfully told my friend Robin, "I'm practically on your doorstep!" I figured this was hyperbole; I didn't know it was just plain clueless.

The space of the Old West was beginning to impress itself on me. Movies and TV shows had made the names familiar but meaning-less—a man might finish his drink in a bar in Santa Fe, New Mexico, and say he reckoned he'd head out to Pecos, Texas, and you'd think, fine. Yet when you ride that space you see how vast it is, more than 300 miles of open desert. The big empty, a space that conceals and exposes. I couldn't imagine looking for anyone out here, but at the same time if a man came by a homestead for food and water he would be remembered, and so if the marshal came along two weeks later and said, "Have you seen anybody?" they would say, "Wahl there was this skinny, pimply faced feller . . ." and the marshal would know he was on the trail of Billy the Kid.

The 300 miles to Roswell felt like 3,000. All day there was a 40-mile-an-hour wind coming out of Arizona and I felt as if I was wrestling with the lat-pulldown bar of a weight machine. After lunch I rode for more than an hour without seeing another car. I didn't see a cow, though the land was fenced. I didn't even get bugs on my visor. Nothing, just the wind and the sage and the yellow-flowered cactus. I honked my horn every once in a while just to feel homey, and talked to myself inside my helmet. "Ain't nobody out here," I told myself, "Nooooobuddy." The day was defined by wind and emptiness.

I did stop in the little towns of Madrid and Carrizozo, and shuffled around the ruins at Gran Quivira, but as in Santa Fe I did not find the New Mexicans particularly friendly. If I mentioned that I was from Canada they would let the statement pass without comment. In Madrid (pronounced *Ma*-drid) I stopped to admire a Kokopelli sculpture in the front yard of a little house. The sculptor came out and we talked about where he had got the stone and how he had worked it, but he wasn't forthcoming. He wasn't hostile; he just answered my questions in short, complete sentences that neatly ended each particular line of inquiry. Polite, but the door stayed closed. Later, reading *The Virginian,* I sympathized with the narrator who gives up trying to make conversation with the laconic hero, sensing, but not quite sure, that there's a sardonic note in the courteous, terminal replies.

In 1947 a flying disc crashed north of Roswell. There were two separate sites, one containing debris and the other a space vehicle with alien bodies. At least that's one story. The U.S. government said it was a weather balloon. Later they admitted that was a cover-up and that the wreckage was a top-secret reconnaissance balloon. Roswell is also the birthplace of actress Demi Moore and the site of the largest mozzarella plant in the United States. I didn't visit any of these things (the crash site, the museum, the mozza plant, the home of Demi Moore); I bought scissors in an all-night drugstore, walking around the fluorescent aisles feeling like an alien myself, and went to the car wash, the heart of America.

I love sitting home alone on a Saturday, but Friday for some reason drives me out to be among people. So I couldn't go back to the motel after buying scissors. I pulled into the bright twenty-four-stall car wash and the friendly ex-marine told me how to get my bike just right, using the final anti-streak spray. I was going to make some excuse for being there—the Monster was just dusty, not dirty— when two Corvettes pulled in that were cleaner than my car has ever been in its life. This was American auto culture, where having your ride *clean,* so clean, is more important than how it handles. That made sense out here, where the closest curve was in Albuquerque. But this wasn't about logic, I realized as I bought a chamois and wiped the water droplets off my tank, the backs of my mirrors, the front forks and fender; it was about showing respect, about the ritual adoration of the machine. Saturday night was date night, Friday night was car night. As I pulled out from the clean well-lit bay into the dark street, I didn't feel lonely anymore. The camaraderie of the car wash.

IN THE MORNING at Fast Jack's, the cafeteria-style eatery at the turnoff to Carlsbad Caverns, I picked up the *El Paso Times.* The headline for the lead editorial read, "Concealed Handgun Permits Lead to a Variety of New Bans." Sounded good to me. Canada was wrestling with new gun laws too. Then I read on. "What's the use?" complained the writer. "Businesses may prohibit the carrying of guns in the work place . . . the carrying of guns could be banned on transit systems and at country parks.. . ." These were obviously terrible developments, proof the country was going to hell and that individual rights counted for nothing. And this editorial wasn't about handguns in general, it was about concealed handguns. Presumably you were free to brandish a weapon anywhere—in the workplace, on buses, in country parks—you just couldn't hide it in your pants. I wanted to hightail it back to Canada, where when you say someone is "carrying" you mean they're with child, not packing a .44 magnum. Yet the Texans turned out to be the friendliest people I had ever met, and I never did see a gun.

After visiting Carlsbad Caverns, and paying homage to El Capitan, right on the Texas–New Mexico border, I headed south on Highway 54 to Van Horne. I wanted to stay true to my resolve to take smaller roads, though it was dead straight on the map, with "Salt Flats" marked on the east side, and no towns, no green patches to indicate parks. It looked as though I would be turning away from the Guadalupe Mountains and heading into flat desert. Ugly.

But no, the mountains followed me, curving round and coming closer, enfolding the road on the west. The sharp cliffs of El Capitan disappeared and re-emerged as rounded hills, creased with deep ravines, and covered with green sage. They seemed less like mountains than great sea creatures, rising up through the earth as out of the sea. My map called them the Sierra Diablo, yet they felt protective, not demonic. The late-afternoon shadows were deepening in the clefts between the ridges, softening them further. I stopped the bike, took off my helmet, and felt the silence settle round me. It was windless and warm, so still I could hear my own breathing: strange, after the roar of the bike; strange too because in the mountains the air, heating and cooling, moves always. Not here, not now.

It was absolutely still. Just me and the sagebrush and these friendly protective hills. Sometimes when traveling you are braced for an arduous passage and instead you stumble effortlessly into beauty. A gift. I looked east, at the desert rolling away from me to the horizon, unbroken by any building or road. I imagined a lone rider, sweat-stained and parched, slowly crossing this land, heading south to Van Horne, or perhaps heading into the embrace of the cooler mountains. The land had not changed in a hundred years, maybe a thousand.

I looked down at the spiky plants, the rough soil, and knew that this country would kill me in short order if I strolled out alone without a water bottle. *Harsh,* the bean-counter part of my mind told me. *This is a dangerous landscape. You are low on gas in a harsh and deserted land. You should be apprehensive.* It didn't work. I turned back toward the mountains, stunned by the peace and loveliness and harmony of it all. No one had told me the desert was like this.

Let's go! Do you want to get caught out here after dark with no gas and no water? I didn't care. I didn't care. I wanted to gaze all day, drink it in through my retinas, through the skin on my face, the soles of my boots.

Finally the moment passed, or it released me, and I climbed back on the bike and motored slowly on, curving through the Baylor Mountains and the Beach Mountains, into Van Horne.

THE NEXT DAY, my last on the road, I zoomed through west Texas on the straight, empty back roads, singing Tom Cochrane's road anthem in my helmet, "Life is a Hiiiiighway, And I want to riiiiide it. All. Night. Long. Gimme Gimme Gimme Yeah!" Luckily, I never hit anything. The biggest dangers in west Texas are the buzzards—they flap slowwwwwly off the roadkill like a fully loaded 747.

"If you hit 'em in your truck, they can take out a windshield," a Texan told me. "Hit one on a motorcycle at a hundred, and it would probably take your head off."

The other things to watch out for are the armadillos . . .

"When they're scared, they don't run. They jump straight up, and their shell is so hard it'd flip a bike jest like that."

And the tarantulas . . .

"Wahl, they won't hurt you, but in migratin' season they stretch for miles. In a truck ya jest go over 'em, and you can hear the *crunchcrunchcrunch* as ya squish 'em. Trouble is, the road gets real slimy. On a bike you'd slide out for sure."

I only ever saw one tarantula on the road and avoided it easily.

"Then thar's the killer bees . . ."

Right. So much for folk wisdom. My source was Jim Haule, a Woolf scholar who lived down on the Rio Grande, but who hailed from Detroit and liked to josh the newcomers to the Lone Star State.

Non-riders would always ask me, "Don't you think motorcycling's dangerous?" in the tone of a foregone conclusion. It could be, I agreed, but I was a conservative rider. Besides, I said, motorcycling is only one of a million ways you can die. You can just as easily go in your La–Z–Boy recliner. In the spring, or when I haven't been riding in a long time, I have a moment of fear thinking about what I'm going to do, but as soon as I'm up and riding, I'm fine. I would give the answer my father gave when people asked him, "Isn't mountain climbing dangerous?" "Sure," he said, "but at least you go doing something you like." Then in *The Stone Diaries* I read about a Canadian journalist named Pinky Fulham who was crushed to death when a soft-drink vending machine fell on him. He had been rocking it back and forth, trying to dislodge a stuck quarter. Apparently eleven North Americans per year are killed by overturned vending machines. The next time I approached a vending machine I did so warily. And the next time someone asked me about bikes being dangerous, I told them about Pinky.

I had traveled 3,700 miles without a hitch. I would be in Austin in an hour. I was exultant, incredulous, and apprehensive. At the start of any journey there's the stage of peevish resentment at the whole project. Home feels good, the routine comforting, friends especially dear. That fades once you're launched, but at the end, as the destination approaches, the anxiety rises. On the road it is so simple because you think only about the next town, the next meal. Traveling itself becomes the job, the road the destination. Tomorrow I would be back at work and, though I knew I would soon find the groove, as I merged with the traffic on North Loop, life seemed infinitely complex.

I stopped to get gas on South Lamar and the temperature read 90 degrees Fahrenheit with 90 percent humidity. My head felt like a steamed dumpling inside my helmet.

"Yer lucky," said the garage attendant. "It's finally started to cool off."

PART TWO

Have Laptop, Will Travel

EIGHT

ReCovering *Ulysses*

I had booked a B&B in a district called Hyde Park. It seemed such a British name for a place so unlike England, and I asked the pump jockey hesitantly if he knew it. "Yes sir, ah sure do," he said. "This here's Lamar, and it winds up along Shoal Creek. You just stay on it till you hit 38th, turn right, and you'll hit Speedway. Y'all have a good day sir." I liked his enthusiasm, and would learn that it was part of Texas. The next day when I asked in a drugstore if they carried ink cartridges for my fountain pen, the clerk said "We sure don't!" with such cheer I thought for a moment it was a good thing.

Speedway sounded like a racetrack but turned out to be a quiet street with large oak trees that arched into a canopy overhead and restored Craftsman-style houses that dated from the 1920s and earlier. I found the address and turned into the driveway. By the time I had turned the bike off and unclipped the saddlebags, the landlady— Martha—was waiting for me in the shade of the broad porch.

"Y'all must be hot, bein' Canadian and all. Would you like some ice water?" Wonderful. "Your room's right through there." My room turned out to be several: first a sitting room with broad-planked floors and a Persian carpet, furnished with a brocade couch, two wingback chairs, a Tiffany reading lamp, and an escritoire. A big ceiling fan rotated lazily, and unnecessarily—the house had central air-conditioning. Then the bedroom with its cast-iron bedstead, a small oak writing desk, and high windows with louvered shutters that looked out onto a green corner of the front yard. I realized I hadn't seen a swatch of deep green since the Guadalupe Mountains and it felt cool on my corneas. Finally the bathroom, with two sinks and counters big enough to sleep on. The bathroom alone was bigger than the motel rooms I had been staying in. I wanted to stay forever.

I took off my leather jacket and hung it on the chair, noticing it was covered with bugs. I should have scrubbed it off at the gas station. My boots were dusty and I could feel my hot dank socks bunched up inside. I wondered if I should change.

"No, y'all come in here and sit down. This here's my friend Mary More Grit."

"Pleased to meet you, Mary," I said.

"Mary More Grit," she said.

Okay.

"What do you do, Mary More Grit?"

I thought "more grit" was what John Wayne had. Mary's Texas twang was broader than Martha's, and combined with the road buzz still echoing in my ear it was hard to understand. She was a social worker, I got that much. They could tell what I was just beginning to figure out, that I was exhausted. You never really know until about twenty minutes after you've gotten off the bike just how bagged you are. The ice water was fabulous. A big fluted-glass tumbler with lots of ice, beads of condensation making the outside cool and slippery, rimming the outline of my fingers.

I sank into the big burgundy couch and listened to them talk. Martha had "just turned fifty-nine for the second time," and though she had gone through a crisis after her husband, Hubert, died, she was doing fine now. I learned that she loved food, poetry, and jazz. Wallace Stevens had sustained her over the last few months, that and the bread pudding at the Hyde Park Grill, and the gospel brunches around town. Hubert had been an engineer for Motorola and played sax in a jazz band on the side. Martha had widow's benefits but worried that her medical insurance was going up. The buzzing in my head subsided and my ears adjusted enough to the accent that by the time Martha's friend got up to leave I said, "Nice to meet you, Mary-Margaret," in a normal accent.

"Whoa! Say 'about the house,'" she said.

"About the house."

"*Aboot* the *Hoose!*" she cried, "Ah luv thet Kyanajun icksint!"

"Pardon? Oh, yes."

We said good-bye to Mary-Margaret, and from the porch Martha saw the Ducati. "Wow, I've never seen a bike like that! It looks like a little demon!" she said, which confirmed her good character. She told me I could park it in her garage.

"It's pretty full of stuff from yard sales. Not all of it's mine. My friend Susan is kind of an addict and she puts stuff here so that her husband won't find it. But Hubert had a motorcycle and I just sold it so there's a space here."

I asked what kind.

"Oh, nothing like yours. It was an old Triumph, a Bonny-ville I think it was? Do they have one like that?"

They did. My heart was starting to thump.

"Yeah, he loved that bike. Took real good care of it. Hardly rode it. But I couldn't bear to keep it around after he died. I never did ride on it."

I didn't want to know but had to ask: "How much did you get for it?"

"Well you know, it's funny about that. I phoned a motorcycle shop and asked them how much it was worth and they said for an old bike like that probably about $1,200. Hubert seemed to think it was worth something, but I didn't know, so I put it in the newspaper and the first afternoon this young man came around, and offered me $1,000. I said no, and we settled for $1,100. He gave me cash right there."

"I bet he did." I was making moaning noises on the driveway.

"Is that low? You know, that young man he never even drove it. Didn't start it up. That's what I thought was funny. He said he was going to ship it to Britain and sell it there."

"Where it would get at least $10,000 if it was in half-decent shape." I hated this rip-off artist who had gotten there first, and tried to concentrate on fitting the Ducati in beside a big chest of drawers.

"Oh it was perfect. Hubert sent away for parts . . ."

"Just stop. Martha, this is the scenario motorcyclists dream of—the widow, the vintage bike, the unbelievably low price."

"Well, you never mind. Maybe we'll find another one. Now come inside and I'll fix you a salad."

This felt good. Garage space for my bike, writing space for me, and a landlady who already felt like a friend. "Do you like music?" she said as she made the salad. "Austin's full of music."

I told her I'd been to Antone's, the famous blues club. That was good, she said, but I had to go to Threadgills ("the old one, out on what used to be the highway to Dallas, where Janis Joplin used to play"), to the gospel brunch at Stubbs ("the first roadhouse in Austin. You have to hear the Bells of Joy, some of them are getting old and won't be around much longer"), to the Continental Club across the river in South Austin ("If you like Django music there's this band called 8 ½ Souvenirs . . ."). She brought me the salad. I would learn that this and waffles from a Texas-shaped waffle maker was all Martha ever cooked. She hated cooking. "And do you like margaritas?" Not really, I admitted. "Well, we'll see after we go to Manuel's. They make the best margaritas in town and the appetizers are all half price for happy hour. You can make a meal out of them. Ceviche, and chicken mole, and gorditas, and blue crab nachos."

THE NEXT MORNING I chose a white shirt and tan cotton pants from the suitcase I had shipped ahead. Strange not to have just one shirt for the day and one for the evening. These were my clothes but my body felt different in them. The street shoes had laces and felt weird on my feet as I walked the half mile to the research center. My stride had changed and for the first block I carried my briefcase out from my leg like a motorcycle helmet.

I had been to the Harry Ransom Center once before. All the big names were there and, equally interesting, the papers of lesser-known writers, literary agents, and publishers. At most archives, you look at one set of documents related to your project and then move on to another library. At the Ransom Center, an obscure reference in one file could lead you to a whole other archive, and then another and another, all contained in the five-floor, windowless building. It looked forbidding, a giant white-marble cube with gun-slit windows for the offices. British archivists hated the Ransom Center. Against Ransom's oil-cash reserves in the 1960s, resistance had been futile and Ransom had assimilated all the best literary manuscripts. Bad enough that the British literary heritage flowed to the United States, but this institution wasn't even Harvard or Yale. Texas was off anybody's cultural map. That was forty years ago. Now, for modernism, Austin was at the center.

The center may have looked like a fort, but the reading-room staff had an expansive Texas hospitality that made anyone who had worked in other archives nervous at first. The curators made it a point to find out what you were working on, and instead of handing out the documents with a squinty sideways glance as if you were a thieving impostor who had not yet been exposed (the way the clerks did in the British Museum Library), they would suggest other materials that could be useful. Every Wednesday the Ransom Center held a "Scholars' Coffee," and at 10:00 A.M. everyone in the reading room, staff and visitors, trooped dutifully across to the administration wing to eat coffee cake and drink watery coffee. I hate enforced jollity, yet these occasions somehow worked. Scholars and reading-room staff did talk to one another, exchanged ideas, developed working friendships. A genuine intellectual community.

The director, Tom Staley, circulated at these events, working the room like a professional diplomat. "Ted, here's someone you've got to meet. He's the best. . . ." Tom could sum up your career in a line and make it sound fabulous. He would grab you by the arm, steer you into position, and move on. He knew what everyone was doing, and at a certain point he would invite you to lunch at the Faculty Club. A spider luring you into his scholarly web. It seemed innocent enough. We drove the two blocks because Tom had a habit of picking up others along the way, cramming them into his black Volvo, and at the Faculty Club he asked us each in turn about our work. He would ask the question and then pay no attention to the answer. He wouldn't even look at you, he would be scanning the club like an air traffic controller, looking for new arrivals, hailing them with one arm then another, like someone doing sema-phore, talking all the while with his mouth full of food—"Fred! *Good* to see you! Get over here, how's that thing goin'. . . ?" while you mumbled about your research project. By dessert you felt like an idiot.

"You all get yourself some dessert. They've got great desserts here." Tom never had dessert. When you got back he was moving away the remaining cutlery and getting his elbows on the table. Tom's cronies had decided to walk back to the library, leaving him and the unsuspecting scholar who thought he or she was getting a free lunch.

As a young man Staley had spent a year in Italy working on James Joyce, and he had produced articles and books on other writers. Now he seemed too well turned out to have ever been a scholar. He wore trim blue blazers, and kept his hair short and neat. I couldn't place the look until I remembered an old TV show, *The Man from U.N.C.L.E.*, and the dapper spy handler played by Robert Vaughn. Later I found out Staley idolized Frank Sinatra. Short and crisp-featured, he looked a bit like Sinatra and his style brought out the resemblance. The correspondences were in more than the look: Staley was a performer, an impresario, an entrepreneur, and a gambler; he was also a handler, always seeking out new connections, keeping his network of field operatives happy, bringing in the good stuff.

And underneath the genial glad-handing you sensed the quick temper, the ruthless streak, and the power. You were meant to. He allowed himself a flash of exasperation at some setback, nothing to do with you, but fierce enough that you wanted to make sure you kept the genial persona in place. And so he got work done, lots of it, and lots of money for the center.

I remembered my first encounter. I had asked Tom why no current publisher of *Ulysses* had produced that beautiful blue cover of the original and, instead of giving me the quick answer I expected, he said we would do lunch.

"So tell me again about your book cover idea," he said.

"Oh, it's not an idea, just a question. Why don't they copy the first edition's cover? Students love it, everybody loves it. And in a way it's part of the book. Joyce said himself that the blue represents the Aegean Sea, and then in *Finnegans Wake* he refers to that "ulyssessly unreadable blue book of Eccles"—it's *Ulysses* and Bloom lives on Eccles Street but the blue book is lost. But you know all this." I realized I was babbling. Staley was one of the original founders of the James Joyce society.

"Ted, this is a great project."

What? "No, it's just a question, not a project."

"I think this is very interesting and you should pursue it."

"No, but . . . see, I don't know anything about this sort of thing. I asked Murray Beja in an e-mail and he said he didn't know and that I should ask you." (Murray Beja was the current president of the James Joyce Foundation and an old friend of Tom's. I've wondered since if he set me up.)

"Murray's great! How *is* Murray? You have a look at those covers. You can write it up and we'll print it in *Joyce Studies Annual*."

"But I'm leaving tomorrow. And there's this other editor who's going to, well, he's going to kill me if I don't get this Woolf edition done. I can't take on another project."

"The reading-room staff will give you all the help you need. They're great people. Just great. Do you know Ken?"

"No, really Dr. Staley, Tom . . ."

"Then talk to Robin in the editorial office. She's wonderful. You've met Robin Bradford?"

"Yes."

"Good. Then it's settled."

I wasn't quite sure what had happened. It seemed that by admitting I knew Robin I'd agreed to take on this project.

"I'm just going to talk to Joe here for a minute and then we can drive back."

"That's okay," I said, feeling slightly desperate, "I'll walk."

"All *right* then." He smiled warmly and shook my hand. "I'm looking forward to this."

I went back and filled out a call slip. I felt sick. I had made a solemn vow to myself not to take on any project—no articles, no book reviews, nothing—until I had finished this edition. My Woolf editor was going to send a man around to break my kneecaps if I didn't get it done. It was already, well, months . . . could it be years? I wouldn't even name to myself how much it was overdue. I had perfected the Zen art of academic denial. I put that project back in the zone where time had no meaning, and looked at the fistful of call slips I was holding.

"Do I have to fill out a separate slip for each book if I'm just getting different editions of the same work?" I asked the new intern on the desk.

"Well, I'm not sure, I don't think so, but Pat's out for lunch."

"Great," I said. I wrote out the slip for *Ulysses* and the call number PR 6019 and in the box for "edition" I wrote "ALL," and put it in the box. Then I went over to the editorial offices of *Joyce Studies Annual*. I had met Robin at one of the Scholars' Coffees. She was slender with short dark hair and her chin tilted slightly upward in easy laughter and ready defiance. "I'm a writer," she had said when I first met her, as if daring me to deny it. She had won an O. Henry Prize for one of her short stories and was trying to find a New York agent for her novel. She was a brilliant editor but worried about pouring all her energy into midwifing other people's projects.

"Robin, what am I supposed to do? There must be at least, I don't know, probably ten editions of *Ulysses* and Dr. Staley thinks I'm going to do this article. I just wanted to ask him about the blue cover and now I have to do this and I'm not even sure what he expects me to do. He didn't give me any real indication."

"Don't worry about it. He won't tell you what to do. Just do it."

"What do you mean?"

"He does this all the time. He does this to everybody. Staley's genius is that he can see the outline of a project. He sees something here," she put her hand down on the desk, "and then says, take it to here," she put her other hand down on the desk. The hands were about a yard apart. "He doesn't get hung up on the details in between. He lets you figure it out."

I went back to the reading room and found Ken, the reading-room supervisor (who, with his broad belly, wide suspenders, and "aw-shucks" manner, seemed like a Southern sheriff) calming an agitated young intern. She looked at me, sniffed, and strode through the swinging door into the back. What had I done?

"Whaale, Ted," said Ken, "It's like this. . . ." He explained that the Ransom Center had over three hundred editions of *Ulysses*—seventy-five first editions alone, plus other later rare editions and forty-two translations, in addition to every trade edition published. "So when you filled out that call slip and asked for 'ALL,' it kinda generated a typhoon back in the stacks." Ken had come back from lunch, calmed things down, and taken the liberty of making up a representative sampling of their *Ulysses* holdings. A first installment of thirty editions was on the "truck" (the narrow triple-shelved wheeled cart with a spine on the top so that books can be placed upright) and being brought out as we spoke. Clearly I had tested the Ransom Center's commitment to serving the scholar. I thanked Ken and moved the truck over to one of the broad tables. Where most libraries would let you have only one book or document at a time, the Ransom Center let you have three at your table, and you were allowed to go back and forth to your truck on your own, able to actually look at them instead of trying to divine from a brief catalogue description what you needed next. However, because I wanted to compare the covers, they were letting me take the whole load back to my table.

MANY OF THE VOLUMES on the cart had been rebound in fine leather; I would look at those later. I reached for one of the plain blue ones. They were big and floppy, and soft like old telephone books. So this was it, the 1922 *Ulysses,* what I would have seen in the window of Shakespeare & Co. bookshop, if I could have pushed through the crowd that cool morning of February 2, 1922. Sylvia Beach, the daughter of an American missionary, had moved from Princeton to Paris, taken a lesbian lover, opened a bookstore, and became as devoted to Joyce as her father was to the Lord. She had gambled the resources of her store on this banned book, and rushed the printer, Maurice Darantiere, to send three advance copies up from Dijon on the train so that the superstitious Joyce could have the book on his birthday.

I ran my fingers over the famous white letters. The serifed type itself was lapidary, part of the chiseled simplicity of the whole design, giving the sense of stone in sea. The quest for that Greek blue was itself Homeric: Sylvia Beach had hung a Greek flag outside the bookshop during the preparation of *Ulysses,* promised to urgent subscribers for October but not delivered until February, and Joyce insisted that the blue of the cover be exactly that blue. A match could not be found and finally the flag itself was sent to American artist Myron Nutting, who mixed the exact color for Darantiere to copy, who then had to travel to Germany to find the right blue, and then, because the paper was wrong, had to have it lithographed onto the cardboard covers. I spread the editions out on the table. The shades varied from a pale turquoise to a deep, almost navy, blue.

Then I looked at my dog-eared teaching edition, the current Penguin. "Ulysses" was squeezed in between "Penguin-Modern-Classics" and "The Corrected Text." There was a drawing of Joyce's face, looking down, serious and intense, at his own name. Under Joyce the publishers announced, "With a new Preface by Richard Ellmann." Ellmann was a name to conjure with in Joyce studies; this was as close as you could get to celebrity-expert promotion. Like having Arnold Schwarzenegger endorse body-building equipment. Ellmann had done the heavy lifting in Joyce studies, with several critical studies and the definitive biography, heavy with learned footnotes. Finally, at the bottom of the cover, a jaunty little Penguin gazed up at Joyce. Even if the letters had been in the Cyrillic alphabet, this would have marked it as a classic. This cover had everything to do with marketing, little to do with aesthetics.

I worked my way through the various Shakespeare & Co. editions. Lists of typos appeared in the back. Every edition was a "corrected" edition, and the scandalous 1986 Penguin "Corrected Text," the most corrected of all. The new top gun of Joyce bibliographers, a kid named Kidd, had claimed the previous editor, Gabler, had garbled the text, introducing thousands of new errors. Publishers responded by issuing an edition proudly labeled "The Uncorrected Text." I was suitably appalled by it all. I didn't know it yet but Kidd's edition would sink in the bog of litigation with the estate, forgotten as a new Joyce editor (named Rose—Joyce editors seemed to have names that leant themselves to parodic limericks that would circulate mysteriously at conferences) hurled himself on the pyre of Joyce bibliographers with a "Reader's Edition" that presumed to fix Joyce's "mistakes." He corrected the grammar in Molly Bloom's famous closing soliloquy, and was flayed in the usual reviews, and then everyone settled back to await the next sucker. *Ulysses* was the big peak, the Mount Everest of bibliography projects: endlessly enticing, inevitably damaging, often fatal. If you made it back only somewhat battered, you counted yourself lucky.

That was in the future, but I could see the pattern unfolding in the early texts. I picked up one of my favorites, the little gray two-volume Odyssey Press edition, paperbacks that would fit handily in a sports-jacket pocket, one on either side if you needed both with you. Much less daunting than the big Shakespeare & Co. edition, it invites you to take it out of the study and down to a café to read. It has blurbs in three languages (English, German, and

French) on the inside cover and the cities of publication are listed as Hamburg, Paris, and Bologna. You feel cosmopolitan and continental just carrying it. The *flâneur's* edition.

Published ten years after the first, in 1932, it declared, "The present edition may be regarded as the definitive standard edition, as it has been specially revised, at the author's request, by *Stuart Gilbert*." Gilbert was a buddy of Joyce's and so ought to have been an authority. Yet he and the proofreaders managed to miss a boldface headline that should have read "Links with Bygone Days of Yore" and instead made it in as "Links th Bygone Days of Yorwi." I liked these assurances that although the text had been faulty in the past, now the editors had nailed it down. The situation reminded me of Italo Calvino's novel *If on a winter's night a traveller,* where the true version of the novel is always one step out of reach, and the Reader keeps encountering a different first chapter every time he gets his hands on a new copy of the book. No doubt it would please Joyce to know that his text would never be "correct." For one thing, it meant more money. If your edition was faulty you had to buy a new one.

WORKING WITH RECORDS from Sylvia Beach's Shakespeare & Co. bookstore, I kept thinking of how often a pivotal moment in your reading came about from an encounter in a small bookstore—and how seldom in a giant university bookstore, where the book is always tainted with the anxiety of the seminar, the aura of the textbook.

I began tracking bookstores that dealt with Shakespeare & Co. from abroad, such as Mitchell's Bookstore in Buenos Aires. I found an inquiry from Gammel's Bookstore in Austin, whose folksy letterhead proclaimed:

THE OLDEST BOOK STORE IN THE STATE, ESTABLISHED 1877. THE
PROPRIETOR, GAMMEL, WAS BORN IN DENMARK RICH AND GOOD
LOOKING—NOT SO NOW.

I wondered how many copies of *Ulysses* he had sold. I found a
listing for the Alexander Cigar and News in Calgary. Were there
discounts during Stampede week? Like Gammel's, this store sounded
more likely to cater to cowpunchers than collectors. Texas and
Alberta in the 1920s were places off the beaten cultural track. I was
beginning to develop a taste for inquiries that led off the map.

They could lead to strange places. In *The Social Life of Information,*
John Seely Brown and Paul Duguid write of working beside a library
patron who sniffed the bundles of dusty letters as he took them out
of the box. The man was, it turned out, a medical historian documenting outbreaks of cholera. In the eighteenth century, vinegar was
used to disinfect letters to prevent the cholera from spreading, so by
sniffing for vinegar he was able to chart the cholera outbreaks:

> His research threw new light on the letters I was reading. Now
> cheery letters telling customers and creditors that all was well,
> business thriving, and the future rosy read a little differently if a
> whiff of vinegar came off the page. Then the correspondent's
> cheeriness might be an act to prevent a collapse of business
> confidence—unaware that he or she would be betrayed by a
> scent of vinegar.

I liked this: an olfactory subtext.

But the inhalations can be dire. I had a professor who developed
an allergy to the ink in duplicating machines—that old purple ink in

Gestetners that smelled like the purple gum that tasted like soap. She became unable to use the photocopy machine, then she couldn't touch print of any kind and had to read with a pane of glass over her book. The last I heard she had moved to the southern United States, where she lived in an old house built before certain additives were included in paint. From print, she had gradually become allergic to all the world.

WHAT GOVERNS ALL archival events is serendipity. We speak of solid research methods and good detective work, but the real discoveries seem to come from nowhere, to be handed to you, after days or weeks in which (it appears in retrospect) the insight has been perversely denied, as if there were not just the curators but some other power controlling the archives. Reading Tom Wharton's fantastical novel *Salamander* about the infinite book, I came across a reference to a goddess of the archives, Seshat. Had he made up Seshat? Surely I would have heard of her. I had found myself wanting to burn incense at a shrine when the work went well, wondering if I should burn a fatted calf in the parking lot when the files had turned sullen and intransigent. If there was a goddess, I wanted her.

As it turns out there is: Seshat (Sesheta, Sefkhet-aabut, and half a dozen other spellings) was an ancient Egyptian goddess of writing, libraries, mathematics, and architecture, as well as archives. Seshat is the only female deity shown writing (though others are pictured holding a pen), yet she has never received her due. Married to the more famous Thoth, she taught him how to write and he got all the credit—lord of books, scribe of the gods, he represented the heart and tongue of Ra, the major deity, and he, Thoth, spoke the words that resulted in the creation of heaven and earth. Thoth had his own followers and his own temples, while Seshat had none. Seshat, however, was no mere bookkeeper. She wrote the names of the kings on the leaves of the Persea tree (a tall pyramidal evergreen associated with the temple of Ra), and—like the middle of the three Fates in Greek mythology—allotted the span of life.

On some New Age internet sites she is worshipped as the Silicon Goddess, protector of computers and software; some devotees view the internet itself as a manifestation of the goddess. In ancient iconography she is pictured in a close-fitting leopard skin with what looks like a sprinkler coming out of her head, a seven- or nine-pointed star that no classical scholars have satisfactorily explained. (Modern worshippers have argued that this star is a cannabis leaf, but really it only looks like one if you've already been smoking the stuff. Yet she can induce what historians refer to as "research rapture.") Seshat appears to be related to Selquet, also called the "mistress of the house of books": a golden, arch-eyed goddess with a scorpion on her head, an apt emblem of the seduction and the danger of the archive.

Maybe she is the one who judges the readiness of books. Long before encountering Seshat I already had my own superstitions: I believe a book knows when you are ready for it. If you are not, you might as well forget about it. You can buy it, sit down with it, try to read it. If the book doesn't think you're ready it resists. It's as if you're trying to pry it open, to heave open a spring-loaded door, but it snaps shut the moment you slacken your effort even slightly. Sweaty, exhausted, your hair plastered to your forehead, you stagger away.

You put it back on the shelf. The book may even lose itself, so that the next time you look for it—you're certain you put it right there—it's gone. You look where you left it; you know it's in that clump of books you bought at such and such a time, or books on such and such a subject. You check the bookshelves in your office, even though you know you never moved it. You just want a quick quotation, or to check a passage that someone else has referred to. No luck. The book has disappeared itself. You curse. You might even threaten, out loud, standing there in your study, conscious of your ridiculousness should anyone hear. *You come out or I'll kick your colophon from here to next week. I know you're there. I'll rip your* . . . No, you stop at the threat of physical damage; you know it would never believe you, or if it did it would be gone forever. You sidle out of the study, *Okaaay, I'll just go get the LIBRARY copy* . . . You pause on the threshold, giving the shelves one last scan. Nothing. Your bluffs have been called.

The library copy is of course out till the middle of next year (they *know,* they work together), and you manage without it.

Then, when you've forgotten about it, when you didn't even know you needed it, you glance up from your writing, not looking, just raising your eyes as you look for a phrase, and there it is. Right there. Within reaching distance. It may even have edged out to the edge of the shelf. It's a bit scary. You know you looked there. You looked there first. Never mind. This has happened before. You are just grateful.

You take it, it falls obligingly into your hand and flops open to the passage you didn't even know you needed, the passage that crystallizes a month's work. Or you begin at the beginning, and, absorbed, realize now how fine this is, seeing it in a way you never would have a year, two years, ago when you bought the book, before you had become ready in the way you are now. And you would have "read" it, you would have passed your eyeballs over the pages, maybe even made notes on the wrong things and underlined the needless passages, and you would have put it aside, satisfied that you had read it. And missed the essential thing. The book has saved you from this.

They do this all the time. Not always in your study either. They appear at the bookstore when you think you want something else, or at the library, or in a review, or very often through a friend who may not even have read the book. But as you are describing the current log-jam in your writing, the one that has you thinking you should just abandon the project altogether, the friend says, "I heard about a book on that . . ." and you get it (it now materializes easily) and it proves exactly the thing. The book comes when you're ready.

NINE

Archives and Honky-Tonks

Signing with a big publishing firm is like accepting a marriage proposal: suddenly your intimate passion becomes the property of the planners. You wanted this wedding didn't you? Well stand back. In 1934 Joyce dumped Sylvia for Random House and *Ulysses* was whirled away by editors, publicists, and lawyers. For publisher Bennett Cerf this was no labor of love as it had been for Sylvia. It was, he said in his memoirs, "our first really important trade publication. . . . a big commercial book—with front-page stories to launch it." Indeed, they got Joyce's face on the cover of *Time* magazine, where, with his eye-patch turned away from the reader and his one good eye, enlarged by his thick glasses, in the center of the photo, he peers out, wary but pleased. He had made the big time, cracked the U.S. market. *Ulysses* too had come a long way from the simple blue and white Paris edition. The slick jacket sported tall spindly letters that turned the title into an abstract design, making it almost unreadable at first glance, but by this point in its history the book needed no introduction. Tourists had been smuggling it back from France for more than a decade. It was still illegal in the United States, banned ever since an episode published in *The Little Review* had been declared obscene back in 1920. Bennett Cerf knew he could make big bucks if he could get the ban lifted, so in 1932 he invited lawyer Morris Ernst to lunch and asked him if he would fight the case if they could get Joyce to sign with Random House. "We haven't got the money to pay your fancy prices," Cerf told Ernst, but "if you win the case, you'll get a royalty on *Ulysses* for the rest of your life."

Ernst agreed. They plotted their strategy. By the early 1930s *Ulysses* had become a monument of modernism, endorsed by innumerable critics, scholars, and writers, but their opinions were inadmissible in court. Only the book could be judged. So Cerf took a copy of *Ulysses* and pasted in reviews by eminent men of letters such as Arnold Bennett, Edmund Wilson, Ford Madox Ford, and Ezra Pound. Then he arranged for someone to take it over to Europe and bring it back to New York through customs. He had one of his staff go down to meet the boat. It was one of the hottest days in New York that summer and the customs officers were waving everyone through. The Random House man intervened—"I think there's something in there that's contraband"—and insisted that the bag be opened. "Aha!" he said, as *Ulysses* was discovered, but the customs agent didn't want to do anything about it.

"Oh, for God's sake, everybody brings that in. We don't pay any attention to it."

But the man from Random House persisted and called over the chief. He too argued against the seizure, not knowing that he was playing a bit part in a great literary and commercial drama. He should have asked for a piece of the action. The book was duly confiscated, and so it was that this particular copy, with the extra reviews piled inside the cover like one of those giant corned-beef sandwiches that you get from New York delis, appeared in court and Ernst was able to quote from the pasted-in material when he presented his argument.

Ernst arranged the timing of the case so that it would come up when Judge Woolsey, known for his liberal literary opinions, would be presiding. Woolsey spent the whole summer reading the book, listened to the arguments in November, and on December 6, 1933, the same week as the repeal of Prohibition (another nice bit of timing), announced his verdict. Cerf had his presses poised and gave the order for the typesetters to begin work as soon as the phone call came through from the courthouse.

I loved this story, remembered sweltering days in Manhattan, dealing with cranky bureaucrats at the New York Public Library. Cerf was writing years after the fact, and no doubt time and countless after-dinner tellings had smoothed the rough edges off the anecdote, but still it illustrated just how commercial a production this was, from start to finish. They didn't respond to demand after the court case— they created the court case, made it part of the advance promotion of the book. This was publicity you couldn't buy.

All this remains as part of the book. The U.S. edition still has three forewords. First Morris Ernst, with no mention that he was the presiding lawyer. Then Judge Woolsey who declares, "I do not detect anywhere the leer of the sensualist. I hold, therefore, that it is not pornographic." He also states, "It is advisable to read a number of other books which have now become its satellites." *Ulysses* thus officially becomes a book that is impossible to read on its own. Then a letter from Joyce himself, testifying that this is the one true edition. This was no spontaneous effusion: Item 6 of his contract with Bennett Cerf stipulated that Joyce must write a letter of "not less than 300" words in which he authenticated the Random House edition.

I needed a coffee and a shot of daylight; the reading room, though well lit, was windowless. I got my bag and umbrella from the locker, took the elevator down, gave my pass to the security guard, and walked across the street to Dr. Quackenbush's Intergalactic Cappuccino Bar. A student hangout that seemed left over from the 1960s, it featured cheap lunches of beans and rice and a blob of sour cream, and giant bowls of cappuccino. You gave your order then sat at one of the wooden tables until they called your name. "Ted!" It was friendly, and made me feel better when I first arrived and didn't know anyone. This was February, the rainy season, when flash floods ripped out bridges in the countryside and in town the water seemed to fill your shoes when you were just running across the street. Quacks, as the students called it, was warm and steamy from wet coats, and was an extension of the library. It was nice to have someone shout your name, like a friend had come in and hailed you. For the price of a cappuccino they would let you read all afternoon.

I finished my coffee and dashed back through the rain. In the reading room I turned my attention to a squat yellowing paperback. There was no introduction, no declarations by Joyce or the judge at the front. The back was another story: there the ads urged me to buy *Four Way Swappers* and *Whips Incorporated,* books of dirty Irish jokes, and a device called UTHAID that looked like a rocket ship, "designed to help married men with certain sexual problems recapture the joys, bliss and harmony which only happy sexual relations can bring to husband and wife." Ah, I got it: Uthaid—Youth Aid. Fair enough, I thought, *Ulysses* is about a guy who hasn't actually had sex with his wife in ten years. Their home is no abode of bliss. The last page of the book featured an ad for ALL MALE NUDES!

Seeing all these different editions together I was beginning to get a sense of how the physical book would change your reading of the text. I didn't know the term yet, but what I was doing was reading the "paratext," the elements surrounding the text—cover art, blurbs, prefaces, introductions—all of those "thresholds," as the French critic Gerard Genette calls them, that we must cross before encountering the text itself. There is no such thing as pure text; we always reach it through the paratext, and though we may try to ignore it, it shapes our reading. Who said, "Don't judge a book by its cover"? We always do.

The reading room was closing, but I had my line of inquiry. Through all these editions the words on the page remained more or less the same, but the paratext turned the text into something different with each edition. Okay Staley, I thought as they flashed the lights to signal readers to return their books, I can do this. I'll have it done in a month. Six weeks tops. I didn't guess it would take me over a year.

THIS WAS MY LAST EVENING in Austin. People were strolling along Guadalupe ("The Drag") enjoying the warm Friday night, and I had to catch an early-morning flight back to soggy Vancouver where the mold was creeping over the windowsills of my sabbatical apartment. I drifted into Tower Records feeling lowdown and restless and picked up Stevie Ray Vaughn's "The Sky Is Crying." Beside the till was a poster for Antone's, home of the blues.

"You'll like it," the young woman told me as she handed me my change. "Antone's is a good scene an' Albert Collins is *great!*"

The place was packed, dark, and smoky when I got there, and the crowd was already moving to the Antone's house band. Then came the teasers. Albert Collins's 350-pound manager/bodyguard took the microphone and shouted, "Ladiesangennelmen, put your hands together for the *MASTER* of the Tele-*CASTER!*" So we did, but we didn't get Albert, we got his rhythm section for a couple of tunes. Then we got the horn players for a couple of tunes.

Some good old boy at a table up front began to chant in a hoarse voice, "al-*BURT*! al-*BURT*!!" but nobody else much minded because this was all great music you would be happy to pay money for any day of the week. The usual $8 cover had only been upped to $10 for Albert so we could hardly complain.

Then out he came—about 5 feet 5 inches, roly-poly, with a balloon head and a halo of frizzy hair, his blue-black skin shining dark against his white rattlesnake guitar strap. He wore a dark blue shirt with Texas longhorn steer heads on it, and had his guitar slung over one shoulder, the Fender Telecaster with slinky strings and a capo halfway up the neck that gave him his trademark shimmery sound. He turned his amp up to ten, dialed in full reverb and gain, and, popping his goggly eyes at the audience, flicked his thumb across the strings. *Whang!!* We were off.

He teased too, not doing much for the first two songs, letting everything start to cook, and just playing rhythm lines. The backup guitarist, a local white boy, took the lead breaks. Then in the third song the local boy got a long solo and he really cranked it. Albert was popping his eyes out, nodding at us and back at his man here, soliciting our approval, telling us this guy is *hot*. Albert gave him twenty-four bars and the kid pulled out all the stops. He was fast, he was mean, he had more licks than a Popsicle. He was here to show us how to play guitar. Albert was smiling and shaking his head like a doting dad—look at my boy go. Very kind. Very generous. Then Albert got this businesslike look on his face, hunched over his axe, and ripped out a cold, wailing lick that froze the room. This is why they call him "The Ice-man." The backup kid's proud smile turned to a weak grin. The crowd howled. Albert was back in town.

Now it was all Albert, and after forty minutes he called for the house lights. The harsh fluorescent bulbs made everybody squint and exposed Antone's for what it was—a bare room with a bar in it. The Greyhound bus station looked like a Hilton compared to this place. But Albert was coming down into the crowd in front of the stage, playing and shaking hands, working his way through. By the time he got to me I could see he had his old roadie behind him with what looked like a two-hundred-foot coil of cord. Albert was going to cover the club. And he did. Playing and grinning and popping his eyes, whipping off a particularly tasty riff for the cute blonde sitting at the bar, playing with his left and shaking hands with his right, he worked his way over the dance floor, through all the tables, and out the front door onto the street. Everyone was smiling and bopping and clapping and there was such joy in the club. As he worked his way back to the stage to end the set, I knew the girl in the record store was right. I had just five hours until I had to catch my plane, but I was glad I had come. And I knew I would be back.

This was part of the strangeness of Austin: the archive and the honky-tonk were on the same street and you could go from one to the other in ten minutes. In London, when you were working at the

British Museum you were in the heart of Bloomsbury; you stepped out into narrow streets full of little pubs and rare-book dealers, and you could wander around the squares where writers such as Virginia Woolf, George Bernard Shaw, Oscar Wilde, and dozens of others had lived and worked. The manuscript room had no air-conditioning, and judging from one visit I made in February no heat either. The outside and the inside fit. In Austin they did not. The reading room hovered around 68 degrees Fahrenheit and when you stepped outside it could be close to 100, the difference between 20 and 38 degrees Celsius. It was like stepping out of a sauna in reverse. Your chilled core would sustain you and you could take four, maybe five paces before your body registered it was under attack. You were in a completely different zone, and the extreme change in temperature mirrored the change in culture. Austin rattled my preconceptions the way London, for all its splendid diversity, never did.

TEN

Readers, Riders, and Shooters

That had been three years ago, when the notion of a motorcycle odyssey was just a wistful dream. Now I was back and on a bike, but Albert Collins had died, Antone's had moved, and Quack's was gone. I hardly knew Austin and already I was becoming nostalgic for the old Austin. Will Goodwin laughed. "You're starting to sound like a local," he said. "Have you heard the joke, How many Austinites does it take to change a lightbulb? Answer: Ten. One to change it and nine to talk about how good the old lightbulb was. And I heard that when I arrived here back in 1984. Austin changes but the unofficial city motto is still 'Keep Austin Weird.'"

When I got to the archives, I expected to have trouble adjusting. Walt Whitman knew about that; his *Song of the Open Road* opens by abjuring libraries:

Henceforth I whimper no more, postpone no more, need
nothing,
Done with indoor complaints, libraries, querulous criticisms,
Strong and content I travel the open road.

Now I was giving up the open road for libraries with their attendant "indoor complaints" and "querulous criticisms." How would I
cope? Making miles had been my job, eight hours a day for two
weeks. But really Whitman was just keeping up the travel writer's
façade. Everyone from Hakluyt to Kerouac exalts the time on the
road, denigrates and minimizes the time in the library. Yet they all
spend their time with the books. The two worlds might seem
opposites—the silence and stillness of the archive after the roar of
the Ducati on mountain passes and desert highways—but the more
I worked the clearer it became that archival work was the inverse,
not the opposite, of motorcycling. For one thing, silence surrounds
them both.

Motorcycling is not noisy. If you're riding a Harley with straight
pipes and you crack the throttle at a stoplight in a skyscraper canyon
of the city, or open it up going through a tunnel, you'll feel the roar.
That's not what I'm talking about. When I first put on a full-face
helmet, I have a moment of claustrophobia. I can hear only my own
breathing and I feel like one of those old-time deep-sea divers. (The
boots, jacket, and gloves feel cumbersome too—they're shaped all
wrong for walking, but once you are on the bike, the gloves curl
round the handgrips; the arms of the jacket flare out and forward, the
wristbands are at your wrist instead of your fingertips; and the boots
are snug onto the footpegs, reinforced toe under the gear lever.)
When you hit the starter, your breath merges with the sound of the

bike, and once you're on the highway, the sound moves behind you, becoming a dull roar that merges with the wind noise, finally disappearing from consciousness altogether.

Even if you ride without a helmet, you ride in a cocoon of white noise. You get smells from the roadside, and you feel the coolness in the dips and the heat off a rock face, but you don't get sound. On a bike, you feel both exposed and insulated. Try putting in earplugs: the world changes, you feel like a spacewalker. What I like best about motorcycle touring is that even if you have companions you can't talk to them until the rest stop, when you'll compare highlights of the ride. You may be right beside them, but you're alone. It is an inward experience. Like reading. In the archive there might be ten other readers, each at a solitary table, yet if you intersect at all it is only at lunch breaks. You may spend two weeks or more together, in silence.

The classical pianist Alfred Brendel once told a *New Yorker* interviewer, "I like the fact that 'listen' is an anagram of 'silent.' Silence is not something that is there before the music begins and after it stops. It is the essence of the music itself, the vital ingredient that makes it possible for the music to exist at all. It's wonderful when the audience is part of this productive silence." He was speaking of classical piano concerts, but he could have been talking of the highway. Some of the best moments on a bike come when you are not moving: roadside moments. You stop, kill the engine, and take off your helmet, and all is still.

On my last day I got on the road at dawn and drove for about a mile before pulling off on the shoulder. I ate my doughnut and drank some juice, and after about ten minutes I heard a semi. I heard it coming from probably 5 miles away, a low rumble, building gradually to a windy roar as it passed me, and then subsiding to a distant rumble once more, leaving me the desert silence. My boots scrunched on the sandy pavement, and my leather jacket creaked as I lifted the juice bottle to get the last mouthful. The desert was fully lit now, though the sun wasn't yet over the ridge beside me. Like reading, when you lift your eyes from the page and then move back, riding is defined and punctuated by silences. What we strive for is a productive silence, a collaboration with the text in which the silence is, as Brendel says, not an absence but the "vital element." I capped and stowed the bottle and got back on the bike. I had an empty road. This was going to be great.

The excitement at setting out is what I've come to think of as the *andiamo* phenomenon. *Andiamo* is Italian for "let's go." D. H. Lawrence calls it the most beautiful word in the Italian language. Certainly, the English "let's go" feels flat-footed in comparison, pedestrian in the worst sense. The Italian is like a whip about to crack; the throb on the third syllable marks the wave that pulses through the word. Both command and response, with a built-in exclamation mark, *andiamo* conveys the exotic, carries the excitement of taking off. It's the word you breathe inside your helmet when you finally clear traffic and the road opens in front of you. It's the feeling you get when you finally clear time and space and settle in with a new book. Heading into the silence, the plenitude and possibility of silence.

I WAS HERE to investigate *Ulysses* again, but this time instead of analyzing dust jacket advertising I wanted to figure out who actually read the book. On my first visit to the Ransom Center a tall, slender man had appeared at my table and introduced himself as John Kirkpatrick, John K as everyone called him. With his bald head and bright eyes he looked like an eagle and the library-school interns whispered that he knew everything.

Observing the first editions of *Ulysses,* he said, "I expect you'll want to see the Saillet notebook."

"Oh yes. Of course," I said, wondering desperately what a Saillet was and why I had never heard of one before. I would learn that Maurice Saillet was the young man who befriended Sylvia Beach in her later years, and who had owned the little notebook in which she listed the subscribers to her edition of *Ulysses.* This was an important link, and not one I would have made on my own. John K would give me several more leads in the course of my work at the Ransom Center, and I began to think of this as the K factor: the intangible influence of the curator (or the person who truly inhabits the archive—it is not always the highest-ranking employee). Without that animating figure the collection is just a heap of books and manuscripts; with him or her it becomes a web of live connections. Watching John K move from table to table, offering a suggestion, pointing out a reference, I realized that the great curators have the whole collection in their heads, and they play it like a conductor with a musical score.

As an undergraduate I had been taught that all the literati of the age had lined up to buy *Ulysses,* but a quick look at the Saillet notebook surprised me. Sure enough there were a few famous names such as W. B. Yeats and Ezra Pound, but what was more striking was how few of the subscribers for the first edition of one thousand were household names. Who were these other people? Now I hoped to find out.

I couldn't wait to really hold a book again, not just thumb a paperback in a diner. In Satyajit Ray's film *Charulata* everything takes place around writing. The husband's favorite smell is that of printer's ink. He prefers the sound of the printing press to the sound of the waves. He calls the press his co-wife. Meanwhile, his wife, Charulata, is falling in love with the handsome young cousin Amal, a poet. She gives him a new notebook and he composes a poem to the virgin notebook, untouched by imagination. Charulata says, "One touch and you're in the mood." The most sensuous shot in the whole movie is that of her taking a book out of a bookshelf and giving it a slight caress. The library assistant brought me Beach's little account book. I gently lifted the cover with the forefinger of my right hand, and let it fall back onto the palm of my left. One touch and you're in the mood.

Sylvia Beach, who had fallen in love with bookstore owner Adrienne Monnier, had published Joyce's *Ulysses* in the same three-tiered format Monnier used for works published at her bookstore. The first 100 were printed on special *vergé d'Arches* paper and signed by the author, the next 150 on good but less fine paper and unsigned, and the remaining 750 on standard handmade paper. The cost at the time for an "ordinary" *Ulysses* was not extreme, about US$50 in today's currency. Now an ordinary, unsigned first edition would set you back $60,000. I had twenty of them spread out in front of me. I wanted to match the books to the subscribers and to compare the books to see if they contained any clues to the responses of the reader.

I admit I was intrigued by the celebrity books. I passed over the Gloria Swanson copy, bound in soft fecal-brown leather and obviously never opened, to the copies of T. E. Lawrence, Lawrence of Arabia. He had bought two of the expensive copies, one of which (#52) he retained in its original paper covers, unread, untouched, in pristine condition. The other (#36) he had had bound in full burgundy leather by one of his favorite binders, C. & C. McLeish, with the pages trimmed and the front and back covers bound in at the end. This was a reading copy, and it was heavily read—more than 150 pages had marginal notes—and it was read casually—many of the pages had greasy smudges on them. These marks suggested a complete lack of reverence for the physical book. Molly Bloom's famous closing monologue was the only episode without marginal notes, but obviously the book had been around the block. I also discovered a shard of biscuit in the second-last episode, just as Stephen Dedalus takes leave of Leopold Bloom, as if the reader were participating in the communion.

I showed the greasy pages to the curator, Cathy Henderson. "Look at these paw prints on the inscription page," I said. "It's as if the reader were eating a particularly buttery muffin and then put his fingers down on the paper while reaching for the marmalade."

"Not butter," she said without missing a beat, "motorcycle oil." Of course, why didn't I think of that? Lawrence is famous for the fact that he was killed on a motorcycle, the very fast Brough Superior, known as the Rolls-Royce of motorcycles. He had a series of seven "Bruffs" (as aficionados refer to them), one of which was bought for him by George Bernard Shaw's wife, Charlotte. It seemed obvious Lawrence was as devoted to *Ulysses* as he was to his bike, making careful, factual notes in the margin and reading it between bouts of working on his motorcycle.

However, such was not the case. When I looked at some of Lawrence's correspondence I discovered that the handwriting was completely different from the marginalia. It turned out they were written by his friend W. M. M. Hurley, and they were mainly factual notes to do with Dublin—nothing to do with classical allusions, literary technique, or exegesis—and they may have been *for* Lawrence, who had trouble getting through the book. Though Lawrence had written to Sidney Cockerell in December of 1925 that "to bring [his own *Seven Pillars of Wisdom*] out after *Ulysses* is an insult to modern letters," in May he was moaning to Eric Kennington, "Arnold Bennett . . . said the perfect word about *Ulysses,* when he swore that Joyce had made novel-reading a form of penal servitude." Another month later, he was no more enthusiastic: "It is even worse to read than I had hoped. Months: and such dull stuff. Joyce is a genius, but an unlucky one. His writing has the architectural merit of Balham. It goes on for ever, and needn't ever vary in spirit."

So who did read the book?

While stationed in the Drigh Road Royal Air Force base at Karachi, where all the RAF aircraft engines in India were sent for overhaul, Lawrence worked in the office of the engine repair section. There he lent books to the "book-hungry men (hungry for more than the fiction library can give them)," he wrote to Charlotte Shaw. "We are rough, and dirty handed, so that some of the volumes are nearly read to death. You can tell the pet ones, by their shabbiness." Even without other volumes from Lawrence's Karachi library to compare with, I found his *Ulysses* certainly qualified as "shabby," and its condition suggested multiple readers, readers who read the entire book. A few months later he returns to this theme: "Everybody reads rubbish when he is tired. . . . So magazines and shockers are read: but my little library of queer books is almost as much used as the thousand-volume fiction library which the H.Q. maintains. It's because I tell 'em about books, and make them see them, as they reflect us."

I wondered what these airmen, on a dreary base 7 miles outside Karachi, some of them obviously reading at mealtime during work, saw reflected of themselves in Joyce. The crumbs and stains leave us only the trail of these anonymous readers, a trail leading off the map. If they'd been book collectors, they would have stolen it, and if they'd been pornographers, the smudges would have been grouped around two famous passages. Yet though I could not track them, the readers were there, and their presence alone unsettled the assumptions I had had about the audience of *Ulysses*.

As for Lawrence, why did he buy the book? Why two copies? Since 1919 he had been working on his own epic, *Seven Pillars of Wisdom*. He would begin printing a draft in January 1922 and produce fine press copies in 1926. He had always dreamt of printing on a hand press in a great medieval hall, and he had a collection of hand-press books, from Kelmscott to Ashendene, which he spread out in his room at Oxford to compare typefaces when deciding on the type for his own book. *Seven Pillars of Wisdom* was far too large to handset, so he opted for monotype. He not only deplored "rivers" (the vertical white spaces that run down ill-set pages), he hated long spaces at the end of paragraphs (which cracked the page across) and large blanks at the end of chapters, so he rewrote to force his paragraphs to end in the second half of the line and to make his chapters close near the bottom right-hand corner of the page. Like Joyce, he wrote and rewrote on the proofs, sometimes fourteen times, but he did so to enhance the balance of the page rather than to improve the text. Unlike Joyce, he wrote with speed. Where Joyce could, he claimed, spend all morning getting the words of a single sentence right, Lawrence claimed that he wrote a thousand words an hour. He wrote the introduction to *Seven Pillars of Wisdom* in an airplane between Paris and Egypt: "Its rhythm is unlike the rest. I liken it to the munch, munch, munch of the synchronised Rolls-Royce engines."

WILL GOODWIN, who in his spare time was also a printer and favored classic typefaces, came over to the table where I was working with the

Lawrence material. "That's a beautiful typeface," he said, looking at the immaculate cover of the #52 *Ulysses*. "Is it Bembo?"

"Hey, that's the name of the brakes on my Ducati," I said. "But I don't know about the typeface."

"No," said Will, "The brakes are *Brembo*." He said it easily as if this were a common mistake, but I still felt like a bumpkin. When Will had gone I got out Robert Bringhurst's *Elements of Typographic Style*. I had picked up my own copy at City Lights bookshop in San Francisco a few years before, attracted by the black cover and the shape, thinking it would be a serviceable reference text. I had flipped it open and read, "If you use this book as a guide, by all means leave the road when you wish. That is precisely the use of a road: to reach individually chosen points of departure. By all means break the rules, and break them beautifully, deliberately and well." I was hooked. Words to live by, and write by. This was not the dry-as-dust list of types I expected. Bringhurst captures the quirks of each typeface, each one as individual as a character in a Dickens novel.

I wondered if there was anything to connect Brembo and Bembo other than the slippage of a letter in my brain. *Brembo*, supplier of fine brakes to Ducati and Moto Guzzi, as well as car manufacturers Alfa Romeo and Ferrari, is located near Bergamo, a walled city whose winged lions in the piazza proclaim its Renaissance subservience to Venice. *Bembo* was a typeface cut in Venice, for Aldus Manutius, the man who invented small-format books for scholars to carry around—the first pocketbooks—to publish a piece by Cardinal Pietro Bembo in 1495 about his visit to Mount Aetna. In the 1920s Stanley Morison supervised the update of Bembo for the Monotype Corporation. With what Bringhurst calls its well-proportioned "functional serifs," Bembo became known for its "high readability" and "quiet classical beauty." Sounded like Brembo brakes to me. Hsing had once caught me down on my knees taking a picture of the silver disk and gold caliper of my front brake. "I swear you love that bike more than me," she said. "Oh no darling," I said dusting off my pant legs. "It's just, well, look at the way it glints in the sunshine."

Why look at brake bits or typefaces? Why would you want to look at a single letter? At a *part* of a letter, for pity's sake? Who cares about serifs (those little lines at the top and bottom of the letter, which originally resulted from stonecutters finishing the letter with their chisels)? Any motorcyclist would understand. Only the uninitiated look at whole bikes. The concept of "garage appeal" is predicated on the notion that you're not going to walk out to the garage, look in, say "Yup, she's still there," and walk away. With a bike like a Vincent Black Shadow—the Mona Lisa of motorcycles—there is almost too much to look at. To be in its presence is to risk Stendhal syndrome. (When the writer Stendhal went to Florence, he was so over-whelmed by the beauty there that he fell into a swoon.) Your gaze glides from the tank, to the engine, and to the exhaust pipes, and then works back, noting the shape of the ends of the pipes, the cylinder heads and rocker covers, and smaller details: the headlight, as impor-tant as eyes in a face for character, the brake cables, perhaps the snakeskin pattern that indicates braided steel . . . and you've just begun.

Before I left for this trip I had taken the Ducati's seat off to get at the battery and Pasquale had said, "Ah, look at that casting."

"What?" I said. He pointed to the bracket for the uni-shock under the seat. I had seen it but never really looked at it before, and I real-ized that the beautiful curve of the piece echoed the lines on the visible parts of the bike. The first time Pasquale rode my Ducati, he came back, put it up on the kickstand, and stood back from it. "You know," he said, "a motorcycle looks different after you've ridden it. I liked it before, but now it's beautiful." The bike looked different to me now that I knew about that bracket; like a detail on a medieval cathedral that no one can see, if you know it's there, it changes your sense of the whole. And knowing its function made me see—of course!—that there were no shock absorbers at the back, which in part gave the bike its clean, airy line. Do riders think about this when they ride? No, but the knowledge becomes part of the experience, suffuses it. The machinist's and the typographer's art are alike; the beauty of functional precision is transparent. We look through type, past the brakes, and only later do the ligatures and calipers move from ground to figure. After an afternoon of reading about typefaces and page design, I came back to T. E. Lawrence's mint copy of *Ulysses*. It looked different.

THAT EVENING at the Dog and Duck, a pub just south of the Ransom Center, I learned Will Goodwin knew about Brembo brakes because he was a motorcyclist. He used to ride a BMW, an R80, the bigger version of Hsing's bike. "I called it Isobar, and it only missed once in 65,000 miles. You know that *chickachickachicka* the engine makes? I was crossing Nevada and it went *chick*—" he cocked his head, "and that was it." He smiled. "The only time."

He called it Isobar because shortly after moving to Texas he took the bike up to his family place in Colorado in the late fall, and coming back he hit a snowstorm. How bad can it be? he thought. Bad. He tried to ride and it was pure ice. He fell over again and again, but the tough protruding cylinder heads (what Hsing called "those sticky-outy things") of the BMW boxer engine took the shock and saved his ankles. Finally he gave up and slept in a café. "So I called it Isobar because it had braved the ice, and because the name would remind me to always check the weather, the isobars, before heading out."

Sitting with us were some other regulars: Leo, a librarian who played a handmade Louden guitar; Ron, haberdasher, poet, and gun enthusiast; Mark, who liked travel books and wanted to go to China where his grandmother had worked as a Methodist minister in the 1920s; Dave Ray, who worked at Asylum Books over on Lamar. They all wore cowboy boots and they all loved books. A nice crew. I would never find this in Alberta. A woman who catered for rock groups ("She started here in Austin and now works for tours like the Rolling Stones") dropped by to say hi. I told Will he should get funding from the Ransom Center. They have the Scholars' Coffees on Wednesday mornings, why not Scholars' Pints on Tuesdays, pint night, at the D&D?

Will was telling Ron about my soon-to-be-published article about the covers of *Ulysses*. "We should have saved that edition of *Ulysses* that we shot," he said. "Ted could have included that in his study."

"You shot it?" I said. "Why?"

"Well, alcohol was a factor, but a number of things came together to produce the event. I had just become the bibliographer for *Joyce Studies Annual* and around the same time Ayatollah Khomeini had issued a fatwa against Salman Rushdie. Ron's idea was that this was the Khomeini school of literary criticism—shoot the book. We were sitting around at my place and as you know it's outside the city limits so I can shoot there. I went in and got my old copy of *Ulysses*. It was an old book, all yellowed, the one I'd had in college, and I didn't need it anymore. I had the new Gabler edition. So we set it up against the woodpile—that's where we always shoot, so that the bullets don't go astray—and I used my .22 rifle. I'm a good shot and I got it dead center, right above the *y* in *Ulysses*.

"The hole is clean going in—just like you see in the movies when they shoot a guy in the head and you've got this neat, round hole—but then the bullet blows out the back. Same with the book. Afterward you could still open it about halfway, say into the 'Circe' chapter, but the later chapters, especially 'Penelope,' were just all mashed together and you couldn't open them. I wish I'd kept it. Ron said I should donate it to the Ransom Center. What would we call it? The *fatwa* edition? The .22 edition?" They laughed.

"So," I said, "Did you feel . . . ?"

"That it was blasphemy? No. I thought about it. But I didn't feel it. I've been a librarian so long that I've gotten over that feeling some people have that every book is sacred. The text is what matters. Of course I would never shoot up a first edition."

"No."

I picked at the label on my Shiner Bock. Austin was shaking up my pigeonholes again.

SCHOLARS HAVE A SHORTHAND for introductions: "She's our Gordimer person" or "He's a Shaw person." Now at the Ransom Center, I was being introduced as "the motorcycle guy" instead of "the Woolf man." On the strength of this an Australian scholar wandered over from his table, leaving his boxes of George Bernard Shaw material to talk about T. E. Lawrence's Brough Superior.

"He actually had several Broughs you know," he said. "They were extraordinarily expensive. GBS was a motorcycle enthusiast too, and his wife had a bit of a crush on TEL. She bought him the motor-cycle he was killed on." I hadn't known. There should be a conference paper here at least: "Motorcycles and Modernism." Lawrence appears, with motorcycle, as Private Meek in Shaw's *Too Good to Be True*. In Evelyn Waugh's *Vile Bodies* the priest, Father Rothschild, rides a motorcycle. George Orwell was a keen motorcyclist, and now I had Lady Brett to add to the list. I could work in Woolf's desire for a motorbike. Maybe there would be enough for an article.

The boundary between archiving and motorcycling seemed increasingly porous to me. I wrote on the bike and I rode in the reading room. I'm sure it's the same in offices everywhere. The guy you see working so earnestly on a report, raising his eyes to consider some fine point of structure? He's not even there. He's on his bike, crossing a high desert. That woman in accounting who's poring over her figures, twisting slightly in her swivel chair? She's gone. She's on a tight little sport bike carving through some canyon.

The most repeated passage in *Zen and the Art of Motorcycle Maintenance* is the one in which Robert Pirsig contrasts riding a motorcycle with riding in a car. You're *in* a car, he says; when you're on a bike you're outside; the frame dissolves. It's an apt metaphor for working in the archive. There you're outside the frame: you read the topography of the texts as well as the linguistic codes; you get a perceptual jolt as well as an intellectual thrill. Responding to hand-writing, looking at the stamps on letters, feeling and sniffing the paper, hearing the crunkle of a heavy parchment manuscript—you're reading with all your senses.

A road too is a text. In a car you read the map, but on a bike you read the road. You look for the shiny black of tar strips; they're murderously slick in rain and they turn to soft goo in the heat and will slide you sideways. Hit one on a tightening bend of an off-ramp, and you'll be dropped before you know it. You watch for ridges clawed in the road by the machines preparing a road for new asphalt. The ridges are usually marked, but if it's a Sunday and the road crew isn't working, you may find yourself juddering through them unwarned. They do the same thing those metal grill bridge decks do—set the whole bike squirming.

You also have to watch out for grooves in the road. Ruts, of course, but also the worn lanes of heavily used traffic corridors in cities. There the road is not flat; it's like the cross section of a double-barreled shotgun. You can pull up to a stoplight in the middle of a lane, go to put your foot down, and find the road surface is a cowboy boot-heel lower than you thought. Instead of steadying the bike upright, you're staggering to keep it from falling over, worrying about scraping the tank, and looking like a fool in front of eight lines of commuter traffic. Out on the highway, the grooves fill quickly in a thunderstorm, providing wonderful potential for aquaplaning.

You learn to watch for oil slicks at intersections or anywhere cars have to stop. As you set up for a curve that runs under an overpass, you peer into the shadow, for the road can be sandy, or still wet, or even have a thin skiff of ice if it's cold out. Manhole covers, cross-walks, the white line, the yellow line, any kind of painted line; railway tracks and tram tracks; glass, sand, gravel, fruit, dung, blood—anything on the road except the road is a hazard.

If you're going to hit anything, you want to hit it straight on. If you have to go over a log or a curb, the technique is to brake just before, to compress the front suspension, then release and accelerate slightly to lighten the front end as it rolls over. Sometimes you can post, like a horseback rider rising up in the stirrups. But that's only if you have time. If you're surprised by a lump or a hole, then you just take it; the last thing you want to do is brake and swerve. Momentum is everything. But after you've had a few big potholes slam your crotch against the tank and grind dust off the bones in your wrists, you learn to anticipate. Even as you're looking at the street signs or the view, your eyes are searching, constantly reading the road.

WHEN I WAS SUPPOSED to be doing research on Joyce, thoughts of riding and phrases for a travel article kept invading my head. Then I spent a guilty afternoon with a file of letters open in front of me, pretending to make notes but actually writing a query letter to *Cycle Canada*. Would they be interested in an article titled "Monster Tour" about riding a sport bike from Edmonton to Austin. I thought the letter would take ten minutes after lunch. Last year I had bought *Writer's Marketplace* (smuggling it back to my office like pornography, shy of my ambitions) and I knew a query letter couldn't be any more than one page, three paragraphs. "Grafs" as a journalist friend called them. The first draft sounded like an academic article and was two pages long. These things were bloody difficult. The lights flicked to signal the closing of the reading room. I had wasted four hours of academic work, and my query letter, down to one page, still wasn't quite right. Should I waste more time tomorrow? Just bag the whole thing?

"How's the work going?" said the Australian as we retrieved our briefcases from the lockers.

"Great!" I lied cheerfully, "How about yours?"

ELEVEN

Continental Courier

T he intern brought the note to my table in the reading room. "Dr. Staley would like to talk to you about your project," she said solemnly, and put down the pink slip with Staley's office number on it. Here we go again. How did Staley get wind of this? I made the appointment and he waved me onto the big leather couch. "Ted. *Good* to see you. How *are* you?"

"Now then," he said drawing a chair up to the coffee table, "Tell me about this project of yours. On the Sylvia Beach notebook."

"Well," I said. I was trying not to slide into the depths of the enormous couch. Leaning forward at the waist just made my bum slide farther back. "It's not really a project yet . . ." You had to sit way back, throw your arm along the top of the couch, and surreptitiously dig your fingernails in. This is justice, I thought. With my own office I had inherited two chairs, one with an upright back, another lower, more relaxed and inviting—except that the back was angled

20 degrees farther back than you would expect. When students came to complain about a grade I would gesture affably toward the nearer, more casual chair. "Oh!" they'd yelp as they fell back in. They'd struggle to find a forceful posture (impossible) and by the time our discussion began it would be with much less rancor than if they had taken the stiff chair. I discovered this by accident and always wondered if the prof before me had set it up deliberately.

Staley interrupted, "Do you know Glenn Horowitz Books in New York? He's a rare-book dealer and his partner, Laura Barnes, has also been working on the Beach notebook."

"Oh." I tried to keep my voice neutral. I was being warned off. A prior claim had been established. Fine. I hadn't gotten very far anyway.

"They deal with a printer in upstate New York, and what we propose to do is to bring out a facsimile of the Beach notebook. Your article on the readers would be the introduction. What do you think?"

Think? A moment ago I thought the project was being taken away from me. Great.

"Great."

"Good. She's flying in tomorrow. I'll introduce you. She's very good, very sharp. Knows her Joyce."

When I came into the office the next day Laura was already sitting in one of the chairs beside the coffee table. Tom made the introductions and we sat down, all three of us on chairs around the coffee table. Nobody sat on the couch. A high-powered New York executive? A fusty rare-book dealer? I'd met neither and had only stereotypes to go on. I liked her immediately. She was short and slender, though she had rowed at Oxford, eyes wide and enthusiastic behind her glasses. "She's all business," Tom had told me approvingly, but it was quickly obvious that books were a passion first.

Laura had already tracked down names for the first eight hundred of the thousand buyers of *Ulysses* accounted for. Like the first 80 percent of a crossword puzzle, doing so had been comparatively easy. Now she was trying to fill in the gaps. Each name might take a week, a month. A reference in a biography of somebody who met somebody who knew someone who had bought a copy in Paris in the spring of 1922. Each scrap of information meant money. The copies were numbered, so even if nothing at all was written in the book you might be able to specify the owner, and if you could establish a narrative about the copy then it would be worth more. "At the end of the day," Laura said, "what matters is not the money, it's the hunt." I told her I was trying to track T. E. Lawrence's cookie crumbs and she was intrigued.

"How much would you need to do this full-time?"

"Well, I'd need money for travel. New York, Buffalo, maybe London. Back to Austin." I named a large sum.

"Double it. It always costs more."

"What I really need is time. If instead of extra travel money we could buy me out of teaching that would be better."

"Consider it done."

I LEFT THE BIKE in Martha's garage and flew back to Edmonton. Laura had already talked to the dean. Classes were due to start soon, but outside money makes even university administrators swift and flexible. A week later I was in Manhattan ("You can stay at our place on East 95th Street," said Laura, "We hardly ever use it."), taking the morning train out to Princeton to sift through the Sylvia Beach papers.

While Laura worked at the account books, I turned to boxes of correspondence. What exactly, I wondered, did these prospective readers think they were getting when they ordered *Ulysses*? After a review in the *London Observer* that stated "Mr. James Joyce is a man of genius" and "Yes. This is undoubtedly an obscene book," 136 readers immediately dashed off orders. What could be better? Sex and genius both. Some of these orders were more curious than others.

Mr. D. Webster, an antiquarian bookseller from Leeds, wrote the day after the review appeared, "I understand you publish James Joyce. Ulysses. I want a copy for a Medical Customer." Four days later, again from Leeds, Henry Walker, "New & Old Bookseller, Stationer and Bookbinder," ordered a copy (had he been talking to his colleague Mr. Webster?) and also noted, "This copy is for a Medical Man & he would like it at the earliest possible moment & the earliest number." If his customer sounds anxious, Kenneth Dickinson, a medical student at Newcastle upon Tyne, was even more so: "I am a Senior Medical Student, and understand that 'Ulysses' is an important contribution to the literature of Psychology, and the study of the individual. I append my prior qualifications, as proof of my bona fides."

Why would he send his bona fides? A 1927 letter from one Norman L. Madson in Los Angeles spelled it out: "I have been informed, not officially, however, that the book 'ULYSSES' by James Joyce can be delivered in the United States by mail, provided it is ordered by a physician and plainly marked as intended for a doctor's use. . . ." It is clear that these readers thought they were buying not great literature but great pornography. My favorite was one R. Burns from the Transvaal in South Africa who, having seen a review of *Ulysses,* said flat out, "Perhaps you will be able to notify me if you have any books in stock dealing on Flagellation or Corporal Punishment in any form."

MY UNIVERSITY COLLEAGUES were happy for me (okay, one was— she got my senior modernism course), but there was the taint of the commercial in what I was doing; I felt myself between camps, a rogue among scholars and a scholar among rogues. I had to admit I kind of liked dropping into Glenn Horowitz's shop on East 76th Street, and, on days when we were in the city, eating Waldorf salads with Laura at the French restaurant up the street. Glenn dashed in and out like a stage impresario, occasionally firing a question at me. "Imagine the ultimate Yeats inscription. What would it be?" I hate quizzes like this. "The ultimate. What do you think?"

"I, uh, I don't know, maybe *The Winding Stair* inscribed by Yeats to his patron Lady Gregory?"

"Exactly!" He produced the dark blue volume like a rabbit out of a hat and gently flicked open the cover. "There you have it." I was hanging out with the books Yale and the Ransom Center couldn't afford. Glenn in action would lean back in his chair, put his feet on the desk, and work his magic on the telephone. "It's a beautiful copy, John. Yes, I'm holding it right here. Of course it's expensive. It's expensive because it's the best." He puffed on his cigar. "It's immortal, John. And you can have it for thirty."

Nobody ever said "dollars." And "thirty" wasn't the ten and the twenty that I would lay down for an expensive paperback. I was now moving in a world in which individuals, not institutions but actual people, had first editions of *Ulysses* worth $60,000 and more. It was very strange. People smile differently above the $10,000 mark. There's a glint in the eye. I saw it even in Sarah, the young assistant, with her Audrey Hepburn fragility and her socialist politics. She hated the whole concept of selling first editions for fabulous sums. I had said I would love to have a plain-Jane garden variety, no attribution, no signature, first edition of *Ulysses*. "Are you kidding?" she snapped. "If I had that much money I'd use it to open a shelter for the homeless." She had grown up surrounded by books; her parents' idea of a holiday was to take the family car and drive around to book sales in the state and come back with a trunk full of old books. "None of them cost more than $50 though."

But I was there when Sarah made her first big sale. A young executive was buying his wife a birthday present, a first edition of Edgar Allan Poe. I bent over the showcases, attending to the Nabokov display, but at $30,000 the smiles glitter. The guy in beautifully tailored pants and casual shirt smiled as Sarah went over the points of the book. There was a throb in her voice as she repeated the inscription. I turned away. Book buying is an intimate act at the best of times, and I was embarrassed to be there. Later I saw an even higher exchange. At $50,000 the smiles are like those of sharks in love.

I never did mention my copy of *The Virginian*.

"I'M FLYING DIRECTLY into Rome," said Laura. It was June, conference season, and we were presenting our findings together at the International Joyce Symposium in Rome. I was stopping in England first. "Could you do me a favor when you're in London? I want you to go to the house of a collector, Quentin Keynes, the grandson of John Maynard Keynes. He has some Ezra Pound letters that I want you to bring to Rome."

"Pound letters? What if I get mugged or something? What if I lose them?"

"You won't. Here's his address. I'll phone and he'll be expecting you."

IT WAS COLD and rainy, and the wind kept whipping my cheap New York umbrella inside out. I found Finchley Road, an unprepossessing cross street in North London, and found number 2 with "Keynes" on the buzzer. This seemed like a bad B&B, not the kind of place you would expect to meet a copy of *Ulysses* worth more than my house. Inside it was a rat's nest, stacks of papers and books covering the living room, folio volumes stacked beside and in front of the fireplace like so much cordwood. A narrow channel down the inside wall had been kept clear so you could get to the kitchen—but only just; I had to hold my shoulder bag in front of me. At the edge of the kitchen stood a low rack of kitchen shelves, full, not of pans but of books.

"You sit here," said Quentin, edging past me to the chair by the sink. I had expected everything to be upright and behind glass in discreetly lit wooden cabinets. This wasn't collecting, this was pack ratting.

On the table was a sheet of notepaper and a cardboard mailing envelope. The letter was from Pound, typed on letterhead headed Rapallo, Via Marsalla, dated 11 November. It began,

I have no objection, but I don't think I have any right to grant permission.

I don't suppose JJ wd object. . . .

Augustus will CERTAINLY never answer. Q was finally disgusted with A.J. and sold him up, i.e. his pictures lock stock and barrel in a orlkonsumin rage.

"Well," I said, "Q. is obviously John Quinn, the lawyer and patron, and A.J. will be the painter Augustus John, but I still don't see what this is about."

"Ah yes," said Quentin, "Q—Quinn. I didn't think of that. I knew it couldn't be me."

"Laura will figure it out," I said.

"Yes, she's good at that. She's sorted something out for me already, as you probably know."

"Mmmm," I said. I didn't. I was just the courier, and Laura never talked about business or her clients.

"I'm sorry I can't offer you a cup of tea. A young woman is coming at ten thirty to look at my materials for a Burton exhibition. I have the biggest Richard Burton collection in the world. The explorer, of course, not the actor."

He picked up a volume beside him. "Look, here's a book signed by both Stanley and Livingstone. Scholars said that's impossible but you can see what he did. Livingstone was giving a lecture so he got him to sign the fly-leaf, then years later Stanley was giving a lecture so he went up and said, 'See, Stanley has signed this,' even though he was now long dead, 'Won't you sign it too?' And he did, and there you are. A very rare book, one of the rarest in the world." He put the rare book back under a pile of others on the kitchen rack.

"Laura tells me you're interested in *Ulysses*. Would you like to see the copy he inscribed to Barnet Braverman? I don't know if I can find it. It's in the bedroom. I'm in such a mess. This is what happens when you're an explorer. In fact I'm off to the wilds of Africa tomorrow."

Quentin set off into the wilds of the bedroom where towers of books teetered beside the bed and against the window, blocking the light. He emerged with a volume beautifully bound in full morocco, blue with a single gold band around the edge. "It's very good isn't it?

They don't have capable binders in America. My binder comes to my house, I don't even have to take it down to his shop." The original blue paper covers, front and back, were gone. A pity. I reached the inscription: "To Barnet Braverman / James Joyce" and the date. Like all of Joyce's inscriptions, at a 30-degree angle in the upper left corner of the page.

"Look at that," said Quentin, "He doesn't even say thank you. After all the help he gave Joyce getting those books into America. You know that story don't you?" I did know the story but Quentin told it to me anyway. Braverman, a friend of Hemingway's, was a copywriter and part-time salesman at an advertising agency in Windsor, Ontario. *Ulysses* had not been banned in Canada, so Sylvia Beach sent him copies and he made forty trips across on the ferry between Windsor and Detroit, each time with a copy of *Ulysses* stuffed down the front of his pants.

"I have an original picture of Joyce as well. Where is it? It's hanging on a wall, I know it is, and there isn't that much wall space ... where is it? You must pardon me. I'm sure it's somewhere ..." We both turned round and round in the little hallway. It wasn't there. We never did find it, but I noticed a copy of *Road and Track* and a model of a Bugatti boat-tailed speedster on the mantelpiece. My first literary enthusiasm had been for Henry N. Manney III who covered the European Grands Prix for *Road and Track,* a fact I hid from my colleagues. "I've driven Bugattis," he said. "I have a passion for them. My own car is very rare. A Gordon-Keeble. Only 99 were made, between 1964 and 1966." I had vaguely heard of it. One of the sixties hybrids?

"Yes! An Italian-designed glass-fiber body with an American Corvette engine assembled in Britain. It will do 140 miles an hour."

I had the feeling I had scored more points for having heard of Gordon-Keeble than knowing about Barney Braverman.

"Tell Laura I'm off to the wilds of Africa," he said shaking my hand and handing me the cardboard sleeve with the Ezra Pound letter. I promised I would. The rain had stopped, and I peered into the cockpit of the Gordon-Keeble, all leather and round Smith's gauges, in the best British tradition. I strode off, glad of the space and the light after the cramped jumble of the apartment, but glad to have met someone who was both a Burton and a Bugatti aficionado.

TWELVE

Ducati Spirit, Roman Circus

I had the letters in my Eddie Bauer shoulder bag, and with my tan cotton pants and crumpled linen shirt I looked like a generic academic. Not worth mugging. I flew to Geneva as all good spies did, and my brother Lloyd picked me up in his minivan. I felt like I was in an Eric Ambler spy novel: the ordinary guy, thrust into the unusual situation. Lloyd had a briefcase exactly like mine. This was good tradecraft. Any operatives following me would not know which was the real briefcase.

"Argentina is the new Chile," Lloyd said cryptically when we got to the house. Was this code? He did not even know I was carrying the letters. "Their wines are now the best deal anywhere," he continued, uncorking a bottle. "Way better than the French." I was reminded how much the Swiss-French looked down on the French-French, those hopeless provincials who lived across the border 300 meters away (his wife, Nicole, was from the Valais and looked down on people in the next canton). He headed out to a birthday party and left me a bowl of fettuccine with sautéed red peppers and grated Asiago cheese; the wine seemed harsh at first but melded well with the Asiago. After dinner I poured myself another glass of the Argentine red—it really wasn't bad—and opened my new novel: "It was late evening when K. arrived. The village lay deep in snow." This was the new improved translation of Kafka's *Castle,* one of those books I had been meaning to read for years. Appropriate, I thought, to be starting it here in Geneva, a European capital renowned for its bureaucracy. I read for a while and then *The Castle* began to be hard work. I poured myself another glass of the very drinkable Argentine red, and switched to *Tennyson's Gift,* a comic novel by Lynne Truss, a writer I had met at my friends Neil and Geraldine's place in London. It was much lighter, but kindred to *The Castle:* the Isle of Wight is populated by characters as bizarre as those in K.'s village, and the young Ellen Terry (sixteen years old and married to the doddering Watts some thirty years her senior) is a self-dramatizing version of K. the land-surveyor, trying to make sense of it all. I liked her advice on not dwelling on insults: "The more you tramp on a turd, the broader it grows."

Lynne, as obsessed with apostrophes as with infielders, seemed an unlikely sportswriter, but she had just been dashing off to cover a soccer game in Spain for the *Times.* I envied her, and my friends Neil and Geraldine. He was a graphic designer who was always flying to places like Moscow for the day to do a photo shoot for a corporate report; she was a book-review editor for the *Times Education Supplement* who was always dashing off to European book fairs. They had renovated their Victorian town house in Sumatra Road and took weekend holidays in Umbria. Though they said they liked my account of Quentin Keynes, their lives seemed so much more interesting than mine. Still, I reminded myself sternly, sloshing just a little bit more of the superb Argentine red into my glass, being a Pound courier and reading Kafka in transit in Geneva could be construed as interesting. I wondered if certain wines, certain spirits, went with certain books, like wine with food. You wouldn't read Hemingway while sipping sherry would you? Or Edith Wharton with tequila? What about Kafka and the Argentine? Somebody should work this out, I thought, and fell asleep.

The next day Lloyd and I took bicycles down into the center of Geneva and sat at a little café by the tram tracks. "The coffee is much better here," said Lloyd, "and half the cost of those places by the lake where you can see the *jet d'eau.*" I'd seen their water spout before, an impressive 140-meter-high waterfall in reverse, but after you'd watched it for thirty seconds and said, "Thar she blows," there was nothing more to do but go for ice cream.

We watched the scooters and motorcycles parade by. Genevans have their own style that moves between the flamboyance of the Italians and the studied nonchalance of the French. You can see it in the way they ride, deftly threading their way through the traffic, parking with a quick flick of the sidestand, poised and precise. Like the young women who tie on a scarf or sling a good bag over one shoulder with quiet elegance. An Aprilia 500 single parked in front of us. "A perfect all-round bike," I said to Lloyd. "I still want to get a single-cylinder. Do you ever wish you'd kept your Ducati?" He rode his bicycle like a Grand Prix motorcycle down the hills of Geneva, using gravity instead of horsepower to outrace the cars. I thought he was crazy.

"No," he said, "it's too dangerous, and riding the bicycle back uphill every day keeps me in shape for ski touring. Besides, the seat on that Mach 1 was like sitting on a railway tie. That's fine when you're sixteen. Still," he said looking at the bright row of bikes at the curb, "mine looked like a real motorcycle, not like these plastic-wrapped things they ride today."

BACK IN THE 1970s when Lloyd bought his Mach 1 the number of Ducati fans in any Canadian city could dine out together on a large pizza. Today Ducati is a fashion statement, an instant evocation of Italian speed and style. Bologna is a short jog east from the Geneva-Rome line so I decided to make my pilgrimage to the Ducati factory. As I caught the bus from central Bologna to the suburb of Borgo Panigale I wondered what could be left of the spirit of the exquisite little bikes my brother and his friends used to ride.

I got off at the cross street A. Cavalieri Ducati, named for the founder, Antonio Cavalieri Ducati. Though he started out in the 1920s making radios, his middle name carried his destiny: *cavalieri*—riders. Walking down the block to the factory you can see the green hills at the edge of the suburb. We were close to the Apennines here, and the bikes parked in the parking lot are, except for a handful of scooters, all Ducatis and all well used. They have scratches and road grime. These people ride.

The tours assemble in the cafeteria where the life-size photo-mural of a bike taking a corner makes you feel, even sipping an espresso, that you're riding in a Superbike race. Alex, the American-accented coordinator (he learned his English from rock videos) introduced us to Maria, who would guide the English-speaking group. Dark-haired, severely pretty, she was dressed in trainers, cargo-style jeans, and a red Ducati T-shirt, and she strode like a pit-crew boss as she led us to the shop floor. She stopped and swiveled: "OK. We have some rules. First of all no pictures. Absolutely no cameras. Second, do not cross the yellow lines around the work areas. Third, of course, you touch nothing. OK? Here we go."

She slightly elongated the accented vowel, as she would in Italian. Other than that she had a neutral, language-school accent. Ducati may be rooted in Bologna but the company is very conscious of its international reach—tours are offered in seven languages, though most visitors take the Italian or the English tour. In 1996 Texas Pacific, a Fort Worth–based financial group, bought a controlling interest in the floundering Ducati. They have begun using Ducati workers—"Ducati people"—rather than models in a sophisticated marketing campaign designed to hail you as a Ducati person.

We stopped first at the engine assembly. No robots in this factory: engines are made one at a time by one mechanic. She—and it is mostly women technicians in this section—moved with the engine and a tray of parts as it traveled down the line. The workers reminded me of typesetters, hands instinctively choosing the right piece from the case. The bikes outside had led me to expect a bunch of lean, mean sport riders, but these looked like moms making money for their families. We moved on to the line where complete bikes were taking shape.

I wondered which person had assembled my engine. Maybe the blond woman with her hair pulled back. And who fit the engine into the frame? Maybe one of the older men tuning the finished bikes. Each bike is made, in effect, by a family of workers. And each bike connected to families. "They spend forty-five minutes just to get the exhaust emissions right," Maria had said. I once spent a summer riding a lawn mower and the sound of the engine and the whirr of the blades became part of the ambient sound in my brain. These men must listen to the soccer matches, talk with their children, through the sound of Ducati engines.

I skipped the gift shop and went to meet Livio Lodi, the curator of the museum. I expected a suit, but Livio, his beard close cropped in the Italian style, was wearing casual cotton pants and flip-flops. My opening query about the museum opened a floodgate.

"You must understand that half my life has been spent with Ducati. My father was a medical doctor with the company. Most of the people I know, the people whose weddings I go to and whose christenings I attend, live here in Borgo Panigale, within 500 meters of the factory.

"So. We wanted the museum to be not just a place where the bikes are on display but someplace that would convey an emotional impact, to remind people of the importance of Ducati to Bologna, and to create something of historical significance. And we feel we have succeeded. This is the most visited museum in Bologna." He paused to let this sink in. "The most visited. Even though it is far from the center. Even though it is in an ordinary suburb."

It is far. You catch the crowded number 13 bus in the center of Bologna and ride west for more than half an hour. The bus passes over the river Reno where people are sunbathing on the gravel flats below, a reminder that this was once a stretch of countryside. Beside the "Ducati" bus stop there is a credit union, a hairdresser (PARRUCCHIERE KING 57), and a shop that sells handbags, flanked by modern low-rise apartments. Neither tacky nor wealthy, just a clean and prosperous neighborhood, and not an industrial park in sight. There is no big sign on the corner saying THIS WAY TO THE DUCATI FACTORY! The barista at the espresso bar on the corner will give you directions. What is remarkable to the pilgrim is how unremarkable it is, how integrated Ducati is into the community.

"Also we wanted the museum to be free. You know Ducati is often called the two-wheeled Ferrari. The Ferrari museum is near here, but to visit the Ferrari museum you must own a Ferrari. And you must make an appointment months in advance. So it is very exclusive. This is normal because of course Ferrari is very high end, but Ducati is still very much part of the motorcycle world. We want that everyone who is interested, all motorcycle enthusiasts, will be able to come."

He spoke of the region and of how there seemed to be something in the air of the Emiglia-Romagna province, "a friendliness combined with the need for speed." Within just a few kilometers are the famous Italian speed merchants: Ferrari, Maserati, Lamborghini, and Ducati. "When you buy a Ducati you are getting, if I may say, the real taste of Italy, like the lasagna or the *ragù*—the pasta sauce— of the region. Even though you may eat lasagna in Canada it will, excuse me, not be the same. It will not taste the same anywhere else in the world. With a Ducati you get the thrill that is like no other. This is a bike that has a soul."

I wasn't quite sure how drifting a carbon-fiber race bike through a banked corner at 250 kilometers an hour related to lasagna, but Livio, the Mike Hailwood of orators, never paused. "As you know, the Ducati factory was bombed by the Allies in 1944." I did: Operation Pancake. The Germans had taken over the facility the year before and turned it into a munitions factory. The Allies were determined to flatten it, and although they did not completely succeed (the cafeteria is in a building that was rebuilt after the bombing) they destroyed enough machinery that the Ducati brothers could not resume their old manufacturing.

"Until this time we did not make motorcycles. Radios, cameras, electric razors, yes. Even jukeboxes. It was a huge factory employing seven thousand people. It was very important for the economy of the region. After the war Ducati applied to the State for money to rebuild. Now we employ about a thousand people. Once again it is an important part of Bologna, of the Borgo.

"You will notice that this room is shaped like a helmet." I hadn't. We were sitting in theater-style seats in a pod in the center of the museum. "The bikes are arranged on the outside like a clockwork exhibit, giving the history of Ducati from 1946 to 2004. We look out here, at the front, as if underneath the visor of a helmet."

We were looking at one of the Superbikes ridden by Carl Fogarty, who ruled for Ducati in the 1990s. "We chose racing over production because first of all we have no room for the more than 150 models Ducati has produced. We decided that racing has had the most impact for Ducati and so we have been collecting the most important racing bikes." But unlike Ferrari, Ducati didn't start with high-performance machinery. When the Ducati family began rebuilding in 1946 they introduced the Cucciolo ("the Puppy"), a 48 cc engine that you could bolt onto your bicycle. Transportation for the masses in impoverished post-war Italy. The little bike became so popular that it had a pop song written about it. Only later did Ducati become identified with speed.

I told Livio (though I was afraid he would think I was not a true Ducati enthusiast) that although the Superbikes were fabulous I had come mainly to see the early street bikes. I also wanted to find out more about the two young men who drove around the world on Ducatis back in the 1950s. Livio smiled. "Ah yes. Leopoldi Tartarini and Giorgio Monetti. They left the factory at the end of September

1957 and returned a year later, traveling 60,000 kilometers through forty-two countries. This was important for Ducati to show that their motorcycles were reliable.

"You see, there was a crisis in motorcycles in 1957 because that is the year Fiat began making their 500, the famous 'Cinque-Cento.' Smaller and cheaper even than their 600, it suddenly gave people an option for weather protection and long-distance travel. This was the nail in the coffin for some of the smaller motorcycle factories here in the region. Also 1957 was the end of the Mille Miglia [the thousand-mile road race from Brescia to Rome and back on open roads], when the Marchese de Portago crashed, killing himself and several spectators. So people began to think differently. To think that maybe a little city car is better than something for racing on the roads. So Ducati sent Tartarini and Monetti around the world on their 175 cc machines."

What he called the crisis for motorcycles lasted over ten years, and the factories limped along. "But then something happened that was very important—the arrival in Italian cinema of *Easy Rider*. People were shocked in a good way by this movie. They wanted to ride down the highway like Dennis Hopper or Peter Fonda. In 1962 Ducati had begun producing the Scrambler model for the U.S. market, but in 1969 it took off here in Italy. It was, if I may say, the Monster of the seventies. It enabled us to survive. I often tell people that Ducati is like the Three Musketeers—there are good times, bad times, but at the end a happy ending."

Odd. I had always thought of Ducatis as the opposite of the choppers in *Easy Rider,* and the endless straight stretches of the U.S. Southwest the reverse of the twisty European roads I dreamt about. Naturally it is always the other that is exotic. There are those

moments in riding that are pure sensation, but motorcycling is insep-
arable from image and desire.

Livio went on. "There is continuity to Ducati. Our great designer
Fabio Taglioni died three years ago, but it is still his vision that drives
Ducati. Things are very different but still the same—the tubular
frame, the L-shaped engine, the Desmodromic valve system, and of
course the sound. Nothing sounds like a Ducati."

Once in Ireland, touring the west country before a Joyce conference in Dublin, I had stopped to take a picture on a mountain pass
in the Dingle Peninsula. I heard the far-off *poom-poom-poom* of a
motorcycle engine pulling against compression as it came down the
steep wet road, and I called to Hsing, "Must be a Duc." Sure enough,
a few minutes later, out of the mist, traveling slowly but with that
unmistakable throb that makes the hair stand on the back of your
neck, came a red 900SS.

"And all the bikes are still built here, on the same site as the original factory. We have produced only forty thousand bikes, where
Honda has produced eight million. Ducati is like the pumpkin at
Halloween or the Christmas tree at Christmas." I think what Livio
meant is that you could not imagine the motorcycle world without
Ducati, that Ducati crystallized the spirit of motorcycling. Certainly
part of the mystique of Ducati is that everything they produce
derives from a race-bred engine and a race-tested frame.

But there was something more, and I was trying to sort it out as
I rode back on the bus. In the museum the gap between the road
bikes and the race bikes defines by an absence another history of
Ducati: one devoted to the street rather than the track, that runs from
the early Cucciolo mopeds, through the round-the-world 175s, to
the Scrambler, and up to the Monsters and MultiStradas of today.

Even the new 999R, Maria had pointed out, has an adjustable seat and pegs, and a frame modified to make it more stable for street riding. Significantly, though excluded from the museum, an immaculate yellow Scrambler sits in the hallway of the executive offices.

As the bus passed through the gates into the old city I remembered what one fiercely partisan historian had said about Bologna—that it was the anti-Florence. He dismissed that city as merely an "open-air museum of rare works," a place to go and admire and leave, whereas Bologna was a city to live in. After Venice, Bologna has the best-preserved historic center in all of Europe, and what gives it its distinctive character is not any one grouping of buildings but the porticoes, 35 kilometers of covered sidewalks, that wind through the city, linking homes, shops, palaces, churches, and university buildings.

The university was Europe's first, founded in the eleventh century for the study of law (one of Bologna's students founded the law school at Oxford in 1144—two hundred years before Chaucer was born), and as the students poured in from other countries they created Europe's first student housing crisis. The government solved the problem by commanding all the homeowners to build on a spare room, extending out over the street and at a height tall enough for a man on horseback to ride underneath. These extensions, fused into a line, formed the porticoes and created a communal civic space, one that blurred the divisions between private and public space, and between classes as well. If architecture was destiny then it was no accident that "Bologna the Red," so named for its red-brick buildings, had always had strong socialist leanings (in fact if you look at them from the university area the two central towers lean left), and until recently Bologna had had a successful Communist city government. Near the end of his discourse Livio had said something about "it all has to do with socialism," and it occurred to me that maybe Ducati was not the Ferrari of motorcycles, it was the Bologna of motorcycles, fusing the aristocratic and the pedestrian.

When I got off the bus I saw two Ducati police bikes—the first I had seen. I scuttled over and explained in my broken Italian that I was Canadian and therefore wanted to take a picture of the motorcycles. The cops smiled and stepped back, but I waved them into the picture and they posed, intuitively standing behind the bikes so as not to spoil the lines. The bikes were beautiful, but they were also workhorses. This was it: you don't see Ferrari police cars. However exotic, Ducatis have always been integrated into the everyday life of things. Like their pre-war radios and razors. And *ragù*. Linking the flavor of Ducati to the pasta of the region, Livio had been talking about the whole community, the people who built the engines one by one, who got married and raised children in the streets surrounding the factory. Their pride in the Superbike champions was less a pride in the racer than in the whole recipe from the Borgo. I was beginning to get it. A Hailwood or a Fogarty was just the final pinch of basil in the long-simmering sauce.

Starting the tour I had wondered if it was all about marketing. The museum had, after all, been founded after Texas-Pacific bought in. Was this the Starbucksification of the brand, a small shop gone global with the inevitable merchandise spinoffs? The answer is, of course. But not only. The last thing I had asked Livio was what he rode (I had him pegged as a MultiStrada kind of guy). "To tell you the truth," he said, "I drive a scooter. For me, whenever I see a Ducati anywhere in the world it gives me pleasure, for it is the spirit of Italy, of Bologna, and the Borgo Panigale. That is what Ducati is for me. Something made at home."

ROME WAS HAVING A HEAT WAVE. By late morning my forearm would be sticking to the page of my notebook. I'd put the conference program under my arm, where it would stay glued as I lifted my hand, but at least the arrangement let me move my pen across the page. The first day in Rome I loosened my leather watch strap one notch, then two, then three as my wrist became stickier and stickier. The International James Joyce conference was a week-long circus with hundreds of papers every day, seven sessions running at the same time. At first I fretted that I could not possibly make it to all the important talks, but by the third day my notebook records, "the palm tree, the orange plaster wall, the curved terra-cotta roof tiles, the swish of wind through the palm leaves, a gust of damp air through the window—rain. . . ." I didn't even manage to get down the title of the session, the rest of the page is blank.

The younger scholars would anguish over why their papers produced no discussion, would blame the moribund Joyce establishment and secretly doubt themselves. The blame was not theirs. At 9:00 A.M. we would have found their arguments interesting. At 10:30, after cappuccino, we would have found them cutting edge, and debated fiercely in the question period. But at 2:30, after a plate of pasta and a glass of crisp white wine to cut the cream sauce, a *dolce* and an espresso to finish off, Rome itself called us to sleep. It was an unnatural act to sit on hard chairs in these un-air-conditioned rooms and subject ourselves to academic arguments. Attendance was sparse. No Italians came at all. Siesta reigned.

I met Laura on the steps of the Campidoglio, told her that I had the packet and that Keynes was off to the wilds of Africa. "So here are the letters." She opened them. Her husband Michael, an investment banker, said, "I've seen better. They're not that interesting."

"We'll look at them later," said Laura wrapping them up again. "I need to concentrate on my paper." That was it. These fabulous documents I had been carrying were not so fabulous after all. No matter. I'd enjoyed the espionage fantasy. My work as courier was done.

Laura and I gave our papers in a morning session. I called mine, "Cowboys, Queers, and Collectors—Who Was Reading *Ulysses*?" replacing the academic colon with a jaunty dash to signify that this would be provocative stuff. Laura's paper, which actually was provocative, dealt with the shifting value of the French franc and showed conclusively that *Ulysses* was never designed as a collector's item, as one scholar had claimed, calling this the new scandal of *Ulysses* (there is always a scandal about *Ulysses*). Afterward we went for lunch with Luca Crispi, the Roman-born *Finnegans Wake* scholar and assistant curator of the Joyce Collection in Buffalo, New York. Luca brought a continental sophistication to Buffalo, but here he was really in his element, wearing a linen Armani suit as casually as a jean jacket.

Walking past the sprawling Monument to Vittorio-Emmanuelle II— which, depending on your mood, looks like a big wedding cake or a giant white typewriter—we picked up other Joyce scholars: Aida Yared, a Persian pediatrician who was exploring the connections between *The 1001 Nights* and *Finnegans Wake,* and her boyfriend Dean, a lanky truck driver from Kentucky who read Joyce in his spare time; Geert Lernout, the tall silver-haired Belgian, and Alistair McCleary, the short cherubic Scot ("An elf and a hobbit," someone smiled); Bill Brockman, librarian and lothario from Illinois. Soon we were a dozen. The café was jammed. We stood in the doorway. "So," said Luca, *"Allora . . ."* and spoke to the waiter rapidly in Italian.

Tables appeared, carried over the heads of the other diners, chairs materialized, a tablecloth flapped, and suddenly we had banquet space on the sidewalk. Luca waved away the menus. "We'll be here all afternoon if everyone chooses," he said. "I recommend . . ." he named a pasta, a salad, a wine. Done. Conversations erupted up and down the long table. "This is the real conference," said Geert. Nobody was going back to the afternoon sessions.

Dean leaned across the table. "I didn't make it to your talk, but I read your new article," he said. I told him I didn't know it was out yet. Robin had said there would be copies of *Joyce Studies Annual* at the conference but I had not seen any.

"I don't know about that," said Dean, "I mean your motorcycle article, the one in *Rider* magazine about your trip to Texas."

Wow! With academic publishing, if you were fortunate, your piece came out before you had forgotten what it was about or changed your mind completely. And, if you were fabulously lucky, one of the six people who read it would want it as more than footnote fodder for their own article. Most often you felt like you were dropping your manuscript into one of those time capsules they used to bury in the cornerstone of a new city hall. You hoped someone would read it someday, but you knew you would probably be dead. But *Cycle Canada* and then *Rider* had published my travel piece in three months, and now someone had read it who didn't have to. Paid money for it! ("Actually I just read it at the newsstand," said Dean.) No matter, I felt like a rock star.

PART THREE

Riding Home

THIRTEEN

Off the Shelf

M y article on the *Ulysses* covers did come out a couple of months after the conference, and I was pleased to see it between the blue hard covers of *Joyce Studies Annual*. This was solid, this would last; it came out once a year and went to all the best libraries. *Cycle Canada* and *Rider* had given me my fifteen minutes of fame and motored on; the only place you could find a back issue was my living room. Yet I remembered the thrill. I never did run into anybody who had read both articles. I wondered if it would be possible to combine the work of Edward Bishop the archive diver with Ted Bishop the rider. Probably not.

Still, some people seemed to manage to break down the bound-aries, manage unlikely combinations. I had heard of Herb Harris, a motorcycle collector in Austin whose living room was full of rare bikes. I had heard that Will Goodwin had left the Ransom Center and was living in a studio apartment with piles of books rising off the floor like stalagmites. It was supposed to be a rare-book business but he hated to sell anything. I heard about lesbian archivist/activist Ann Cvetkovich who had published a book called *An Archive of Feelings* and wrote about, among other things, the Lesbian Herstory Archive that was not contained in a building that looked like a fort but was in a house in Brooklyn, with the photocopier next to the sink. She too, it turned out, was in Austin. Good reasons to go back. I needed to look up a few things in the Ransom Center, and I wanted to look *at* the Ransom Center because they had finished their dramatic renovations. Also my Ducati was sitting in Martha's garage. I needed to drive it back north before the summer heat put a lockdown on all of Texas.

LIBRARIES OFTEN LOOK like bunkers set up for defense, not access, for a last-ditch stand against invading hordes. Whatever their professed mission statements, architecturally they remember the Alamo. Yet this was changing. When I had been in London I had noticed the British Library, formerly housed behind the sentry-guarded gates of the British Museum, not only had bigger quarters but welcomed you with an expansive plaza and a cappuccino cart out front. The Ransom Center now had what the architects called glass lanterns at the corner of the building—glassed-in rooms with yard-high images from the collections etched into the panes. I liked the whimsical quality of it, a mix of graffiti and scrapbook. Each time I climbed the stairs I noticed different combinations, the long nose of a caricature next to a snail, or Lytton Strachey looking at a raindrop. The designers had captured the heart of archival work: the discovery of surprising connections between disparate artefacts. Most arresting was the pair of eyes at head height as you walked toward the stairwell. Brooding on dark days, amused in the morning sun, they always seemed to be examining you. "Quite the orbs," I said to the curator one day when we were leaving. "Yes," she said, "Picasso's." Was he turning us into cubist collages or one of his sinuous line drawings? It's all in the gaze.

The reading room, once a windowless room on the fifth floor, now spread across the whole second floor, and in each wall were windows. "Look," said Cathy Henderson, "we think this is the only archive in the world where you can look out in four directions and see trees." She was right. The giant live oaks that surrounded the Ransom Center, formerly visible only through the gun-slit office windows, and not at all by the readers, now seemed part of the building. Spacious wooden tables and chairs replaced the steel standard-issue office furniture. In the old room you felt you were in some secret room of the CIA or MI5; here you felt like you had been invited into the study of a benign and cultured collector. No longer were we sealed off.

"I DON'T DRINK COFFEE," said Ann Cvetkovich on the phone from her office, "but there's a new bubble-tea place on the Drag, why don't we meet there?"

"Fine," I said. "How will I know you?"

"Well, I'm kind of tall and have long red hair . . . I don't know, I'll find you. It's a small place." She looked like Bonnie Raitt and strode into the little shop like she should be carrying a Stratocaster instead of a book bag. She gave me a wide smile, a firm handshake, and stopped me when I started to give my prepackaged explanation of where Alberta was. "I have Canadian roots," she said, "My mother married one of Andy Russell's sons—have you heard of him, the writer and rancher?—and though they separated a long time ago she still has a place in the foothills near Waterton Lakes." I told her I had been reading her book, *An Archive of Feelings,* and that I admired the direct style. She smiled. "That's kind of a family expectation. Have you heard of Roderick Haig-Brown? He was my grandfather. He was a conservationist who wrote books about things like fly fishing on Vancouver Island. He had a very pared-down style. I don't think anyone reads him anymore." I had read *Timber* in graduate school, and knew that he got kicked out of his elite school in England, came to the West Coast to work for a logging company, and settled on Vancouver Island. He produced more than twenty-five books, winning a Governor General's Award for children's literature, and the ongoing admiration of fishermen for *A River Never Sleeps.*

"He's getting a bit of local fame now," Ann said. "His house on Vancouver Island has been turned into a historical site. A kind of archive, I guess. The opposite end of the scale from the Ransom Center. 'The history of any archive is a history of space,'" she said, quoting her book, and laughed. She had written about the Lesbian Herstory Archives, whose mission was to preserve documents that might have been destroyed by indifferent or homophobic families, or left to neglect. The collections are housed in a house deliberately: the living room is the reading room, pointedly blurring the distinction between institutional and domestic space.

"There's even a motorcycle connection," she said. "They took the lesbian archive on the road."

"A motorcycling archive?"

"Well, not the whole thing. They had a slide show of the main items in the collection and my friend Alexis Danzig drove across the country showing this slide show at women's music festivals, community centers and such, and she would tell people how to set up their own grassroots archive. She hates the idea of big centers with a board of directors. It has to come from the bottom up, she says. 'You need to do the hard work of inclusion.' I should connect you two."

Alexis told me, "I was a disgruntled queer ex–AIDS activist and educator in search of adventure and romance. I bought my brother's Yamaha Radian and signed up about thirty communities from New Jersey down to the Florida Keys and back up again out of Florida, across the Southwest, through Texas, and on up to San Francisco. The most beautiful stretch of road in America is down through the mountains from Flagstaff to Phoenix. I was never harassed, I never ran out of gas and I never fell asleep while riding. The only time I ever almost ran off the road was in a rainstorm I hit leaving Santa Fe. After the tour I moved to San Francisco and re-invented myself as a house painter. If you know how to load properly and tie decent knots, you can get a lot of gear on a bike. Even ladders. Just short ones." I asked her if she had written about this. "No," she said, "too many other things to do. Now I'm in law school. I want to specialize in Queer Elder law—its queer seniors who fall through the cracks of the judicial system. Like short people. I told Erik Buell he should make a bike for under 5 foot 6. Then I'd ride again." Just talking to her felt like a ride.

IT SEEMED THAT EVERYBODY at the library had a motorcycle story for me. Rich Oram, the head librarian, stopped me on my way back from lunch. "Hey, I've just been reading the correspondence between Albert Camus and his publisher Blanche Knopf. Camus writes in the summer of 1948 asking if the sales of his novel *La Peste* are as good as the reviews, because, *'je voudrais m'acheter une motocyclette'*—'I want to buy a motorcycle!' I figured you'd want to know that."

Inside the reading room Pat Fox, who doled out the manuscripts, told me she used to ride motorcycles. "Just little ones, Honda 50s and

90s, and then we got a 125. We lived up in Michigan and my parents always put one on the back of the trailer. I hardly ever rode on the street, I just liked following trails to see where they would go. Often I wound up in a mud hole and fell over. Those little bikes were heavy when you tried to get them up. We were crazy in those days. We never wore helmets and what I loved best was riding through the woods, feeling the wind. I'd never do that now. Of course I can't ride, with my leg and all."

She had an artificial leg. Since she brought it up I asked her how she had lost her leg. I wondered if it was a motorcycle accident. "Oh no," she said, "It was a drunk driver. I was with my dad and our car stopped and we got out to try to fix it. It was at night and we were parked behind another car. I was standing at the side holding the flashlight when a drunk ran into the back of our car. He hit us, backed up, and hit us again. My one leg was pinned, but my dad who was in front had both legs pinned.

"I woke up lying on the ground and I could see my leg just hanging by a bit of tissue and I thought 'Well, I guess I'm going to have to learn to walk again.' But my dad was unconscious and he didn't know till he got to the hospital. He asked my mother for a blanket, he said, 'My feet are cold,' and she had to tell him both his legs had been amputated." Later I would meet a biker with a titanium leg, learning how to walk again. He had stopped in the park lane on a freeway to adjust the tie-down straps on his motorcycle trailer and a drunk had plowed into him and sliced his leg off.

WAITING FOR MY DOCUMENTS, my eyes wandered to the wooden bookcases surrounding the room. They were not yet full, and though I knew they would be at some point I enjoyed looking at the empty spaces. My own were crammed, with books slotted in sideways on top. These had beautiful smooth boards. If I had money I would donate a wall of bookshelves with the proviso that they never be more than one-quarter full so that you could always see the shelves, and the space. Seamus Heaney knew about bookcases: in his poem "The Bookcase" he speaks of shelves "planed to silkiness," of how the "vellum-pale" boards never sagged, were themselves emblems of virtue, and how he could feel their measure in his own limbs. He remembers the volumes of Yeats, McDairmid, and Hardy, and the blue-white dust jacket of Elizabeth Bishop, but comes back to bookcases, these planks that are at once a "bier" and a "raft for books."

I knew you could never endow empty shelves, unless maybe you paid an artist a fabulous sum to designate them an art installation. The bottom line for libraries was space, that is what it always came down to, what they were always fighting for, and over.

At some point the books become, as they say, a relationship issue. Just before I left for Texas I walked into the house to find Hsing standing in the hallway, hand on hip, holding a brown paper package, "What's *this*?" she said as I came through the door. The problem with the shape of a book is that it doesn't look like anything else.

"Research," I replied gamely, but had to clear my throat before I could get the word out, which diminished the effect.

"So what are libraries for?"

"Well, they didn't have this."

"And you have to have . . . let's see, here's the invoice on the front [damn, why do they do that?] . . . a first edition, a *first* edition? of Robert Fulton's *One Man Caravan,* 1937?"

"He, he went around the world in 1935. It's a classic of motor-cycle travel."

"I'm sure it is. And can you not get it through interlibrary loan?"

"Well . . ."

"You don't have to own every book you read you know."

"Well . . ."

"Anyway, the point is we don't have enough space."

It's always the space.

ALEXIS HAD TAKEN HER ARCHIVE on the road. Will Goodwin was living in his. I met him for coffee at the Metro café, a new place on the Drag done in industrial bleak, everything gray steel and hard angles. "CC's is gone," Will said, "and this is the only place that lets me smoke." CC's coffee house, which had a covered portico where smokers could sit at wrought-iron tables and watch the street from the shade, had come, thrived we thought, then suddenly disappeared. There had been more changes on the Drag, not only had CC's gone but Europa Books had disappeared, and the university bookstore had morphed into a Barnes & Noble. I thought about how good the old lightbulb was.

Will's hand shook a little as he brought the match up to the unfiltered Camel. He was wearing jeans, a white shirt, and a striped seersucker sports jacket—his standard uniform—but his face had acquired a pebble-grain texture and deep grooves since I had last seen him. He had inherited his parents' extensive library and was setting up a rare-book business. I told him that I had ridden his old motorcycle, Isobar, that weekend.

He had sold it a few years before to the acquisitions manager in the main library, Glen Worley, who lived out near Elgin on the rolling plain east of Austin. Someone had introduced me to Glen because I was the motorcycle guy. We hit it off, and because he had a new BMW he invited me out for a ride on the old one. I told Will it was amazingly smooth, steady in the crosswinds even at 75.

"I used to take that bike to library conferences every summer. New York, San Francisco, all over the place. I visited my family in Colorado. Long rides. But no saddlebags. I liked the look of the bike just as it was, and I used to just bungee a small pack to the backseat and put on a tank bag. That was it. And it was stable. One time coming back from the coast through the desert in Nevada—you know the Big Basin?—you come over a rise and you can see the road stretching away for miles and miles. No turns. Well, I'd always wanted to ride at 100 miles an hour for an hour. To cover 100 miles in one hour. And I did, I put my head down on the tank bag and just held it at 100. No one else out there. Straight across the desert." Will smiled, and for an instant I could see the young librarian speeding into the empty space, stretching the moment to an hour he would have all his life.

He still had his house in the country but spent most of his time in the narrow studio apartment he had rented in a limestone build-ing tucked into a hill just off Sixth Street. He showed me a travel book by somebody named Kathryn Hulme called *Arab Interlude,* about driving across northern Africa in the 1920s; a copy of Woolf's *Orlando*—first U.S. edition with dust jacket, but fourth printing; a book by Christopher Morley, *Parnassus on Wheels,* about a horse-drawn caravan full of books. My first independent reading had come from the bookmobile; in my memory it was always winter and my snowboots clunked on the tall steel steps, and I would sit on the wheel hump that curved up out of the floor and look through the books I had collected, choosing the three I was allowed. Edmonton had been the first place in North America to have a traveling library, an electric streetcar that traveled out along the river. I asked about *Parnassus on Wheels* and Will became uneasy. In fact whenever I showed the slightest interest in anything he said, "I haven't priced that yet," or, more firmly, "I'm not ready to sell that."

I picked up *Arab Interlude* again. Will told me how Hulme had become famous later in life with *The Nun's Story*. "The book was a huge success, became a film, got picked up by the Book-of-the-Month Club, made into a *Reader's Digest* condensed book. Remember those?" My parents had bought them. As an undergraduate I was ashamed of them, their greasy brown bindings, fake class, and when my mother died we sold them in the estate sale for 10 cents each. Now I wish I had them. They were part of the sensibility of the era, along with Sputniks and speed-reading courses. I looked at the deep black wood-cuts in *Arab Interlude* and read Hulme's opening disclaimer that there was nothing heroic about two women spending four months driving 3,000 miles across northern Africa in the modern 1920s.

"I'll take it," I said.

"Dang!" said Will, jumping up from his chair. "I really love that book."

"I've just been to the bank machine. I've got cash."

"Dang!" he said again, as if I'd pulled some particularly devious bargaining trick. "Dang."

I TOLD GLEN WORLEY about Will's 100-miles-an-hour run as we talked over margaritas out at the Hula Hut on Lake Austin. "I don't know," he said, shaking his head. "Even with your head down you'd take a beating. There's a lot of wind at a 100. But Will's a purist, he never would use a windshield." He pulled out a book that I had been trying to track down, *The Last Days of T. E. Lawrence* by Paul Marriott and Yvonne Argent, not so much a narrative as a report of his crash, with pictures and diagrams, quotes from witnesses, and analyses of the skid marks. I sipped the margarita. My Texas friends, appalled at my backwoods attitude toward tequila—in Alberta it had been one step down from rubbing alcohol—were trying to educate me. The pure agave tequilas were so smooth they were dangerous. I now thought I could tell the difference between Herradura Silver and Patron Anejo in a margarita (on the rocks, no salt). "You know," said Glen, "it was that movie *Lawrence of Arabia* that made me want to be a motorcyclist. Watching that opening sequence where he's on the Brough I thought, *That's what I want to do*—ride a motorcycle like that through the hills. And not crash of course."

My reading on Lawrence and *Ulysses* had naturally led to a little research on Lawrence and motorcycles, and in one sense his death on a bike seemed inevitable. "It's my great game on a really pot-holed road to open up to 70 miles an hour or so and feel the machine gallop," he wrote to George Brough in a letter praising the firm's motorcycles. He told Charlotte Shaw how he rode down from Edinburgh averaging 65 miles an hour, hitting 90 miles an hour for 2 or 3 miles on end, "leaping" past Morris Oxfords doing a staid 30 miles an hour. He called his motorcycle Boanerges—"sons of thunder"—and the thunderous riding was a compulsion: "When my mood gets too hot . . . I pull out my motor-bike and hurl it top-speed through these unfit roads for hour after hour." Like the pilots after the Second World War who formed the biker gangs in the United States, Lawrence felt his nerves "jaded and gone near dead, so that nothing less than hours of voluntary danger will prick them into life." He poured money into motorcycling, always buying the latest and fastest Brough (he sold his Fourth Folio Shakespeare for £80 to make up the £150 necessary for his second Brough). The only thing that brought him comparable pleasure was writing: he wrote to his editor Edward Garnett of the "frenzied aching delight in a pattern of words which happen to run true." Yet he always doubted his writing. (He wrote an article about racing an airplane on his Brough and sent it anonymously to a motorcycle magazine. They rejected it, which fueled his conviction he was only being published because he was "Lawrence of Arabia.") Ironically, after all his wild rides, Lawrence was killed at about 40 miles an hour on a familiar road near home, when he swerved to avoid two boys on bicycles.

LAWYER AND COLLECTOR Herb Harris often rode his Brough through the limestone hills not far from where we were sitting. Austin had surprised me again. While the Harry Ransom Center had been acquiring the prize documents of British modernism, Harris had been collecting the prize examples of British motorcycling: the most historically significant Vincents in the world, nicely bracketed by some Broughs from the 1920s and a few Triumphs and BSAs from the 1960s.

One of the first things Harris said to me as I settled into the couch in his living room, between a BSA Gold Star and an AJS cutaway engine, was, "You've got to have an extensive library if you're going to collect motorcycles." He has a complete run of Vincent shop manuals, and he has also collected sales pamphlets, "so you can see what the factory thought was important at the time." On his website he speaks of the importance of having the original title certificate, and he told me, "I like what I call 'history bikes.' When I buy a bike I take along a tape recorder and I make an audiotape of the owner. I want to get everything I can about the bike, all the stories." He is happy enough to have a fine example of any Vincent, but what really excites him are bikes with a past; as he's fond of saying, "It's not the hardware, it's the history." Reviewing Harris's website later, I was impressed by his advice to collectors. He speaks of the importance of provenance, and he knows where to put the apostrophe in "Collectors' Guide." "Never surrender an original title without keeping a photocopy. Much history is on an old certificate of title which the State will kindly shred for you when you register your motorcycle," he writes, sounding just as cranky as Nicholson Baker on the destruction of newspapers.

Philip Vincent was an engineering student at King's College, Cambridge, in 1928 when he sketched his radical motorcycle. The first Vincents rolled out of the factory in 1937, and after 1940 when Brough ceased production they became *the* bike to own. If T. E. Lawrence had not died in 1935, he surely would have owned one: he loved speed and the Rapide would do 110 miles an hour, the Black Shadow 125 miles an hour, and the Black Lightning 150 miles an hour. Vincents were notorious for developing speed wobbles, "tank slappers," which are less hilarious than they sound: an oscillation in the frame increases in amplitude until the ends of the handlebars are hitting the tank, sometimes so violently that they leave dents. More frequent in older bikes, tank slappers rarely happen to newer motorcycles with modern frames and suspension, but other factors such as unevenly loaded saddlebags, a tall windshield, or steering head bearings in bad condition can cause small vibrations to increase, like feedback from a guitar amplifier. Beyond a certain point the bike implodes and bike and rider go down.

Vincents became icons. Richard Thompson sang about them, Hunter S. Thompson wrote about them, and what is probably the most famous motorcycle picture ever—of a guy named Rollie Free in nothing but a bathing suit, shower cap, and sneakers stretched out on a seatless bike racing across the desert—immortalized a

Vincent Black Lightning. I had, quietly, always been a little uncertain of the aesthetics of Vincents. The engine is undeniably beautiful, with the two exhaust pipes curving out, forward, and then fusing into one before entering the muffler. It is erotic and echoes, softly, the straight-edged triangle of the front suspension, and it catches the eye because it curves into empty space—there is no front frame member to box it in. What has never quite worked for me is that seat perching over the shocks like a bridge across a canyon, as if Vincent didn't really want a seat at all but grudgingly realized that his beautiful creation had to have a rider and that this rider had to sit somewhere. Maybe that's one reason the picture of Rollie is so compelling—the seat is gone and he lies groin on fender with his belly dipping down into the space above the shock absorbers.

The Harris Vincent Gallery looks less like an art gallery than an Edwardian library, with heavy burgundy drapes, dark wainscoting, and wooden shelves, and it displays documents as well as motorcycles: Phil Vincent's elegant original drawings of the motorcycle, and the one-page contract transferring the assets of the HRD motorcycle company to Phil Vincent's father. Harris showed me an early Brough that had been used by a hunter in Africa, and a couple of early Vincents, and then directed me to the most famous bike in his collection, the "bathing suit bike" on which Rollie Free set the world speed record of 150.313 miles an hour at the Bonneville Salt Flats in 1948. I said the name was almost laughably symbolic: "Rolling Free," like those nineteenth-century novels in which a man with many children is called Mr. Quiverfull. "It's better than that," said Harris, "there was a journalist who thought that's what the picture was about—'Rolling Free,' the state of Nirvana that you reach at high speed."

Harris rides all his bikes. That too is history. "These bikes dictate a certain pace, one that reflects the pace of life at the time. You can't just push a button and go like on modern bikes. If you're in a hurry to get it started it's going to be a frustration. If you look at it as a task in itself it's satisfying. Like that BSA Gold Star in the garage. If you get it started in three kicks you feel you've accomplished something.

"For the Brough it's even longer. The fact that you have to oil the rocker arms before starting out tells you something about the way they lived. Including getting his leathers on and everything, a man would need maybe half an hour to get ready to go on a ride." I thought of T. E. Lawrence suiting up. "On an old bike the world of the past becomes reality. They say the brakes were bad on those old bikes, but they were just fine for the time. There wasn't a lot of traffic on the road and people weren't going 80 miles an hour. Those old brakes did the job."

He'd put his finger on something I had felt when chuffing through the countryside on the twenty-five-year-old Isobar, following Glen on his new BMW. He had sophisticated suspension and ABS brakes, I had forks that turned the bike into a rocking horse if I shifted down too quickly. We were riding on the same road but in different eras. I was cruising in a time warp. On old bikes you not only move at their pace, you move into their space.

Harris appreciates history, but some riders in Britain feel he is plundering their heritage. He owns a supercharged Black Lightning that was built in 1949 to try to bring the motorcycle speed record back to the United Kingdom. It was dismantled and mailed out of the country in boxes before it could be designated a historical artefact. At some Vincent rallies Harris was treated like the Prince of Darkness (that isn't precisely what he was called), but over the years

British collectors have acknowledged that the bike is probably in better shape than it would be if it had stayed in Britain. I told Harris about how British librarians had resented the way the Ransom Center had made off with their literary heritage, but how the writers and their heirs appreciated both the cash and the care that the manuscripts were given.

In fact the rivalry between the Ransom Center and the British Library was giving way to a new spirit of cooperation. Later that week Staley said, "You have to meet Chris Fletcher. Great guy. You'll like him. He's the curator of modern manuscripts at the British Library, over here to work with us." I expected a hunched, tweed-encrusted academic with food on his tie, and instead was greeted by a tall, improbably young man who said, "I hear you have a Ducati. We must talk. I ride a KTM Supermoto." He thought I was adventurous to have ridden all the way to Texas; I thought he was insane because he roared into central London every day, lane-splitting at 70 miles an hour. "You're expected to," he said, referring to the practice of riding between the lanes of moving traffic. "The whole point is that a motorcycle doesn't take up the space of a car." But what if someone opens a door, even slightly, say, to adjust a snagged seat belt? "Well you just hope they don't." His first weekend in Austin he had rented a huge Harley and taken it out into the hill country. "I once rode a Harley in London but you feel bloody ridiculous. Sort of like you're riding around in quotation marks the whole time. Look at me, I'm a 'Biker.' Here they make more sense. You're out on the open road, in the desert, no people around, and the Harley handles surprisingly well." We talked about motorcycles and national character, and I wondered what the reaction would be if the rarest and best Harley-Davidsons wound up with a private collector in Manchester.

I CALLED HSING because she was coming down to Austin at the end of the week to spend a few days with me and Martha—mainly Martha, mainly for yard-saleing—before I started back on the bike.

"How's the work going?" she said right away. Which is not something you ask an academic straight out, just slapping it down on the counter like that. You ease up to it, test the waters, and if you sense unease you don't broach the subject at all. "Have you finished your *Jacob's Room* annotations?" Not completely, I admitted, nor the Joyce work, and told her I had discovered some fascinating things about the archive itself, and about obscure bookstores. It didn't seem necessary to mention Herb and the Vincents. I did tell her that Jim, my editor who had warned me about killer bees and tarantulas, had emailed me that the editorial committee was ready to make other arrangements if they didn't get the draft soon. I hoped Hsing would say something consoling.

"How can you *do* that. How can you work this way? I don't understand. Why would you even take on a project until you'd finished the one you're working on? I'd just say to the editor, 'No, I can't do that until I've finished this.'"

"You're probably right," I said.

"I *am* right." I tried to mount the "different-doesn't-mean-worse" defense. The last time she had been in Austin we had gone together to Central Market, where she'd looked at the array of yogurts available and said, "Fruit-bottom yogurt. That's just wrong. You have to mix it up anyway." I told her I didn't mix it. She said that was wrong. Our discussion became fairly animated. I pointed out there was a reason that manufacturers made both mixed and fruit-bottom yogurt, that just because *she* mixes up fruit-bottom yogurt before eating it didn't mean *I* had to, that I didn't insist that she *not* mix up the fruit-bottom yogurt, and that maybe she ought to just sidle down to the other end of the yogurt section and buy her low-fat low-rent mixed yogurt and eat it and shush up and recognize that there was a *reason* they made it this way and it was for people like me, *lots* of people, who liked a vertical shaft of pure white yogurt with a dollop of, say, peach on the end, who didn't want to homogenize, who wanted the tartness *and* the sweetness simultaneously, the metaphorical clash as it were of yogurt and syrupy fruit, but it was *okay* if others wanted it mixed but it was *also* okay if they didn't.

I paused for breath and she said, "Yes, but it's wrong."

And so I began to explain softly (we were in the checkout line now) that *this* was what was wrong with *her,* and with her mother, and with the entire Taiwanese civilization, which would be justly swallowed up by the even more rigid mainlanders who would make her eat yogurt with chopsticks and there wouldn't be any fruit in it at all, not on the bottom, not swirled in, and everyone would have to wear those jackets with the stupid collars . . .

"See? You're ranting. Why can't you be reasonable like me?"

For sure my editors wished I could be more like her. I could have used the freelancer's argument, which is that you have to take the work when it comes, that you don't say "No" to anything, and that, like the guy who renovates your house, you say "Two weeks" and do an enormous amount in the first ten days before you disappear into the mists leaving the kitchen looking like Sarejevo. But it's only partly that. I could have reminded her of my "terror of the page" theory. Not the blank page—I may dance around it a little, resist getting down to it—my terror is the published page. I will have projects fifteen-sixteenths complete and walk away from them. Even when I finally get them done I'll sometimes let them sit—in an addressed envelope, proofed, ready to go—just sit, on the floor of my study so that, for two weeks before I send them out, I have to walk by the envelope every time I go to the bathroom. So that makes finishing difficult. The real problem though is that I can't write unless I'm playing hooky. I never skipped school, was a dutiful student, yet when it comes to writing if you give me a studio, unlimited time, and one thing to work on I'll dither. But if I have something else to do I'll work like mad on the forbidden one, the adulterous project.

Part of the attraction is that all writing projects look easy at the beginning. You can practically write them in your head on the half-hour drive or walk to work. When you get there all you'll have to do is type them out and *ecco!* there they'll be. Done. Alas, it seldom works this way. Actually it *never* works this way. That doesn't stop me from thinking it *might* work this way, this time. And so I take on "little" projects, which then grow like the blob that ate Chicago, consuming time, energy, and enthusiasm, taking me away too long from the other writing that languishes like cold half-eaten dinners on the counter of my mind. They become unappetizing, and it's then so hard to get back into them, to do the mental microwaving that will put some heat back into them. So they sit, until an editor comes in with a flame-thrower. Hsing was probably right.

I said, "My work is like yours in the emergency ward. I stabilize one patient-slash-article, hop to another and put in an IV, get back to the first, put it on oxygen and active verbs, call for a CT scan and syntactical analysis of the second, then turn to a third that's just come in with massive trauma and paragraph defibrillation . . ."

"Yeah, but we don't let them die in the corridor."

I'm thinking there's a reason nobody rides motorcycles with sidecars anymore.

FOURTEEN

Bad Chain

"That's a *baad* chain," said Vern. "Yessir that's the *baddest* chain we sell. You won't find a badder chain than that."

"Uh, good," I said, and shelled out the equivalent of Can$210 for the new bad chain. I wondered what to call my old chain, which was bad in the conventional sense—I'd overtightened it on the way down in my eagerness to perform the one act of motorcycle maintenance I was capable of (two wrenches! grease on my fingers! move over Pirsig), and it had stretched in one spot so it would never be right again. "It's happy loose." said Vern. "It'll slap the swingarm if it's loose but it's happy. Won't hurt anythin', it's when it's too tight you've got a problem."

I could have got the cheaper one but the weather channel was announcing brush fires in New Mexico and snow in the Cascades, and I had three days of empty desert before I even got to where there was foliage enough for a brush fire. I knew I wouldn't have problems with a cheaper chain but I wanted everything ticking over more than perfectly. I would be riding 3,500 miles alone. I wanted a margin of error as big as the continent. They wheeled the bike out of the shop. I hadn't been on it, hadn't seen it, in over six months. I wished other people weren't around. What if I forgot how to do this? I pulled on my helmet, settled on the bike, hit the starter—*roar!* Whew. I'd forgotten how loud those new pipes were. I clonked into first gear, eased out the clutch, I was off. I swung into the main road, hit second, snapped the throttle to make a lane change, and felt my grin poking the sides of the helmet. Back on the Duc. There's nothing like it.

Heading west from Austin, out through the hill country, the big live oaks—like giant broccoli stumps—gradually give way to low bushes and fat succulent cacti, and then to scraggly brush in a rocky white soil. I stopped in Llano, drawn by the bright red, white, and green Italian ESPRESSO sign as I rode through the historic main square. I parked the bike by the church and walked in. The place was made of rough-hewn boards and looked like it should be selling shots of bourbon, not espresso. It had a long wooden bar, and the *barista* and the two older men in the place were plainly ranchers— checked shirts, cowboy boots—but the guy made a mean espresso. I drank it standing up at the bar. (Maybe Clyde Barrow had smashed back a bourbon here. The Bonnie and Clyde gang used to stay at the Dabbs Hotel because of the quick access to the gullies out back where they could hide.) We talked about the weather, and how these little ten-minute spits of rain didn't do anything, didn't even dampen down the dust for long, and then I thanked him and got back on my bike. It turned out to be my last decent coffee for almost a week. This was the end of the hill country and the gentrifying influence of

Austin. As the land heated up, the sky changed from bright blue to a dull silver like unpolished aluminum. The glare scattered the sunlight and the rays came from everywhere, sliding under my sunglasses, hitting my eyeballs in little needle jabs. The road flattened out like a dead snake and headed straight northwest, through San Angelo and Big Spring toward New Mexico.

THE SEVENTH EARL OF AYLESFORD, a drinking buddy of Edward VII's when he was Prince of Wales, came to Big Spring in the wake of a divorce scandal. The hotel didn't have room for his entourage so he bought the hotel; when he wanted to give a party for the town he bought a saloon. After a year of hard drinking he threw a fabulous party in his hotel, got up from a card game saying "Bye, boys," and died. He was thirty-six.

I knew this because I was sitting in the public library in Big Spring, trying to stay awake. It was 90 degrees Fahrenheit outside and still only one in the afternoon. It would get hotter before it cooled off. I learned that Big Spring was used in 1942 to train cadets in precision high-altitude bombing. I learned about a project to take bats with incendiary devices attached and drop them from aircraft at 1,000 feet. The idea was they'd spread out and eventually land, creating brush fires. Would the bats themselves be burning when they hit the ground?

Fascinating as this all was, Big Spring depressed me. I cruised the town center: nothing but pawnshops and boarded-up windows. The giant Wal-Mart at the outskirts of town had sucked the life out of the core. There was the old Settles Hotel, a 1930s wedding-cake-style skyscraper. It was sandstone colored, and its edges worn, as if it were gradually dissolving back into the desert. It was boarded up, and the only place to stay was at a Motel 6 or Best Western out on the highway. If I was going to have to stay on the highway I figured I might as well make a few more miles, and before I'd given it much thought I was barreling along the deserted back road from Big Spring to Andrews. The sun sat low now, smudging land and sky together in a purple haze out over New Mexico. I knew this was unsafe. I was ignoring my friend Pasquale's injunction: "Never try to make that extra 100 kilometers at the end of the day on a bike. It's not like in a car."

My hours in the library had stored up some coolness in my body so I didn't feel the heat so much when I first went out. But then I found I had lost my map, which rattled me, then that I had lost my sunglasses. I have accepted that it is my destiny to leave a trail of sunglasses through this life, but I never lose my map. My *map*. What could be a worse omen for the first day of a trip? Bad karma. Starting a journey you should be calm, centered, complete, like a samurai, at one with his sword, totally focused on the task. Not flailing about like a man trying to pick up an exploded bag of marbles. It was all Hsing's fault.

She had come for her visit and was mad that I was leaving this morning at dawn and not seeing her to the airport at 2:00 in the afternoon. 2:00 P.M.? At which point I was supposed to head out into the blazing sun that not even the rattlers ventured into?? She conceded my point, but she was miffed because I had discovered Highway 93, leading all the way from Las Vegas to Lake Louise. "Won't that make a great ride?" I asked, thinking she would share my enthusiasm.

"No, I think it will be a terrible ride. I think you should wait and do it with me and Matilda," she'd said.

She'd been fine after that, I thought, but that morning when I bent to kiss her good-bye she had flicked her head aside, then lay rigid as I kissed her on the forehead. Saying nothing.

"Good-bye," I said.

"Good-bye."

"Well, have a good trip," I said (this was what *she* should have been saying to *me*).

"You too." That was it. I grumbled inside my helmet. She had taken the motorcycle safety course too, she *knew* you were not supposed to ride when you are angry or distracted. If I hadn't been so annoyed this morning I never would have forgotten my map and sunglasses. She had deliberately cursed my trip and now I was going to hit an armadillo and die.

I didn't of course. I hit Andrews at seven and the sun was still high in the sky. Maybe I should go on, make it over the border into New Mexico, get all the way out of Texas in one day. I would gain an hour as soon as I crossed the border, so actually it wasn't really seven at all, only six. I knew this was just the road-mode part of my brain talking, the tempter who lures you on, but I needed gas. Andrews did not have much to recommend it. Even the caption on the visitor's guide said, "Ain't nothin' out here *on* the ground so God put all that oil *under* the ground." The only thing moving on the harsh land outside of town seemed to be donkey engines. The first oil well had been discovered just after Christmas in 1929; the rest of the country was crashing into the Great Depression and Andrews was staking its claim to be the largest oil-producing county in the state. Midland, a few miles south, had lured George Bush down from New Haven. I wondered idly how growing up on this scorched plain would affect your perspective.

Once off the bike I knew I should stop. I got directions to the Energy Park Inn, and walked out to the bike already thinking of how cool the room would be and forgetting how top-heavy the bike becomes with a full tank. I swung it off the sidestand and— aaurghh . . . *thump! tinkle-tinkle*—I dropped it. The brake lever knob skittered across the tarmac. The saddlebags kept the bike from coming down on my leg, but gas was spilling out around me. I struggled but couldn't get the bike up (which way do you turn the bars? there's a trick to getting bikes up but I couldn't remember).

"Excuse me?" I called to the guy at the next pump. He had his back turned and I was muffled by my helmet. *"Excuse me! . . ."* I said louder (god how embarrassing—it's like those commercials: "Help, I've fallen and can't get up"—maybe they should have emergency beepers for elderly motorcyclists). *"Help!!"* I shouted.

"Oh . . . *oh* . . . sorry," he said, grabbed the handlebar, and together we got the bike up. I was really shaken. Not because of the bike falling over but because the fall made me realize how far gone I was. I had no business riding around the block, much less blasting into the desert sun at 80 miles an hour with my brain completely poached. I was lucky I had fallen over at a gas station. And it wasn't as humiliating as having a pop machine fall on you.

The brake itself worked fine, and as I drove to the motel I could feel the jagged end of the lever through my glove. The extra 100 kilometers. This one I couldn't blame on Hsing.

THE NEXT DAY I faced the Llano Estacado, the "staked plain." Nobody knows exactly why they call it that, perhaps because stakes were used to mark the trail, to tether horses to, or to tie up enemies for torture; and it too is desolate and bursting with oil underneath.

It is part of the great plain that runs from Canada to Texas, and the Athabascan Indians came through here in the 1500s on their long trek from the prairies of what would become Alberta. They weren't my ancestors, and Canada hadn't been invented yet, but I was heading back to a cabin close to the Athabasca River, and it made the plain seem less empty to know that these folks, neighbors in a sense, had come through here.

I had a lesson in aerodynamics that morning. As a car driver I had always laughed at semi trailers that sported swooping curves on their mammoth fenders or those spoilers on the top of the cab that made them look like bald-headed wrestlers. As if that would make a difference. Yet one of the first things you discover as a motorcyclist is that it's the shape of the truck, not the size, that makes a difference. Cube vans throw a fat blast of air that feels like it could punch you straight back off your bike. Somewhere west of Artesia I met an old moving van, completely squared off, like a brick wall chugging across the plain at 55 miles an hour. I hunched down a little, as I always do, when *poum* his draft hit me like someone swinging a sandbag. If I had not been holding on tight I would have been in the ditch. Those rounded corners on modern vans do make a difference.

From Cloudcroft to Ruidoso in New Mexico I got my first bit of tasty road since leaving the hill country—"slow to 45 . . . to 30 . . . to 25"—swinging the Duc through the S-bends in high pine forests. I had to watch for cattle guards in the corners, that was all; there was nobody but me on the road. For the first time I was listening to the engine again, watching the road and shifting on the exhaust note. "Such sweet thunder." Who coined that phrase? Though appropriated by Duke Ellington, maybe it was in fact a translation from the Italian. It was first used at the Ducati factory on the outskirts of Bologna in 1970

to describe the sound of the new Desmo twin: *"Che dolce tuono!"*—
what sweet thunder—said Taglioni reverently as the unmuffled
prototype thundered past on the banking. Some detractors claim that
actually Taglioni was looking at his sandwich and had really
murmured, *"Che dolce tonno!"*—"what sweet tuna." This is a vicious
slander perpetuated by manufacturers jealous of the Ducati sound.

Up Silver Spring Canyon, through the Apache Indian reservation,
and too soon you pop out onto the freeway for the last couple of
miles into Ruidoso. I checked into the Pines Motel, a charming
fifties-style ten-unit place by the river, with red screen doors on the
units that make them seem like summer cottages. Very clean, very
cheap, with a staircase behind the office that runs down to a deck by
the little river out back, and there I saw an old guy in hip waders
who reminded me of my grandfather, hefting a fish he had just
caught. In the room there were good reading lights and a little table
under the window, perfect for writing.

As I sat at the desk I could feel my face still glowing. I had been
riding in my short desert boots, with just a T-shirt under my half-
open leather jacket. I knew the wind had been drawing moisture out
of me, and reminded myself to drink more. It was early evening and
I just wanted to watch mindless TV, but I forced myself to record a
few things in my notebook. My pledge to myself, along with staying
off freeways and eating in nonfranchise diners, was to write every day
for an hour. I wouldn't let myself go on in the morning if I hadn't
done the hour at night, because the new impressions would overlay
the old ones and they would fade, unrecoverable though only a day
old. My mind was like one of those kid's slates where with the flick
of a lever you wipe it clean. You can write over it as many times as
you want, but you only get one page.

Main Street was mainly deserted. This was the off season, between the winter skiing and summer tourism. Ruidoso has no center; it snakes along the canyon, one shop deep on either side of the road in and out of town. I rode through, taking note of places I might like to investigate or eat at, and stopped near the far end of the commercial strip. An ugly modern flat-topped building caught my eye: RARE BOOKS said the sign in the window. Posters and signs in red and black also proclaimed ART GALLERY, BILLY THE KID ROOM, GIFTS, NEW BOOK ON RUIDOSO OUT SOON! LOCAL MERCHANT, MONEY TALKS! 30% OFF RAKOCY WATERCOLORS!

It was so astonishingly tacky that I had to look in.

"Howdy," said the deep voice.

I nodded.

"Everything's 30 percent off."

"Okay."

He let me look around and settled back in his armchair. I appreciated that. I hate it when they follow you around the shop, telling you the percentage off of every item you look sideways at. I didn't see any rare books.

"I don't see any rare books."

"Well these ones here I've published myself are pretty rare, but I guess you mean old books. C'mon over here. He led me through the gallery into a cluttered studio with a shelf of books on U.S. history that dated to the 1940s.

"So . . . are all these paintings yours?"

"Yep. Most of 'em. These over here are by a friend of mine. Very good work. Everything else in these rooms is by me. Those books on the rack out front are by me too. That's just a sideline with me. I'm no great shakes as a writer—and I've got five books to prove it!" He delivered the line like stock riff, used hundreds of times. Still, I was intrigued. Everyone wants to be a writer and I respect anyone who actually follows through on a work, no matter what it is. I picked up a bright yellow volume: *THE KID: Billy the Kid, With Rakocy Watercolor Sketch $14.95, Without $12.95.* "So how do you go about writing?" I asked. He paused and thought for a minute.

"One day I heard the writer Paul Hogart talking about how he writes. Do you know his books?" I admitted I didn't.

"No matter. Anyway, he says the biggest problem with writers is *material*. Most writers don't have enough material to write from. They just try to write out of their heads and there isn't enough to go on. So when he gets an idea for a book—just a subject, he doesn't even know what it's going to be yet—he gets a big box, about, oh, so long by so wide . . ." He held his arms out a little wider than his shoulders, then his left hand on his chest and the other about a foot and a half out and looked at the space critically, then adjusted the right hand out 6 inches.

"And he starts throwing things on the subject into that box. He does this for about a year. Say it's Apaches. Everything related to Apaches goes into the box. Then when the box is full . . . no, half full. Well maybe two-thirds full. Anyway, then he starts gleaning, you see, writing nuggets on 5-by-7-inch note cards. And he doesn't even know *what the book is going to be yet*. But," he lowered his voice, "he's getting a marvelous research bank. You see? He's getting the *material* he needs to write, that other writers don't have."

He paused to let this sink in. I nodded.

"Then he starts shufflin' those cards. Oh he shuffles and shuffles, gettin' them in the right order. Mind, he hasn't written a bit yet. He's absorbing the *material* though.

"Then when he starts to write he puts up a card [he placed an imaginary card on an imaginary rack] and he looks at it [he looked]. And then he thinks of a story and he starts to write [he turned a quarter turn to his imaginary typewriter]. See, he can do this because he's got all this *material* to draw from."

I waited, but Bill was finished.

"So, is that how you work?" I asked.

"Oh," he waved a hand dismissively, "sort of. I kind of model myself on him but I come at writing from painting. I like to write *about* something. I'm what you may call a historical writer, I'm not the kind of writer who can just make something up out of his head. No, I'm no great shakes as a writer but . . ." He remembered he'd said that and changed tack, "but if you're interested in that Billy book I can let you have it for $12. No tax."

"I'd like it but I'm traveling on a motorcycle and I'd hate to wreck it up stuffing it in a saddlebag."

"We ship."

"Ah."

"Just write your address on this slip of paper." He rummaged. "Here."

"Well. Okay." I wrote the address. "By the way do you take MasterCard?"

He reared back like I'd pulled a Colt 45 on him. "MasterCard. No *sir*. No credit cards. No."

"It's okay, it's okay," I said, a $10 bill already in my hand. "Here's cash."

He relaxed, and harrumphed like he hadn't really been disturbed at all. I wondered briefly if he would really send the book and was instantly ashamed; of course he would, and it was waiting for me, with my genuine Bill Rakocy watercolor sketch, when I got home.

FIFTEEN

Hunting Kokopelli

When I stopped for coffee in Socorro at ten thirty it was already 86 degrees Fahrenheit, but I had had a wonderful cool run out of the mountains, starting at seven thirty. Up over the pass, dropping first one knee then the other deep into those uphill curves that always make you feel like a racer. I whooped as I came over the summit, the pine forest disappeared, and gravelly hills like those of Greece spread out below, while the hot bare ridges of Tucson Mountain and Carrizozo Mountain glared in the distance. I was heading back into the desert. Down on the valley floor I passed through Nogal and connected with the highway that cut through Lincoln County to Roswell. Now that I knew more about the Lincoln Range War and Chisum and Billy the Kid I wanted to stop. I had seen all the BILLY THE KID road signs on the way down but talking to Rakocy had made it more real.

Pat Garrett, the sheriff of Lincoln County, shot the Kid on a hot night in July 1881; nine months later he gave birth to "The Authentic Life of Billy the Kid, The Noted Desperado of the Southwest, Whose Deeds of Daring and Blood Have Made His Name a Terror in New Mexico, Arizona & Northern Mexico," and the accounts have not stopped since. The Kid was supposed to have been a pimple-faced psychopath, but I knew him as an amalgam of Michael Ondaatje's shard-like images and Kris Kristofferson in Sam Peckinpah's *Pat Garrett and Billy the Kid* (in which Bob Dylan plays a scrawny printer and, on the soundtrack, sings the beautiful "Knockin' on Heaven's Door" as the Latino sheriff bleeds to death by the river). I had been reading an article by Fintan O'Toole in *The New Yorker* about how the Kid was an Irishman, maybe from Limerick, probably from the slums of New York, and that the fight in Lincoln County was not whites fighting Apaches and Mexicans, it was Irish Catholics against Protestant Britishers. The Kid became famous for avenging his friend John Tunstall, which oddly enough aligned him with the Protestant camp: Tunstall was a Londoner, and his partner Alexander McSween was a Scot. At least he called himself a Scot and may have been born on the Isle of Skye but more probably in Canada of Scottish parents. Myth and history were impossibly tangled.

I TURNED LEFT, the sun behind me casting a long shadow of my bike down the road in front of me. The desert rock was burnt orange and the highway itself had a pinkish hue. The road ran straight now, notching the rock ridges, like a gunsight framing the empty sky. These 8 miles were the only ones where I was traveling the same road as last fall. As I passed the Four Winds Café at the Carrizozo intersection I remembered the exotic Tex-Mex special. Now I felt like an old hand. I paused briefly at the stop sign, then blasted through onto the fresh road. Like skiing in powder snow, it's fun looping other tracks but what you really want to do is cut new ones of your own.

West of Socorro the ground turned brown and ugly, the country less welcoming. I crossed the Malpais Lava Beds, horrible sharp black lumps of rock, encrusted with cacti. Repair crews were working on the road so I rode through it at a walking pace, looking at the evil splinters, wondering how you would get a horse through that. The construction zone itself was a rough enough track. The front tire of the Duc skittered sideways off the rocks embedded in the roadway. I'd learned that if I just gave it its head it would get me through, though the wiggles and shudders of the headset were unnerving.

In Gallup I stayed at the Colonial Motel. It was cheap, and the faucet and taps in the shower jutted 3 inches out from the cracked tiles as if someone had tried to rip the fixtures out and given up. I showered quickly, careful not to touch the shower curtain or the wall. I had tried my bank card and the ATM spit it out. Why wouldn't it give me any money when my balance was $750? I tried again. It was because I had a *negative* balance of $750. Over my overdraft limit. Traveling for me always seems to involve these sickening lurches at a teller's wicket or a bank machine as I find I'm in the hole and thousands of miles away from home. So I deserved the Colonial Motel.

It's easy to be depressed in Gallup. Everyone looks seedy and though they don't actually scowl they look at you suspiciously. I went for a bit of a stroll around Dominic's and confirmed that there is no downtown core, only pawnshops. I had been reading Hillerman's *The Dark Wind* as my lunchtime book and the opening murder takes place in Gallup. Well, I thought, that's one useful thing about this excursion: I'm getting a feel for the locale. As usual when I tried to cheer myself up I wasn't convinced. I visited the mall, which depressed me more, and then walked over to the cinema at the little strip mall back of the hotel. I watched Uma Thurman and Janeane Garofalo in *The Truth about Cats and Dogs*. When I came out I met the same panhandler I had seen on the way in, still asking for $5. Everything about the town seemed sad and ineffectual and greasy. I met a biker across the parking lot from me, an Aboriginal guy from Arizona on a 750 Suzuki. He had been biking for thirty years and was intrigued by the Ducati. Very friendly, he shook my hand and introduced himself. I hoped he was not going to suggest going for a beer or anything. He seemed nice enough, but he had a weak handshake and, though smiling, always looked aside.

I GOT ON THE ROAD early and by nine I was in Window Rock, Arizona, capital of the Navajo Nation, and settled into a big break-fast at the Navajo Inn—huevos rancheros, scrambled eggs with green chilies, and grated cheese on a corn tortilla, with pinto beans and hash browns on the side, plus a flour tortilla with butter and jam. It cheered me up and it was cheap. I was going to have to watch my cash for the rest of the ride. I looked around the dining room and made some notes. The Navajo men are often described as barrel-chested; what they are is barrel-torsoed—an upper body like a keg, then a tiny butt and thin legs. Most of the men wear white shirts. The busboy sauntered by in Bolle wraparound sunglasses and a black shirt, glancing in over my shoulder. If you write while you eat it makes people very uneasy. They think you're a restaurant critic, or a health inspector, or maybe (if you're wearing a black leather motor-cycle jacket) a corporate scout for the Hells Angels looking for new businesses to muscle in on. ("Hey buddy. What if that tortilla was to get . . . hurt?")

On my way out I picked up a pamphlet about the Navajo people. The first thing it told me was that in greeting they shake hands softly, with eyes averted. Not to do so is a sign of rudeness, even aggression. I thought of that nice guy I'd met in the parking lot of the Colonial Motel in Gallup, of my hearty eye contact and firm handshake. Oh god. I must have come across as some kind of Tarzan—Me ride Ducati. Me come from Canada. Ooh. Ooh. The visitors' center fell away as I stood there in a hot pillar of shame. I hoped the Navajo had pamphlets explaining that the retinal-bruising stare and finger-crunching handshake of white guys in fact signifies good fellowship.

I cut north to Canyon de Chelly (the name does not rhyme with "jelly"; it's a Spanish corruption of the Navajo word for canyon, *tséyi,* and is pronounced "shay"). Ever since buying my Kokopelli T-shirt at Taos Pueblo I had wanted to see the actual image of the wily flute player scratched on the rock, and Canyon de Chelly, a spectacular thousand-foot gorge of pink-orange sandstone with ancient multi-storey cliff dwellings carved into the walls, was famous for its petro-glyphs. I went into the visitors' center and was looking at a sign that said (amazingly) that you could drive your own SUV into the canyon as long as you hired a guide, when a voice from a purple Grateful Dead T-shirt said, "Ah've got a four b' four. We could share." He looked rough and his old Suburban looked worse, but his Texas accent reassured me. A Navajo guide appeared, shook our hands (softly, with eyes averted), and we climbed in. The Suburban slewed as soon as we hit the sand at the entrance to the canyon. The canyon was once filled with water and the surface is still soft, even though motorized tours have been going in there since the 1940s. I wondered about the cumulative effect of the noise and exhaust, but when we stopped at a Kokopelli and a chain-link fence kept us back from the wall I was disappointed.

We parked in the shade of a cottonwood tree and the guide explained that all these trees, cottonwood, tamarisk, elder, and others, were planted in the 1930s. Then he began to describe the Kokopelli in a loud voice as if he were lecturing a group of thirty, a sure sign of a pre-packaged answer. He told us how Kokopelli would make the corn grow and impregnate the young maidens, and then play his flute again to ease their pain in childbirth. I looked at the little guy lying on his back tootling away beside the handprints, the snake, and the leaping figure. It figured. He probably would lie on his back while his woman, his for a night and now his again for a single night, nine months later, shuddered in pain. She cursed him but the music helped. "What a great job," said my new Texas friend. "Ah'd sure like to be Kokopelli. I heard that his big flute was actually a big penis until the Spanish missionaries taught the Navajo that that was nasty."

At Antelope House the guide showed us riders in the rock, light spaces in ruddy stone that looked like kids' drawings to me. I was struck more by the rock than the figures, how the bands across the top caught the light so that the rock seemed to glow from within, and how below the dark patch the figures on the rock seemed to run away as if it had melted. Then as the crick in my neck distracted me further my peripheral vision captured what the direct gaze missed. The three separate scratches coalesced into a three-figure grouping: the two horsemen and an antelope formed a scene. I looked at it now. The horses with their elongated necks and hairbrush tails seemed to take on speed, driving down on the antelope, cutting it off. The tendril-like legs of the horses, back legs forward, front legs back, carried them swiftly, the top rider's open, the second rider's more angled, and the antelope's legs bent most of all, back and front hooves almost touching in frantic flight. The top rider was less defined, but on the second rider I could now see a headdress and in his upraised hand a spear. He was closing in. The antelope's antlers, like sprigs of coral, were precisely etched, and if you strained your eyes you could see the cleft hooves. It was closest of all, thundering past. For the briefest of moments I got it.

IN HIS BOOK on the Anasazi, *In Search of the Old Ones,* David Roberts tells of meeting Fred, a curmudgeonly ex–Bureau of Land Management ranger who has developed what he calls his Outdoor Museum. If he finds an artefact he refuses to bring it in or even notify the archaeologists. Instead he leaves a note in a Ziploc bag identifying it and asking others to leave it where it is. His credo is, "It's not the artefact, it's the geography." A basket or a wooden doll left under a ledge has more power and more value than it does resting under glass in a display case or, worse, sitting in a storeroom of dusty and vaguely catalogued pots. In his museum the artefacts stay united with the landscape, and the visitors have to do the background reading, the hiking, and the discovering (and Fred would often build little walls of rocks around fragile exhibits to protect them).

It was the old question of use versus access. I sympathized with his position of leaving objects in situ. Archaeological techniques were inevitably disruptive, often destructive. In the 1960s Brigham Young University had called for the collection of all the shards from individual sites. They were bagged and tagged and taken to a lab in Provo, the sites stripped bare. Then at one point a novice researcher took out bags of pottery shards from different sites, dumped them all together on a table and sorted them out by style—immediately destroying the provenance and the chronology of hundreds of artefacts. The same way the well-meaning librarians in Pullman had destroyed the Woolf library. What's the balance? I knew I would not want every tourist who went to London pawing over Woolf's suicide note, but if Fred had his way I would not be looking at this petroglyph at all.

As we walked back to the truck my Texas buddy (who turned out to have read widely and traveled all through Central America visiting ancient sites) told me, "*Anasazi* means 'ancient enemy' in Navajo. The Hopi and the Navajo have never got along. The Navajo still resent having the Hopi in the middle of their reservation." As we drove past the Canyon del Muerto the guide told us about the Long Walk, the forced migration in which American troops under Kit Carson drove the Navajo out of Canyon de Chelly. "My grandmother remembers how her mother was on the Long Walk, how they shot the pregnant women who fell behind, how women and children who couldn't swim died when they crossed the rivers. She cries when she speaks about it."

"Rough," said the Texan quietly when our guide got out to lead us to another site. "But this was Hopi land before the Navajo came, and the army moved the Navajo out because they were exterminating the Hopi."

I felt out of my depth. Part of the attraction of historical sites is that everything seems nicely settled, and of course it is not. In the formal archives in which I worked the tensions were muted, papered over, but there was always a struggle over whose narrative would win out. I had been going to ask our guide about the Hopi, but instead told him I heard that the Navajo originally came from what was now Canada. "Yes," he said. "My cousins went up there to a rodeo and they can understand some of our language. No other tribe in the United States has a language like ours, but they could understand. We call ourselves 'Dineh'—the People—and they call themselves the same."

"Dene," I said. "Yes, some of the Athabascans went north and called themselves the Dene, some walked south and became the Navajo. That's where I'm going, actually, past the source of the Athabasca River. My family has a cabin near that river."

"Oh," he said flatly, plainly not interested in a white guy's summer cabin. Fair enough. The small Hopi reservation sits right in the middle of the Navajo reservation. Hopi politicians always campaign on the program of more land, and that morning in the *Navajo Times* I had read that the Navajo were arresting the Hopi for trapping eagles without a permit, claiming they were not really using them in religious ceremonies. I bought a pair of silver Kokopelli earrings for Hsing from a guy selling jewelry from a blanket and got back on the bike. Heading west over the broad-topped mesas, through Walpi, Oraibi, and out to Tuba City, I realized this spare, ethereal landscape was serene only if you did not live here.

SIXTEEN

Route 66

I stopped for coffee at the Grand Canyon, which seemed like a theme park after Canyon de Chelly, and then followed the road south to Williams on what used to be Route 66. I checked into the Red Garter Bed & Bakery (coffee and all the pastries you can eat in the morning); the place used to be a brothel, so I immediately wrote a batch of postcards making the obvious puns about tarts. The town had hung on to Route 66 as long as they could, fighting the completion of the freeway. Now that Interstate 40 blasts by they've got to have something to lure people onto the exit ramp. I could not imagine Nat King Cole singing, *"It groooves to the coast, and it's really rorty / Get your kicks on Inter-sta-ate Forty,"* but I liked the town. I walked down to the end of the four-block historic center and cut up into the residential area behind it. Williams is built on the side of a hill, and you're immediately in pine forest. The houses are mixed, lots of little clapboard bungalows, nothing too sprawling. Like all

205

travelers I was always looking for a Town I Could Live In, imagining myself in the most improbable places. I liked Williams. It was like Rosslyn, Washington (where the TV show *Northern Exposure* was filmed). Hilly and folksy. I would open a little bookstore that would effortlessly net me $50,000 a year. I would live up on the hill and I would play my guitar on the porch in the evenings and sound like Eric Clapton unplugged. I would have a golden retriever and maybe a pickup truck. It was a wonderful town, you could feel the warm spirit.

Coming down, I saw the flashing lights by the beat-up white Camaro at the corner when I reached the commercial strip. A young woman was sitting outside her jewelry shop taking in the scene.

"What happened?" I asked, "Did the guy shoot the stop sign?"

She stared at me. Probably "shoot the stop sign" means something different in Arizona. "He's been sitting beside a red curb talking for about an hour," she said, lips pursed in disapproval. "Wetbacks."

"What?" My mother taught me never to say "what" but I'd also learned somewhere never to say "wetback."

"Wetbacks. Illegals. We got a lot of problems with them up here. Most of 'em don't have driver's licenses." The penny dropped: she was the one who called the cops.

"I'm surprised you have many," I said and told her I was from Canada.

"They come straight up from Nogales. We're close to the border eh?" She spat the words out, spittle flying. Clearly I was not showing the proper outrage. Probably she had said "eh" because that was how you talked to Canadians. Frostbacks. Williams didn't seem like such a swell town anymore.

I rode Interstate 40 to Seligman and then got off onto "Historic

Route 66." Seligman is what Williams feared it would become, a sad backwater, trying to coax anybody off Interstate 40. I stopped to take a picture of an abandoned gas station on 66 and a guy on a brand new Harley Wide Glide rumbled up. Wraparound shades, a white polo shirt, white cotton pants, and immaculate sneakers. No helmet, perfect tan, perfect teeth. I looked like roadkill in comparison. "Need any help?" The reason Gerry (for that was his name) was dressed like a golf pro was because he was. Somewhere just 15 miles down the road from here the miracle of irrigation had created a golf course, and he ran it or owned it. He didn't say, but looking at his immaculate hog, with its sparkling spoked wheel, I figured he owned it. He had fringes on his handgrips, but you knew he didn't have RIDE TO LIVE, LIVE TO RIDE tattooed across his back. I asked him about helmet laws. "Don't need 'em in R-zona." (Only the foreigners pronounce the *i* in Arizona.) "They make you put it back on across the line in Nevada." I had considered going topless myself, but those desert bugs hit like bullets.

LATER, AT A POPULAR CULTURE CONFERENCE in Albuquerque, I would learn that helmets were not just a choice, they were a cornerstone of American freedom. The last session was "Biker Stigmatization" and by this point in the conference the room was divided: bikers on the left, riders on the right. I had already learned that I wasn't a "biker." I'm a "rider." Maybe just a wannabe writer who occasionally rides. I wasn't sure. These distinctions were becoming difficult.

The presenters talked about bikers being abused and exploited, mocked "hand-wringers" like Mothers Against Drunk Driving and other safety groups, and argued that bikers were still the victims of systemic harassment. Then the big bruiser in front got up to respond. He had sat quietly through the whole conference, but at well over 6 feet and 300 pounds, with a Mohawk haircut slicked into a long ponytail, and a face that looked like 20 miles of bad road, he'd been hard to miss. He wore his riding boots outside his jeans and a leather vest commemorating past rides and dead comrades.

"Ah jist wanna thank y'all for havin' a Dumb-Ass Biker to one a these here academic conferences," he drawled. I missed his name. "That's Sputnik," someone whispered behind me. He was head of the Motorcycle Rights Association of Texas. A Texan and a biker, you can't get more independent than that. He began denouncing mandatory helmet laws—which Texas had recently repealed—and told of government harassment. Of how at the conference of Motorcycle Rights in New York the delegates were under constant surveillance by the FBI, the local police, even the chambermaids. One delegate was arrested for possession of cocaine, and then released.

"Why? Because she, like I do, brushes her teeth with baking soda and salt. She was guilty of possession of baking soda! And then it came out that the maids had been paid $50—*$50!*—for each item that they found that might be illegal. A clear violation of the Constitution." Americans are always talking about the Constitution. Sputnik was warming to his point, "Ain't no such thing as a biker-friendly politician. And these new rich bikers? They ain't gonna help us. They don't care about motorcycles. They're just toys to them. If the government puts too many restrictions on 'em, why they'll just go on to their next toy—a . . . a *hayng*-glider or sumthin'." We all laughed.

"The only good thing 'bout these born-again bikers is it means more hardly used bikes on the market for Real Bikers to pick up at cheap prices." Muttered *yeahs!* rumbled through the audience and we all had visions of picking up a Harley soft-tail for ten grand from some soft-ass dermatologist. Yeah!

"We don't need biker-friendly politicians, we need *Bikers* in office. We need the fire in the guts, the *Fire-In-The-Guts* of the *real biker*." He clenched his fist on the upper slope of his belly. "Because if there's anything that's going to save America, to stop the decline and save this country, to save this civilization, it's the *Spirit of the Biker*."

He sat down. We applauded wildly. I wanted to sell my Ducati, quit my job, grow my hair, get tattooed, and ride back to Texas to fight the Feds and Save America. It was only later that I realized I'd just witnessed the most polished talk of the conference. Anyway, I was not about to give up my helmet. I liked the quiet, and at 65 miles an hour the vents kept my head cool.

ROUTE 66 REJOINS the freeway at Kingman, Arizona, and that is where I picked up Highway 93. The sign was like a homing beacon. I had traced the line on my map and knew that 93 ran all the way from Phoenix to Jasper. It starts out as a two-lane road and I had to pay attention. The wind was coming hard from the west, over the mountains. Usually steady, it sometimes played slingshot, momentarily drawing you to one side then shooting you to the other. Tricky. Not enough to throw you off the road, not quite enough to suck you into the path of an oncoming semi, but enough to make life interesting.

This was a different wind from the Texas winds. Those were hot fat winds, big bricks of molten air that threatened to knock you flat before they melted you. This wind had currents, warm, and hot, and fiery. I could feel individual tendrils of air curling round my neck. Like a lover's hot breath under my ear, they would tease and disappear.

Neat.

The road switched to four-lane. I was traveling at 80 miles an hour, holding hard to the bars, and the wind was now a blast, not a caress, like that first blast that makes you cower when you open the oven unthinkingly to check on a pizza and you put your head too close. I'd better drink something, I thought. I stopped at a gas station, not one of the big mini-mart/car wash/KFC Express kinds of places but a dilapidated Shell with a small cooler in the back and two guys, one with his shirt off, watching TV and making change in a don't-give-a-shit way. It's the kind of place Gary Oldman winds up in at the end of *Romeo Is Bleeding,* only worse.

"How hot is it out there?" I asked.

"Cooled off to 98," laughed the short one.

"She's supposed to make 110 today but shit she ain't gonna come close," said the other, spitting into a bucket, disgusted with the desert for not hitting them with its best shot. I looked at the map.

The winds were coming over the Hualapai Mountains, well, they were giving me a wallop, and now I knew why they were so hot. On the other side was the Mojave Desert. So these winds, already dry, lost whatever last shreds of moisture they had in the mountains, swept angrily down the other side, winds with less-than-zero humidity, eager to suck the fluid out of your eyeballs.

I began to feel little shivers inside, weird spasms of cold. I didn't think this was healthy.

LAS VEGAS 35 said the sign. Less than thirty minutes away. I can do this. A person can put up with anything for thirty minutes. Only I wasn't so sure I could. I knew the buffeting was draining me, and there was not a drop of sweat anywhere on my body. Not behind my ears in my helmet, not behind my bent knees, not between my toes in sweat socks and desert boots. It was like the wind had a line right into my tissues, under the skin, and was sucking my juices directly into the desert.

HOOVER DAM 10. I'd stop there. I strained my eyes to the horizon. I could see no break in the desert, no whiff of humidity from this alleged lake. Abruptly the desert floor cracked open and the road dropped into a narrow gorge. Red rock. Shards of poetry I didn't know I remembered muttered in my mind. *If there were only water amongst the rock / Dead mountain mouth of carious teeth that cannot spit.* The heat doubled and redoubled, pulsing back and forth between the red rock walls. Traffic crawled as the motor homes picked their way down through the tight corners. Cars now in a solid line, snaking slowly toward the parking lot below. Angry faces in hot metal boxes. *There is not even solitude in the mountains / But red sullen faces sneer and snarl.*

I know about cold. I know that in the spring there's still likely to be ice patches under highway overpasses, where it's always cooler. My spine knows instantly when the car I'm driving hits black ice. You can't see it—it's so clear the black asphalt shows through—yet the car goes light in a certain indefinable way, and you don't turn, don't hit the brake, don't lift off the gas, don't breathe. You become very still. The Zen of winter driving. Your only chance is to ride it out. Those who react are lost. What if there's something comparable that happens with extreme heat? What is the Tao of desert driving? And there's the corporeal knowledge that comes with prairie winters. Knowing the difference between minus 27 and minus 30 degrees Celsius just by the bite it makes in your nostrils. Knowing your own stages of hypothermia, feeling the body go numb. For me it starts with my cheeks—cheekbones freezing first—then my nose, on the left side, frozen hard one winter and now always the first to go. Everyone has a spot like that, and every kid knows the toe that was cold and painful but now doesn't hurt anymore, and feels warm, is in fact frozen.

You know about things you've never had to use, you know that parkas have funny periscope-like hoods, shaped to protect your face from the wind that whips away the layer of warm air that lies close to the skin (Yellowknife in a blizzard seems to be full of two-legged stovepipes scuttling down the street). You know that a hood trimmed with coyote fur won't build up with frost, that goose down is the best kind of down, but that caribou skins, fur side in, are best of all. In my country every child is warned against licking the sparkling frost off an iron railing: your warm wet tongue will weld instantly to the metal. You mustn't pull back—you'll rip the top layer of skin off your tongue. What is the equivalent here? Am I doing it? In the desert I know nothing.

Robin had told me to wear a bandana. I thought these were just to wipe the sweat off, or so that cowboys could rob trains without having to go back to the ranch for their balaclavas. "You soak it," she said. "Soak it and tie it around your neck and the water evaporates, cooling the veins in your neck that take the blood to your head. They're close to the surface there. It's not like taking a plunge in Barton Springs but it takes the edge off, and if you stay still it's bearable."

I suppose I was still, frozen to this motorcycle rocketing across the desert at 90, braced rigid against the steady crosswind, but I had no bandana. "I love the heat," she said. "I mean I hate it too. It's so humid here, but when summer comes and it's so hot you can't move all day, and you lie around, and you just wear one thing, maybe two things . . . I love it. Then in the evening it cools off enough so you can go out and everybody moves slow and you feel so free." Me, I felt like I was drowning in hot lard. In Austin the air gets so thick you can lean on it. Here in Nevada this hot wind seemed to have no substance, a spectral wind that is terrifying. I remembered the Dolce Vita café in Austin air-conditioned down into the sixties. So cool, so cool. I love that word *cool*. Even when you say it fast it stretches out in front of you like Lake Louise. Cool.

Pow! Another blast that nearly knocked me off my bike. Hang on. It's only 5 miles to Hoover Dam and Lake Powell. How there can be a lake there I don't know. It should be fizzing up in one last vast cloud of steam, like a test droplet on a frying pan. I could see the water now, a flat patch of blue with a sail boat skimming across it. *A painted ship upon a painted ocean.* Still I could feel nothing. Unreal. *All in a hot and copper sky, / the bloody Sun, at noon . . .*

I found a covered parking space with a sliver of shade. I fingered the broken end of the brake lever, and put the bike carefully on the kickstand. I thought through every move, imagining a clipboard, a pilot going through a pre-flight check. Unlike in Texas, this time I knew I was at the end of my rope.

Lake Powell is a nightmare, a hideous fraud. The boat's sail a mirage. From the concrete parapet you can only look, like Tantalus, at the water; nowhere can you touch it. I walked as quickly as I could without walking quickly over to the gift shop. No place to sit down, so I bought a V-8 juice and drank it standing, pretending to be looking at the amazing curios—cherubs with wings and black cowboy hats labeled WYATT EARP. Unbelievable. As I sipped the juice

I could feel my pulse pounding. I looked at the wrist holding the bottle, expecting the bulging vein to burst and spurt boiling hot blood all over the little winged Wyatt Earp statues.

I was freezing. Typical. It's 100 degrees outside so they air-condition it to 55 inside. Idiots. And no place to sit down. Maybe I should just sit on the floor. Sprawl there and let them tell me to move. I had worked my way around to the front door again and noticed a thermometer on the wall. It wasn't 55, it was over 70—a summer day in Canada. If it felt this frigid what was happening to my body? The staff glared coldly. No one was buying their Wyatt Earps. They knew we were just sucking up their air-conditioning. Hot desiccated bodies seeking cool and fluids. I loitered, watching the heat waves coming off the parking lot tarmac, afraid to go out there.

I could see the sign, LAS VEGAS 20. Twenty miles, twenty minutes. You can do this, I told myself. If I could just close my mind off, hold the cold in as I crossed the parking lot and got the bike going, once up to speed I could handle another twenty minutes. I finished the V-8 juice, put the bottle by a cherub, and strode out. Like a skier from a sauna into the snow (I remembered the old sauna at Mount Assiniboine, the miracle of lying naked on crusty drifts, making snow angels while the ice crystals rasped your bum), I felt the envelope of my body temperature protecting me. Heat bouncing off, then being absorbed but not quite getting through ("Shields are down to 30 percent, Captain"). I slung on the jacket and helmet. Out of the parking lot, across the dam (sightseers strolling in the sun! mad!), still not a hint of humidity from the blue water below, I joined the line of traffic climbing slowly out of the canyon. Trapped. No wonder they shoot people down here. Be calm. There's no way back, no shortcut, no end run. Twenty minutes. You can't die in twenty minutes. At least I didn't think so. Can you freeze to death in twenty minutes? I concentrated on the corrugations in the siding of the motor home in front of me. Refused to look at the red rock. This would take more than twenty minutes. Forget about it. Live for twenty minutes. Don't think beyond it. Then figure out where you are. You're not allowed to complain, not allowed to go insane, for twenty minutes.

Second gear all the way up. Then the motor home began to pull away. Third gear. Fourth. We were up to 60, the gaps widening between the cars, out of the canyon, the desert spreading away. The hideous rock walls gone. I could look around now. I checked my speed, settled into the seat. We were coming over a high ridge, looking down to a jumble of shapes on the flat valley floor. Cubes, oblongs, and a spire in the middle. Las Vegas.

I pulled into a Motel 6. Sidestand down. Soft asphalt? Do you need your crushed pop can under the foot of the stand? No. This is Vegas. A soft asphalt parking lot would be glue for half the year. Okay. Off the bike. You made it.

I SHOWERED AND FELL INSTANTLY into an exhausted sleep. I came to an hour later and struggled to the top of consciousness a couple of times but couldn't pull myself over the edge into wakefulness, and fell back in. At last, after another hour, I made it. I was groggy but this was Vegas and I had to see it. It was still light and still hot when I went out. I felt if I tried to walk too quickly I would just shrivel up and rattle on the pavement like a dried pea. The place felt strange and I couldn't say why. I walked into a casino and looked around. It started to sink in. No mafiosi, no showgirls, no high rollers. No sharkskin suits, no Versace gowns. I looked in vain for a reeking drunk pounding a slot machine in demented rage. Or a worn-out whore with smeared lipstick leaning a sagging breast into a business-man's indifferent arm and pleading with him to have a good time. Everyone looked . . . ordinary. It was all distressingly familiar. The noise, the lights, the compulsively spending throng: this looked like West Edmonton Mall on a Saturday afternoon. I had made my ride through hell to reach the scintillating Sin City, the Cesspool of corruption and concupiscence, the spawning ground of VLTs—and it turned out to be a shopping mall with slot machines. I ate at an enormously mediocre buffet, visited the famous car museum that seemed to feature death machines (Hitler's limo, Kennedy's Lincoln, Mussolini's Alfa Romeo, James Dean's Porsche Spyder—more mausoleum than museum) and went looking for a bookstore.

"Oh, I don't think so," said the helpful young woman at the Bellagio.

SEVENTEEN

The Idaho Kid

I left at dawn, happy to put Vegas behind me and curious to see
Ely, four hours north. I knew of Ely from an old copy of *National
Geographic* with a photo of a woman leaning against the doorjamb of
the Big 4 Bar and Bordello, photographed from inside the dark bar
so that she's backlit, her thigh outlined in a sheer translucent dress
against the bright frame of the door. The caption (does anyone read
the articles in *National Geographic*?) told how prostitution was legal in
Nevada, and it all seemed wonderfully romantic. Ely proved to be the
most family-folksy dog-on-the-porch place I'd been in all my travels.
"Go to Elko," advised the ladies I met outside the café. I thought of
asking them about the bordello, "for research purposes," but instead
asked about the road. "And take Highway 229 through the mountains. It's beautiful. Very scenic." I doubted it. I had been riding all day
through the empty sector, Nevada's Great Basin, conscious that
somewhere off to my left was the hidden air force base that is not on

any map, is top secret except that it is featured in any film about aliens. Unrelievedly bleak.

Still, when I got to 229 I cut west, over Secret Pass in the Ruby Mountains, suddenly on a twisty road in green forest, real green, not just the dusty silver-greens of the desert. I began to get cold, a forgotten and now wonderful sensation. I stopped and got out my jacket liner. My leather jacket felt bulky and cozy again, no longer a loose shell hanging against my T-shirt. Familiar. I reached Elko at dinnertime, and on the edge of town I found an Italian restaurant. Instead of settling for my usual Mexican combo-plate special I ordered scallops Provençale, fresh green beans, and linguini marinara. And they had a sturdy little Rancilio espresso maker behind the bar, the first I had seen since Llano. This boded well. The waitress turned out to be from Thunder Bay and had grown up in Saskatchewan. Her husband, the chef, hearing I was from Edmonton said, "Yeah, we used to go to David's Bar in Saskatoon and watch Gretzky. We were there at his first game when he got, what, seven assists? Those were the days, before he left the Oilers and became Bruce McCall's bauble." We had a moment of silence for the Great One. The light was fading pink on the tops of the mountains as I walked back to the motel, feeling happy and tired and Canadian.

Marshall McLuhan says that TV is no good for resolving things, for settling issues, and hence is useless for real debate and shouldn't be expected to do well at that. What it *is* good for is *process,* the ceaseless flow of information, always changing, never reaching a resolution. The ultimate TV show is thus the Weather Channel. McLuhan also says something about the first weather satellite being Canadian. In any case, down in the States they blame us for everything:

"A *Canadian* high pressure system is generating extreme distur-
bances ..."

"A *Canadian* cold front today brought unseasonable temperatures ..."

"A *Canadian* blizzard totally disrupted ..."

I had turned into a Weather Channel addict. I would grab the
remote as soon as I came into the motel room and watch as I tugged
my boots off. I might flip around the dial occasionally in the hope
of some soft-core porn, but always came back to the weather. Back
at the room I turned it on. I had toyed with the idea of crossing over
to Oregon and taking Highway 1 up the coast to Vancouver. The
Weather Channel settled the issue for me: squalls were battering
the coast, the rain had been constant for days and was moving
inland. No chance of the coast now; I would be racing the rain
through Idaho.

PEOPLE ARE PROUD of Papa in Ketchum; they're not too sure about
Pound in Hailey.

"Where is Ezra Pound's house?" I asked when I checked into the
room above the bar.

"I dunno about him." said the owner. "Best to ask at the library
across the street."

"I'm an English teacher," I said to the librarian, trying to strike the
right note, though I hadn't cleaned the smeared bugs off my leather
jacket, "and I'm interested in Ezra Pound. Do you have any displays
of his work and could you tell me where his house is?"

"Oh. Ellen *once* put up a display of his work but she's not here
today. I think we have some of his books. No idea about his house."

"Isn't there anywhere I could find out?"

"I don't know."

"Doesn't anyone keep records?"

"I really don't know. Maybe the phone book."

Clearly she didn't know, didn't want to know, and didn't want to be the sort of person who would know. Another librarian looked up from where she was shelving books. "You might try the Chamber of Commerce. Just go down the alley here and turn left. They might have something."

The woman there smiled when I said the librarians suggested she could help me.

"Of course. It's just over a couple of blocks—here, I'll give you a pamphlet—they haven't restored it yet so you can't go inside, but you can go by and have a look. It's a white house on the corner." She gave me a pamphlet with the address, and a blurb that carefully distances itself from the anti-Semitic and Fascist broadcasts Pound made during the Second World War. I remembered at the bookstore they had some of his poetry but no biographies. "Thanks," I said, and took two of the brochures. I walked back down the alley to the library, where they were just about to close.

"Hi," I said, "I won't keep you. You were right, the Chamber of Commerce was very helpful, and look, here's a brochure with the address of Pound's house right on it. I got an extra one for you to keep in case anyone else comes in asking about Pound." I smiled helpfully. The librarian snarled thank you and put the brochure in a drawer under the counter. Waiting until I left to transfer it to the garbage pail. She knew where to file Ezra. Here it was, Second and Pine. A white clapboard two-storey on a big corner lot, with an elegant wrought-iron fence running around it. Pretty classy. I checked the pamphlet. So Pound's grandfather had interests in the

silver mines in Hailey and used his influence with the U.S. president
to get his son a job out here during the silver boom of the 1880s.

Ezra left before he was a year and a half old ("15 and 1/5 months,"
said the pamphlet), but carried with him some kind of memory:"the
vastness of the Saw-Tooth Range, 5,000 ft. above sea-level (and five
million or five thousand miles from ANYwhere, let alone from civilization, new Yorkine or other) . . . the scenery, miles of it, miles of
real estate, 'most of it up on end'. . ." The Idaho Kid he called himself.
For sure he was the gunslinger of modernist poetry, shooting off the
flabby bits of Eliot's *Waste Land;* like Billy the Kid, pushing his luck
till they put him in jail. Though they found an excuse not to hang
him, they locked him up in a mental hospital for twelve years. He
must have dreamed of this place, enfolded by quiet, maternal mountains. I looked up. The Saw-Tooth Range isn't very toothy at all, but
I guess you couldn't call something the Mammary Range and expect
miners and gunslingers to live in the place.

The pamphlet recounted how Pound had made "incoherent . . .
sometimes obscene . . . anti-American and anti-Semitic" broadcasts
from Italy during the war. The last thing it quotes is his mea culpa to
Allen Ginsberg in 1967: "Any good I've done has been spoiled by
bad intentions—the preoccupations with stupid and irrelevant
things . . . But the worst mistake I made was the stupid, suburban
prejudice of anti-Semitism." Fair enough, I suppose. It did take guts
and love even to produce the pamphlet, to somehow celebrate while
seeming to explain away Hailey's most notorious citizen. (I'm sure
they would have preferred a real outlaw with six-guns blazing. Billy
the Kid died four years before Pound was born. He could have dodged
Pat Garrett that night, ridden north, got a job working security for
the silver mine, bounced Pound on his knee. Billy would have been

twenty-six the year Pound left with his parents for Philadelphia, with a memory of the real Idaho Kid.) Yet people usually read only the beginning and the ends of pamphlets, if they read them at all, and the Chamber of Commerce could have ended with the lovely words from the last canto that they quote in the middle.

They had set them in italics and centered them like a greeting card inscription:

> *Many errors,*
> *a little rightness,*
> *to excuse his hell*
> *and my paradiso.*
> *To confess wrong without losing rightness:*
> *Charity I have had sometimes,*
> *I cannot make it flow thru.*
> *A little light, like a rushlight*
> *to lead back to splendor*

It seemed wrong. When I got back home I took down my copy of the *Cantos,* that terra-cotta brick from New Directions. There was nothing pretty about the poem. The spaces in the original captured the halting breath; the charity does *not* flow through; each line is complete, weighed before the next:

> Many errors,
> a little rightness,
> to excuse his hell
> and my paradiso.

Then seven lines that the pamphlet had left out, probably because they were full of Italian, and the closing:

To confess wrong without losing rightness:
Charity I have had sometimes,
            I cannot make it flow thru.
A little light, like a rushlight
            to lead back to splendour.

The poem now captured the pain of recollection, of writing as penance. More than that, it brought home again the iconic power of the page. A frilly typeface could make the most tough-minded sentiments look like drivel; vary the type size, the space between the lines, the placement on the page and your aphorism could look like a want ad or a road sign. Maybe T. E. Lawrence was obsessive about not having rivers on the printed page but his instincts were right. My favourite aphorism was "Authors do not write books." Because they don't: books are not written, they are manufactured, whether by scribes or printers or technicians, on parchment, paper, or cyberspace. And form effects (not just affects) meaning. Pound had given precise instructions for his famous "In a Station of the Metro" haiku; if he could have seen this pamphlet it would have put him in "a orlkonsumin rage."

THE ROAD GETS SERIOUS out of Salmon, Idaho. It takes you up a canyon on smooth two-lane blacktop, the river high, rushing beside you, the walls narrowing, the road winding deeper and deeper into the gorge, tempting you faster and faster until you find yourself shooting straight toward a cliff face at 75. What to do? Shut it down?

Or trust the road markers, and hope that some local salvage artist hasn't sawed down a sign that says SLOW TO 25. You hang on, and at the last possible moment the road breaks right in a fast sweeper that takes you deeper still. You can practically feel the walls on each side of the road, and the air is cooler here. The sun probably never gets down to road level, maybe on one mystical day of the year. There's nobody out here at all, just the odd ambling cow in the ditch that shows no sign of bolting, that looks up with a look that says "I won't tell if you don't." I won't, and soon I'll be over the state line into Montana where there are no speed limits.

But there I found hardly anybody drives more than 65 miles an hour anyway. Clearly the lack of limit is distressing; they have nothing to pit their hatred of regulation against. Fortunately, between Hamilton and Missoula the government has put up signs proclaiming DAYLIGHT HEADLIGHT USE ZONE. *This* they all flout, driving lights out with pleased determination (No goddam bureaucrat's gonna make *me* burn out the durned sealed beams).

I HAD LUNCH at Ravalli, on the Flathead Indian Reservation. Long before you get there signs appear for the Buffalo Gallery—HOME OF THE BISON BURGER. I had ham and potato soup to take the chill off, and the special, a flatbread pizza with sausage, mushrooms, green peppers, and onions, followed by huckleberry pie. As I ate I read the menu. Menus are important archaeological texts; maybe I should write an article about menus. A menu in Salmon had advertised local services for everything from dead batteries to mastectomy fashions. Here at the Buffalo Gallery I learned how the bison were sold off and then Teddy Roosevelt, a devoted sportsman and outdoorsman, realized the folly of it all and established the National Bison Range.

Not that exciting really. What made my heart leap was that he sold them, it said, to *Canada*. Canada was back on the map, not just the mythical place where blue northers come from.

The Grand Hotel in Kalispell is grand, except my MasterCard was declined. I cashed the worn traveler's check in the back of my wallet. I went to move my bike, and when I came back the clerk said, "Get over here! Where's your receipt?" Oh-oh. What now? "We've got a special on for our Canadian visitors, and even though you paid in American dollars you should get the at-par discount." Kiss me, I'm a Canadian! But best of all, just before dropping off to sleep, flipping the remote up to channel 33 for the weather, I hit a commercial with the red upside-down triangle: Canadian Tire! *Amazingly low prices. Everyday quality. Canadian Tire Dollars. Think of all the money you save.* Yes, I did, yes. I was almost back in the land of the free.

For dinner that night I'd punished myself by eating a baked potato at the mall ($3.75 with iced tea, no tip). Since Gallup I had been reading the prices on the menu before looking at the food choices. Nobody talks about money in traveling; we all know that spending a foreign currency is not spending at all, it's just playing with Monopoly money, and your credit cards seem infinitely elastic. Then coming back you wonder whether you'll make it home, running on empty. I bet Marco Polo wound up a bit short in Constantinople on the way back.

EIGHTEEN

Scene of the Crime

At the border the Canadian customs official showed no interest, didn't want to see my registration, check my saddlebags, or dismantle the tube frame, which could have carried at least a couple of kilos of uncut heroin. Who's protecting this country? I could be a risk! In Cranbrook I stopped at the visitors' center on the outskirts and asked for directions to a good espresso bar. It turned out to be across the street from the police station. Clearly this was fate. I tossed back the double cappuccino, wiped the foam from my mustache, slung my leather jacket over one shoulder, and strode across.

"I've come back to the scene of the crime," I announced to the woman behind the no-doubt bulletproof glass at the reception counter. I told her that I'd been arrested and done time here thirty years ago for stealing a pack of Kraft Gouda Cheese. Did they have records going back that far?

"We're not supposed to show them." I could tell from her tone that an exception might be made. I explained that I had rehabilitated myself and was now a respectable English professor. My allusion to "Alice's Restaurant" was lost on her, though she was old enough to have got it. Maybe she got it and just didn't think I was very funny. Big, stern, dark complexion. She didn't crack a grin but her eyes, well, they didn't exactly soften, but they seemed less hard. She asked for my driver's license and said she'd see what she could find. I was used to dealing with crusty librarians; this was a different world. The smell, some industrial cleaner strong enough to obliterate blood, urine, vomit took me back. This whole idea didn't seem cute any more. I cooled my heels in the anteroom, pleasant enough; with its pastel vinyl chairs it could be a dentist's waiting room, though instead of old *People* magazines they had pamphlets on How to Prevent Car Theft. Finally she came back, smiling now, "There's nothing on the system. Nothing at all."

"Oh well. Thank you." I smiled too. But I was disappointed. It was bad enough that the old building was gone, but that there was no record. I'd been given ten days! Not in jail, exactly. In fact it was a suspended sentence, so I was allowed to go free, on condition that I return to the store and pay for the cheese, and stay out of bad company for six months. Surely they should have kept that on record? I mean, what if I relapsed?

What if I started having flashbacks?

What if later in life I suddenly started stealing Gouda cheese again. Hip-checking little old ladies into the dairy cabinet and running out with an armload? Coshing workers on the head with a crowbar at the loading dock and grabbing a crate of it? Hijacking a Gouda-filled semi with a machine gun and a band of live grenades across my chest? Taking hostages and demanding to be flown to Holland? Hey, I could be a *danger to society* goddam it. I felt mean as I stomped back to the bike, and I scowled at the cappuccino quaffers sitting out under the awning. I was a rebel. See that jail over there? Yeah, well I know it from the *inside,* buddy. I've been fingerprinted. My record's so bad they had to lose it. You look at me sideways and you'll have to answer for it. Actually nobody looked at me at all. I gunned the bike to life. Still nobody looked. Wankers. Even Brando couldn't have woken this place up. I'm gonna blow this hick town. Rebel without a cheese.

I reached Lake Louise at five and though Jasper was only another 225 kilometers I decided to stay. There was leftover snow in the shady spots among the pines, and fat chipmunks running around. What was the rush? This was a road to be savored. I got a bed at the hostel and ate at the Post Hotel pub, where the nightly special comes from the expensive dining room upstairs: grilled salmon on a bed of lemon linguini, with sourdough rolls and a mug of Big Rock Traditional Ale. I phoned Hsing but she was out, so I went for a solitary stroll along the Bow River. The sun warmed the trail and made the fresh snow on top of Mount Temple glow. It was almost nine and there was still a ton of light. I had forgotten how magical these northern latitudes are in late May and June, the way the light lingers like a hawk riding a thermal, effortlessly on and on.

In the morning I hit the road before the sun did, and I froze. I stopped at Bow Lake, gorgeous green ice ringed with snow. I put on my thick ski gloves and the polypro liners, my balaclava, the detested but now-welcome rain suit, and wired myself into my electric vest. Ahh. Heat again. My fingers were still numb but I could feel the vest warming the blood in my chest. I was now a true cyborg, my life support linked to that of the machine.

THE LAST TIME I had been through here it had been with Hsing, our first motorcycle excursion. She had just bought Matilda and we were riding the loop—every place has a loop, and in Alberta it's the foothills-mountains-prairie loop: Edmonton-Calgary-Banff-Jasper-home. We had driven it dozens of times, now we were going to do it on motorcycles.

We took the freeway from Edmonton to Leduc, and then turned onto the old highway. Suddenly all the towns that were only letters on the big green exit signs were real: Kavanagh, Millet, Wetaskiwin. More amazing, the road had curves. They took the kinks out of prairie roads a long time ago, and the freeway rolls out from Edmonton to Calgary like a long black Therm-a-Rest pad, insulating you from the landscape. But on the old highway you still swing around sloughs, drop down for creeks, and curve through stands of aspen; you follow the shape of the land. It was warm and we were hot in our leathers and full-face helmets, and our wrists were getting sore because we still hung on tight. The farthest we had been was the Devonian Gardens 30 kilometers outside of town. This was the first time we'd spent an hour and a half straight on the motorcycles. At Lacombe we pulled into the Dairy Queen, ordered two grilled chicken burgers, a side of fries, a Crispy Crunch Blizzard, and slumped at the table. "I wish we could just sleep right here," said Hsing.

"Yeah," I said. "On a bike you can't take a nap while the other one drives. There's no passenger seat to recline in."

"No, you know what it is—you can't *snack* on a motorcycle. *That's* what the problem is." Afterward we went out and lay on the grass in the shade of a Dumpster. I looked out across the highway to the fields of ripe wheat and then up to the wide blue sky and then flopped back on my leather jacket. "I can't believe it," I said. "I dreamt of this when I was sixteen. I have a leather jacket. I have a motorcycle. I'm on the road. And I'm with a *babe*. What could be better?" Hsing rolled over and kissed me.

"C'mon baby, let's make some miles," I said. I had always wanted to say that.

When we next stopped for gas I asked Hsing how she was doing. "Fine, though my toes are starting to tingle a bit, and I sometimes hug the tank with my knees to give my feet a rest. How about you?" I was ashamed to admit that my computer-balanced water-cooled in-line triple with paralever suspension and rubber-isolated footpegs wasn't giving me so much as a single vibration. This was the new BMW I had bought before the Ducati.

To start her old BMW you had to turn on the petcock for the gas, put on full choke, and hit the starter two or three times. It would cough to life—*whumf! chucka chucka chucka*—and you'd have to ease back on the choke and give it some throttle until—*chicka chicka chicka*—it was running more or less smoothly, with a throaty rumble through its long chrome pipes. My bike was fuel injected so there was no petcock to turn on and everything was computer set at the factory. Touch the starter button and *vrimmm!*

"I like the sound of yours better," said Hsing. "It sounds like an electric motor."

Oh great. Bikes are supposed to have a "throaty rumble." I knew that because it said so in the cycle magazines I'd been reading for years. I had to face the truth: at idle mine sounded like a Water Pik, at full throttle it sounded like an angry blender. Imagine, in that closing scene of *Casablanca*, if Ingrid Bergman hadn't been getting onto a propeller aircraft ("If you don't get on that plane—*whumf!*

chucka chucka chucka—you'll regret it . . .") but onto a Learjet ("Maybe not now, but—*vrimm! vrimm! . . .*"). It would not have been the same.

At Airdrie, Highway 2A disappears (like Route 66, covered over by the freeway), and you find yourself in six lanes with others merging and demerging. Like saddle horses that could smell the home pastures the pickup trucks were really booting it now, nipping back and forth in pointless lane changes to gain a foot or two, while the semi trailers just upped the ante to 140 and bored on through. My wrist was killing me and the knot between my shoulder blades was as big as a cabbage, but I was more worried about being ground up by an eighteen-wheeler or smucked by a pickup truck racing in from the job site to get the first cold one at Rusty's Tavern. And the wind was cold now. There was probably beautiful lingering foothills twilight but I was too busy looking at the lug treads at eye level beside me. The crosswinds had picked up, broadsiding us with shuddering blasts that moved us over half a lane. Hsing's windscreen was shaking her handlebars, and the sleeves of my leather jacket (who needs an expensive motorcycle jacket? I had thought) fluttered so hard they hurt.

We reached Hsing's friend's house bagged but happy. Three hundred kilometers! Our longest ride. "Look at this—bug guts on my knees! Yuk!" said Hsing as the pizza arrived. Our ears were still ringing and we were probably shouting. My wrist creaked as I lifted the mug of ale. Hsing was talking now of the wobble that started in the wind on the final stretch, and how she'd run out of gas going 100 kilometers an hour and had to reach down and switch the petcock to reserve on the fly. We were real motorcyclists now.

We had taken the motorcycle safety course and spent the better part of a week doing figure eights around pylons, learning to shift gears smoothly through a turn, executing panic stops and evasive maneuvers. At the end of it we felt pretty good. After the test the examiner lined us all up, made a last note on her clipboard, and said, "Congratulations. You all passed. You are now qualified to ride—in a parking lot." True, we had spent a whole week and never gotten out of second gear, but our balance had improved and our shoulder checks were second nature. Now, though, we had taken it to the road and survived.

In Banff the next day we ate corn chowder at the Coyote Grill and recapped the ride up the old Banff Coach Road. "Remember that corner by the reservoir?" she said. "And the wind off that lake just as you enter the mountains, where they ice boat in the winter?" You can't talk on the bikes so you fix images and sensations to talk about later. It's sometimes frustrating ("We need to develop hand signals," said Hsing, "Or get walkie-talkies—*yeah!*—then I could talk to you all the time and you'd have to listen"), but in many ways it's better, and it's part of what makes motorcycle touring unique. You know that if you turn your head to look at something the person on the bike behind will turn too, a shared moment that's stronger for not being tracked over with words. As we drove into the parking lot of the Lake Louise strip mall some guy came to the door of his motor home, gave Hsing the thumbs-up sign and shouted, *"I love your bike!"* I was envious. Everyone loved the classic shape of Hsing's bike, the sweep of the long chrome exhaust pipes, the big funky carburetors. My new BMW just did not cut it.

I had gotten used to this. I had had to.

If you have a woman sitting on the back of your bike this confers studliness upon you. The men look at her but look at you with respect; the women glance at her and immediately check you out.

But when a woman rides her own bike, you're immediately converted to chopped liver on wheels. You pull into a gas station and there's chaos, pump jockeys leaping over each other, begging to check her tire pressure, fill the tank, change the oil, anything.

You, you get nothing. No attention, no service, no chance. Of course you could rob the till if you wanted and be halfway into the next province before anyone noticed, but somehow it doesn't seem worth the trouble.

And the women! Unbelievable. Hot-blooded heterosexual women without a Sapphic bone in their bodies (you thought!) go gaga. They come tripping up to you, eyes wide—and go right by you to caress the tank of your woman. Ooh, it's so *big,* they say, all warm moist and trembly. How do you *manage* it? No, they're not talking about you, sport. You're just backdrop.

She takes off her helmet and tosses her long black hair. She peels off the tight leather gloves and lays them on the tank. She bends over her saddlebags so that the crease of her Levis dives even deeper.

By this point you would think the station was giving away free gas. Jocks in four-by-fours are doing U-turns across the median, mothers in minivans are careening across the tarmac, geezers in motor homes, pacemakers in overdrive, lurch up the exit lane, even boys on bicycles, paper routes and vandalism forgotten, race in, flaunting extravagant wheelies. Mine's highest! Pick me!

She heads toward the washroom, taking short, tough steps in her 3-inch-heeled motorcycle boots, tugging down the zipper of her snug bomber jacket, which then sighs in and out with the undulations of her hips. The whole place is on its knees.

Bitch! the overlooked male rages. I've spent thousands on this BMW (Ducati/Harley/Honda/Triumph)! I will *not* be upstaged!

Rage on, sport, ain't nobody watching. And while she's freshening up? You can pay for the gas.

WHAT CAN YOU SAY about the Icefields Parkway except that it is the most beautiful road in the world? The best that Switzerland has to offer, with its bridal-veil waterfalls and cottages perched on precipices, is mere prettiness compared with it. Even my brother Lloyd says so, and if he admits it it must be true. Fifteen years ago he married a Swiss woman and went off to Geneva. The next summer he came back with an accent that sounded like Inspector Clouseau ("It is, how do you say it? 'amazing'"). We saw him through this difficult period, though there were times when we wanted to smack him with a Toblerone, and he emerged with believable accents in both French and English and a new appreciation for his homeland. He's been to the Himalayas and he's been through the Andes and he can see the Mont Blanc *massif* from his window, and he says the Icefields Parkway is still the best.

Back in the thirties my father had hiked this road, before it was a road. He'd been working in the Park Information Center in Banff and knew that work crews were already starting at Lake Louise and Jasper to cut a road through. He came to the mountains because he'd read about the Columbia Icefields in Monroe Thorington's book *The Glittering Mountains*. A picture of Mount Castleguard, rising "like a ship out of a sea of ice," Dad said, had caught him. It was his idea of what a mountain should be. That summer in Banff he learned to climb, working double shifts at the information center and taking every second day off, trading with his co-worker, a passionate fly fisherman. He progressed from scrambles on Cascade to slab climb-ing on Mount Louis, scaling that spire with a hemp rope and high-top sneakers. Standard gear in those days. But in the back of his mind was always Mount Castleguard and that sea of ice halfway between Lake Louise and Jasper. If they had to hike all the way up there anyway, he reasoned with his climbing buddies, why not just go on through to Jasper? It was the same amount of food—flour (for bannock) and rice and raisins for two weeks.

Hsing and I wanted food now, and we wanted to stop at Num-Ti-Jah Lodge, a three-storey log structure built by Jimmy Simpson in 1940, the year the parkway opened, on a spit of glacial sand jutting out into Bow Lake. They made a wicked bumbleberry pie with fresh whipped cream. "You burn up a lot of calories on a bike," Hsing said as she lurched her bike onto the center stand, "All that vibration and wind buffeting. We need sustenance." I remembered Dad telling us how one night they wound up with an extra piece of bannock and they flipped for it. Dad lost. Fifty years later he still remembered that warm bannock on the rock by the fire and marveled at how much he had wanted it.

"Maybe I'll have the double-chocolate cake," I said to Hsing, "and you can have the bumbleberry pie."

We looked at the old pictures on the walls. The lodge in winter, high drifts against the walls. A guy with long hair and a big hat sitting in a saddle on a buffalo. Jimmy Simpson with his crinkled face and pipe smiling into the camera. The Native people had given him the nickname Nashan-esen, which meant "wolverine-go-quick" because he was so fast on snowshoes. I'd met him when I was around eight years old and I remember him as looking like his picture, a slight but tough man; I had never seen that kind of suntan before, his skin looked like beef jerky. My father was almost shy with him. "He's a real pioneer," he said as I shook Mr. Simpson's hand, and though

Jimmy Simpson scoffed and said something self-deprecating, I sensed it was true.

The cool air from the glacier sharpened the smell of the juniper and scrub cedar; the late-afternoon sun deepened the texture of the rocks across the valley. The rest had been a long one, a bit too long, letting the stiffness creep back into our backs and wrists. At the same time, we didn't really want to leave. The tour-bus hordes had abated and you could hear the slap of the little waves on Bow Lake. As we got closer to Jasper the sun moved behind the mountains, casting the road into shadow. The evening bugs came out. Great for fishing, I thought as we passed Horseshoe Lake, but lousy for riding. Our visors were pocked and smeared, it was like looking at the road through a Jackson Pollock. We took a quick break and I told Hsing my best road joke ("What did one bug say to the other bug after flying into the car windshield?" "Bet you haven't got the guts to do that again!"). The orange cliff bands of Mount Kerkeslin glowed above us, but we were getting chilled. The temptation is to ride fast, make those miles, get on home. But the animals come down to water in the evening, and the thought of hitting an elk at 140 kilometers an hour kept me honest. I looked at the scenery and tried not to think of my wrist. The blade of Mount Edith Cavell, the round forehead of Whistler looking out over the valley, the ruddy-pink arrowhead of Pyramid Mountain rising behind the town.

At last we reached the intersection with the Yellowhead Highway. We geared down and flipped up our visors. Suddenly the wind noise was gone and the mountains were sharp, without bug smears, and I loved motorcycle touring. We cruised slowly along the Jasper bypass and turned off to Lake Edith. As we pulled into the cabin my nieces and nephew tumbled out to meet us, and before I had the sidestand down Owen, the cheerfully terrible two-year-old, was poking at my spark-plug wires. Chris corralled the children. "There's some roast lamb left," she said, "but would you like a gin and tonic first?"

We creaked as we clambered off the motorcycles. "A gin and tonic would be great."

"I love seeing a woman on a big bike," Chris said, watching Hsing stow her helmet and explain to the children that her bike was called Matilda. I waited for them to ask why, but they didn't. "How about I just leave Norman with the children and come with you?" said Chris. I think that's what everybody wants. They want to come too. The lamb, barbecued with garlic, rosemary, and fresh olive oil, was fabulous.

Now, AS I PULLED into the deserted cabin I knew I would be going into town for takeout. I did like riding alone. Even when Hsing and I made trips I tended to lag 50 meters back. "It's like I'm riding alone," she complained. But I liked being together at the end of the ride, and the stillness of the cabin, which I always loved, seemed a little empty. My grand Alberta-Texas odyssey now had ended— shouldn't there be something more dramatic to mark it than my flicking down the kickstand and searching for the cabin key?

HSING WAS WORKING that summer in the hospital in Yellowknife in the Northwest Territories. She phoned to tell me that her friend Ken, also a physician, was getting married, "His background is East Indian, his fiancée Margo's is European, the families are in Calgary and Edmonton, and the friends are scattered all over. So they've decided to get married in Vancouver. That way no one can be offended. It's perfect."

"And . . .?" Something in her tone told me there was more to this.

"Don't you see? I haven't had my motorcycle trip this summer. I'll go out on Matilda as soon as I get home. You can come later with the clothes and all the shoes in the car, and then we'll come back together. I'll even let you do some of the riding." How could I refuse? A last ride through the mountains before fall term started.

The wedding defied all categories. Ken and Margo delivered their vows in the Dr. Sun Yat-Sen Classical Chinese Garden in Vancouver's Eastside heroin district, laid out a multi-ethnic feast with samosas, pyrogies, spring rolls, and tortillas, and hired a mariachi band in big hats and silver-spangled boots to play beside the Zen garden. "They love Mexico!" Hsing explained over the trumpets.

"Mmmm!" I said, my mouth full of spicy meatballs, a pork satay stick in one hand and a tempura shrimp in the other. "This is fabulous!"

I DIDN'T KNOW that the next dinner, and every other meal for several weeks, would be out of an intravenous bag.

EPILOGUE

Riding with Rilke

The next thing I heard was the *crunch crunch crunch* on the gravel of boots coming down into the ditch. Someone new moved in beside me and said, "Hello, this is Dan. We're from the team. Can you hear me? What's your name? Good. What day is it? Good. Do you know where you were going? Good. Do you know what happened to you?"

"Yup. I was trying to pass and the bike went into a wobble and I crashed."

"Okay."

I would answer those questions a dozen more times that day, as each paramedic, each nurse, each doctor assessed me.

They were saying, "We'll have to cut your boots off."

I could feel the power of their shears—*kachuck kachuck kachuck*—five snips and they had my boots off. Next time, I thought, I must buy the kind with zippers up the side.

And then, "We're going to have to cut your jacket." I loved this jacket. For a motorcyclist a jacket is more than a garment. It's a badge, it's a shelter, it's a companion. Of course you know it makes you look cool as you stride into the bar, but that's the superficial pleasure. Zipping in you feel like an astronaut suiting up. A good jacket is a climate control system, with snug neck and wrist zippers to keep out the wind, and for cooling, zippered vents in the chest and back. As you put on miles together it forms to you, acquiring wrinkles and memories, and when you sling it across your shoulder your pulse quickens because it's part of the ride. Ultimately, however, it's there to save your hide when you go down.

"Go ahead," I said, but the shears, quieter now, were already munching through the soft thick leather.

IT'S HERE WITH ME in the hospital room. It has some ground-in dirt on the back, but the leather is barely scraped. I wondered if I could get it repaired. Hsing said forget about it. My helmet is here too, bright yellow on one side, and on the other gouged down to the grey carbon fiber. Graphic proof that without it my head would have split and smeared my brains along the road.

"So you think you want to ride with the wind in your hair?" the safety instructor had asked. "Go down without a helmet and your head will stick there on impact, soft, like a ripe peach, and your body will slide away." I've never really liked that word "impact." When I was fourteen and trying to persuade my parents to let me have a scooter, my buddy said, "Listen, tell them statistics show you're 87 percent safer on a bike up to the point of impact!" Dad didn't go for it. Now I'm a helmet zealot, telling anyone, "Buy the best helmet and jacket you can first, then see how much money you have left over to buy the motorcycle. It's your peach against the asphalt."

THEY GOT A BOARD under me, strapped me on, and staggered up the steep ditch. The lurching sent pain screaming through my back, and for the first time I felt like I was in pieces, bits held together with loose open nerves. Then I was in the ambulance. The attendant put a mask over me, squeezing the attached bag to help me breathe. The cool oxygen flowed in, and I began to doze. When we got to the hospital they unloaded me, each jolt firing off little flashes of pain. Falling off a motorcycle was the easy part—*boom!* and the lights go out. Being carted about, that hurt. They cut off my jeans, bloody and stuck at the left knee.

"You've got rocks in there," said the doctor. "Quite deep." He was picking them out, like raisins out of a pudding, dropping them with a clink into the steel kidney basin. "I think there's enough skin to make a flap though, once we're finished."

At some point they gave me the score. Actually they spoke to Hsing, because she is a doctor, and discussed me in the third person. I caught what I could:

"We have fractures of T5 and L2 as well as [damage to the stuff surrounding the spinal cord], fractures of the medial malleolus, and of the distal radius and ulna. The impact also induced paralytic ileus, hence the engee tube, and pulmonary contusion. We'll be checking that out to make sure there's no embolism, but in the meantime we'll stay on oxygen [x litres per something-something-something] until he [expands his lungs by blowing that ball up the tube]. There's a full thickness laceration of the knee and though it's [oozing pus and gunk] there's no other damage."

Hsing translated: "You broke your wrist, your ankle, and your back in two places—cracked one vertebra between your shoulder blades and shattered one just above your bum. The impact also mashed your lungs, which is why they bagged you in the ambulance and why you're on oxygen. Also your intestines are temporarily paralyzed. No big deal, they'll come around, but that's why they stuck that tube up your nose and down into your guts—to take off any fluid. So you can't eat or drink for a while. Oh, and your knee has road rash."

"So the 'engee' tube is an 'NG' tube—nose and guts?"

"Close. Naso-gastric. But don't worry about it. Though I hear they're uncomfortable."

"All doctors should try it. You know that scene in *A Fish Called Wanda* where they stick french fries up Michael Palin's nose? Well, it's like having a long crispy french fry up your nose and down your throat."

I RENTED A TV in the hospital. One of those little boxes on a boom that you swing over in front of your face. I signed up for everything, full cable, fifty-two channels. Friends predicted I'd come out hooked on daytime television, become a slave to Jerry Springer. Yet I only watched the CBC news. I needed to read. I do mean *need*. Adrian Johns, in his immensely learned *The Nature of the Book,* has a chapter titled "The Physiology of Reading: Print and the Passions." This sounds promising, but it's full of seventeenth-century diagrams of the eyeball and talk of the emotions of the soul. I wanted something that talked about what reading feels like. In her article "Turning into Talent: A Writer on TV," Marni Jackson talks about trolling for text. Like a baleen whale ingesting its daily quantity of plankton, she needs her quota of print and will read the notices on boards in supermarkets, anything. I felt this too.

If I don't get it, what I feel is a kind of scratchiness on my scalp and an overall agitation that extends through my whole body. It's like the feeling runners get—or anybody who exercises regularly—when they miss a few days in their workout schedule. The mind won't focus because the body, inside, is leaping around like an unwalked dog. You read at first just for the sensation of reading, hardly knowing *what* you're reading, throwing yourself into it, bolting it down—like eating when you're starving, you don't even taste it until you're halfway through. Or like when you've gone too long without sex. Then you have it, the real thing—copulation, consummation—and what is wonderful is not the ragged shattering climax (though that's okay), no, what's great is the sense of release, the peace that suffuses your whole body, from your earlobes to your toes, afterward. That's what Adrian Johns should have written about.

I read magazines and mysteries. I tired easily and could not read more than about twenty minutes before falling back into a doze. The reading was physically demanding. I was still weak, on tubes for food, for oxygen, not allowed to sit up or even tilt my bed up. My broken right wrist was still in a cast and though the tips of my fingers were free to wiggle they were too weak to hold anything. So I read flat on my back, holding the book above me with my left hand.

My reading had to be, literally, light reading. And I soon learned that those nasty pulp paperbacks, though light to the heft, were the worst. The tiny type goes right into the gutter (the central seam between the pages), and the cheap inflexible glue they use for the binding holds the pages in a rigid block. You pry it open, your thumb and little finger splayed out, and the whole thing threatens to sproing out of your hand.

You read trying to ignore the muscle tension, feeling like you're using one of those Charles Atlas grip enhancers that promise you after ten weeks—"Use it while you're on the phone or watching television"—you'll have a grip so strong you can crush beer cans lengthwise and deliver promotion-winning handshakes.

After a while I would just give up, lie back, and enjoy the morphine. Friends would come to visit and ask, "How are you?"

"Fine!" I'd say. "Fine! How are you?!"

I wanted to reread Eugene O'Neill's *Long Day's Journey into Night*, the play in which the morphine-addicted mother slips further and further into the fog as the night wears on. I loved that fog. For now I realized it wasn't a fog but a shimmering mist that kept you safe yet let you see everything with unhurried precision. I had dictated fifty pages of notes for this story in that fog, yet I knew I could never convey the lovely clarity of my 3:00 A.M. shot. I knew I could become a hophead in a heartbeat.

Michael Ondaatje in *The English Patient* figures morphine as a vehicle of travel: "He rides the boat of morphine. It races in him, imploding time and geography. . . ." I had wonderful dreams that I can still almost recall, and I thought maybe I could use the drug as a portal of discovery. I asked Hsing to bring in my edition of Samuel Taylor Coleridge's poems. *Kubla Khan* was written under the influence of opium; maybe if I read it under morphine it would become clear. I got the shot and as soon as the nurse left I picked up the book.

In Xanadu did Kubla Kahn a stately pleasure dome decree.
Where Alph the sacred river ran
Through caverns measureless to man . . .

Man, this book is heavy. And there are all these footnotes, like gray fuzz at the bottom of the page. Why do they use such tiny type?

I forced myself on to the juicy part about the woman wailing for her demon lover but it was no good. By the time "this earth in fast thick pants [was] breathing" so was I. I'd been hoping for a vision of a damsel with a dulcimer but all I was getting was a sore wrist and a stiff neck. Forget that sunny dome, those caves of ice. I went back to my Minette Walters mystery. Still, I was disappointed that the Coleridge had not worked out. The book had gotten in the way of the reading. Or more properly, my body had. I was used to text slipping in seamlessly as air. I'd been a reader as a kid, scrunched in the back of the family station wagon on road trips.

"Look at the scenery, Ted!" my mother would call. I didn't get motion sickness; I could read on buses and trains. Reading was supposed to be an out-of-body experience.

"The material book," I had lectured my students, "is a zone of transition and transaction between the reader and the text within it." It hadn't occurred to me that the body of the reader was also a zone of transition and transaction. I felt like I was reliving my life from infancy all over again, in fast motion, like the time-lapse photography you see on those nature shows. I was immobile, fed by tubes and drained by tubes. Then one by one they came out. The oxygen tube—I could breathe on my own. The catheter tube—I felt like a real boy when I got to pee on my own. A few days later I took my first steps: four one way and four the other, between balance bars. It exhausted me and I slept the rest of the day.

Then my first drink: a small sip of iced tea, trickling down the side of my tongue. Incandescent. You know how oenophiles talk about tasting the wine on five different places on the palate? I think I discovered twenty-seven. And the next day, my first solid food: a green Gummi Bear. I thought the roof of my head was coming off. The world turned lime.

THEY TRANSFERRED ME to the rehab hospital. There I learned how to put on my back brace, how to walk with a crutch, and how to read in a way I had forgotten. I now had no tubes and was allowed to lie on either side, as well as on my back. I still had to be turned by a nurse at night, but during the day, after I had wormed my way into my fiberglass clamshell, I could turn by myself. This was glorious freedom and infinite variety, and it meant I could read fatter books. I could rest them on the bed and open them at right angles.

Of course it meant one page was in the light, and the next one, when I shifted the book up on its edge, was in a dark tent, but I got used to this. I would read the dark pages faster to get out of the shade, linger over the lighter ones, and the alternating rhythm of light and dark gave me a sense of progress. I took up *Fall on Your Knees* by Ann-Marie MacDonald, a ripping yarn of 566 pages. The type went deep into the gutter, and if I opened the book too far it flipped up and hit my nose, but I finished the novel in three days.

People came to visit, bringing flowers, books, or, best of all, food. Cappuccinos from the Italian Center, Belgian chocolates that I did not share, and homemade southern-Italian cooking from Pasquale. He and Dave also brought me new reading material: European motorcycle magazines.

"So you can plan your next trip," they said.

"Uh, thanks guys, but I dunno," I said.

"Hey, you'll be fine. Once you're out of that brace you'll throw your leg over that Ducati and *budda-boom*"—Pasquale slapped and slid one palm off the other—"away you'll go."

"Yeah," said Dave, "It's very rare that anyone has two *serious* accidents."

"Thanks guys," I said.

Pasquale had spent time in a hospital in Prague after catching the front wheel of his BMW on some tram tracks. Dave used to roar down cutlines out by Devil's Lake on his Husqvarna dirt bike. Crashing was part of his job description.

I wasn't so sure. I pushed aside the German motorcycle magazines and took up my little volume of Rilke's *Elegies*. Rilke, the German poet born in Prague, had walked the same cobblestones Pasquale had crashed on. In the "Eighth Elegy" Rilke speaks of the pure space that animals and children move into, that flowers bloom into: a space without the consciousness of death. We sometimes almost glimpse it, he says; it opens to lovers but they miss it because the beloved blocks the view. We are always turned back to the world. He tells us,

> . . . the beast is free
> and has its death always behind it and God before it,
> and when it walks it goes toward eternity,
> as springs flow. Never, not for a single day
> do we have pure space before us in which the flowers
> are always unfolding.

Actually, I thought, if Rilke had ridden a motorcycle he would have modified his poem. There were moments that came unbidden when the bike seemed to disappear under me. I remembered times at night, on an empty road, with the moon at my shoulder and the headlight beam ahead, when I seemed to be riding that beam, to *be* that beam, streaming down the open highway. Pure motion. Pure space.

I did not think I would feel that way again.

I sat up and ate the dinner Pasquale had left, interrupted often by nurses drawn by the smell of Calabrese sausage, Roma tomatoes, goat cheese, fresh basil. Then I settled back into a book. One of the books I read in my recovery period was Greg Hollingshead's novel *The Healer*.

I took the dust jacket off so I wouldn't get Jell-O on it. It was a hardback, with burgundy boards, good paper, and generous margins. Margins may be essential to the aesthetics of page design, but their function is practical as well: they're there to provide space for your thumbs. The trouble with cheap paperbacks is there is no place for them, so you feel cramped and don't know why. If you're reading with a splayed hand, you'll be covering a hundred words of text.

So Hollingshead's book was easy to read. Hollingshead's text was not so easy. The novel captured the physicality of psychic phenomena better than anything I had ever read, but I was hoping for the zany humor of his short stories (*those* would have been good on drugs); the prose was chiseled:

> The shock of her white gaunt frame fixed him as she stepped
> from what he could not see because of the slope but knew was
> a ring of old-man clothing.

But I read one hundred pages the first day and I was hooked. I read one hundred the next, and finished it on the third. Unless I'm reading professionally, my novel reading usually consists of five pages a night before bed. Okay two pages, and sometimes I quit in the middle of a paragraph. If I *am* reading professionally I read thirty pages and then turn to something else. And there *is* always something else—critical books, student essays, administrative memos—that must be read simultaneously. In time this pattern becomes internalized.

I've heard that most academics—most professionals—read in chunks of thirty pages or less. The average length of a professional article. So even when you have the time, on sabbatical or on holiday, after your thirty pages you feel you should be turning to something else. Or if you do consume a mystery novel whole, it's with the guilty pleasure of a binge chocoholic, or more likely it's not pleasure at all but a desperate avoidance that you throw yourself into because you have an uncompleted project staring you in the face. And you graduate from guilty pleasure to guilt *in* pleasure.

On a sabbatical I started *War and Peace* with a satisfied sense of earnest resolve, drudgery faced. I would bag a big one on my backlist of Books to Have Read (for I didn't really want to read *War and Peace,* I wanted to Have Read it). One thousand, four hundred pages. A worthy task. Then I found to my dismay that it was a wonderful read. I couldn't put it down. Tolstoy was *way* easier than Hollingshead. I carried it into the kitchen, the bathroom, uptown to do the shopping. If I had a minute I wanted to get back into it. But this wasn't *work*. So I tempered my pleasure with Joyce's *Finnegans Wake,* a book I had been reading in, reading at, reading around, for the last three years. I began each day with the *Wake*. Up at seven, at the desk with coffee by quarter to eight. This was Art. This was Work. The book could often be fun, even funny, but it was *heavy*. Each sentence was like bench-pressing your own weight, while someone tickled you and babbled in your ear in a foreign language. But at least I read at them straight. I finished both books on the same day, exhausted with a double sense of pleasure and of virtue.

Before my time in the rehab hospital it had been years since I had read a book without thinking about how I might *use* it: put it on a course, write about it in an article, work it into a conference presentation. Like a musician thinking always of his or her set list, I could not just enjoy the tune. Now I was letting the novel pace me, the way I had not since I had read Hardy Boy mystery novels as a twelve-year-old. And I was reading for the pure experience of reading. So I had lost Rilke's pure space to *ride* into but had recovered that pure space to *read* into. This, I thought, is the real rehabilitation.

My reading coincided with another change. When they let me out of rehab Hsing and I went back to Jasper to pick up the motorcycle. In the morning, before Hsing woke, I strapped the forearm cast to my broken arm and hobbled alone down to the lake. After the smooth lino of the hospital the pinecone-strewn path seemed like a boulder field. I sat upright on a bench, cinched into the two halves of the plastic clamshell, and when I wanted to look around I turned like RoboCop.

Sitting carefully on this bench, looking at the deep turquoise reserved for mountain lakes in certain lights, I felt that I had died and returned. My body now seemed separate. Nothing mystical, it was just that where we had always been fused, my body and I, now we were not. The physical world itself seemed wonderful, a wonder. It was one of those fall days in the mountains where the air is so clear it seems to act like a magnifying lens, separating each needle on the pine trees across the valley. But I didn't need the whole jagged ridge of mountains, or the yellow aspen beyond the narrows. That line where the sand met the water, it was enough. Maybe this was the ultimate motorcycle experience, the post-crash clarity.

THE NEXT DAY we borrowed a pickup to retrieve the bike from the wrecker's yard out on Highway 16, past the crash site. The weather turned sour, cold rain that just wanted a dare to turn into snow, and clouds so low they tangled in the treetops—the usual weather for Thanksgiving weekend. I'd planned to have Hsing take my picture beside the ditch, me posing with my shirt off in my orange plastic body cast, grinning. "Yah, I'm alive!" When we parked the truck I wasn't feeling quite so jaunty. True, it was cold. I had to put on a down vest as soon as I got out of the cab, but the chill didn't come from the weather.

Hsing ran ahead, looking into the ditch every few yards; I followed at my best pace. Then she stopped. "I've found it," she called back. "It's deeper than I remembered," she said as I drew near. No kidding. "It's 6 feet deep," said Hsing. I looked down.

"You could drop two Chevy Suburbans in here and the traffic would roll by without noticing," I said.

"It's not *that* deep," said Hsing.

My final offer was one and a half Suburbans, but she was already scrambling down the steep bank. "See this little creek? You were lying here right beside it. This stump," she stomped to show me how hard it was compared with the moist ground, "was under your back. That's probably what shattered the lower vertebra. And see where the creek bends in an L? That's where your head was. That's why I had to hold it after I took your helmet off. Your head would have been in the water."

I remembered. Forty-five minutes she held my head to keep it dry and to keep my neck and spine aligned. One of the others offered to take over but she said she was okay. I shifted my attention to a big ugly rock, sticking out like a rhino's tusk about a yard below where

I was standing. If I had hit that when I left the road we wouldn't be having this conversation. I had had an excess of luck. The people who stopped after Hsing were an internal medicine specialist and his wife, an intensive care nurse. The guy in the car after that was an ambulance driver. Clearly it had not been my day to die.

"Hey!" Hsing was holding up what looked like a crumpled chrome flower. "Here's a mirror from Matilda." She looked at the back. "Yup, it says BMW on it. And here's some latex gloves left by one of the paramedics." She tiptoed around the flattened grass. "It's really squishy down here. The creek keeps it soft."

A semi roared by behind me and the blast made me stagger a bit where I stood. I shivered. The idea of me posing for a photo shoot by my ditch seemed worse than stupid now. An insult to the gods who would say, So you think this is a joke, wise guy? Next time we'll flop you the other way, into the wheels of the truck. Hsing puffed up onto the roadside, still holding the mirror. "Maybe we can fix it," she said. Half the shattered glass still hung in the frame in pie-shaped shards.

"Yeah, maybe."

A friend told me, "The French have a phrase for when you're driving very fast— *'rouler au tombeau ouvert'*—rolling with your tomb open." It turned out I had been doing just that. When the mechanic took the bike apart he found that the bearings in the steering head had almost seized. Little vibrations that should only send a tremor through the bars would be transformed into waves through the whole frame, surges that under the right conditions would flop the bike from side to side. I had met those conditions.

I wasn't so sure I would keep riding. On the one hand, life is chance, maybe we're always rolling *au tombeau ouvert,* so why not?

On the other hand, I thought, there's no need to climb into that tomb early.

I MET MY FRIEND ROBERT (he of the wobbling Norton) at O'Byrne's Irish pub, and the first thing he said when I walked in was, "You're slower."

"Yeah," I said, a bit miffed; I'd been doing splendidly at physio and was used to daily drafts of praise.

"Is there any virtue in slowness?" he went on. "Anything we should attend to?" Oh Christ, I thought, can't I even get a drink first? Robert begins every conversation with a probing question, like he's leading a graduate seminar. I did know there was no virtue in the slow service of this pub. I also knew that once out of the hospital I had stepped into the country of the old. I sympathized with those shuffling head down on icy sidewalks, trying to make it all the way across a broad street before the light turned to DON'T WALK. I told him of my epic combat that morning with my new jar of Seville marmalade.

"My wrist was too weak to undo the cap. Fine. I expected that. I stuck the jar between my knees, but the smooth glass just slid against my sweatpants. I clamped the jar in the crook of my arm and twisted; all that did was yank out the little hairs. By now the toast had popped. I got out a knife and started rapping on the cap. The lid was sealed like the door on an Apollo space capsule. The toast was getting cold. Frantic, I started bashing it on the counter, wobbling on my crutch and screaming *'Open you motherfucker!'* The cap was now bent like a roadside beer can. I put the jar down on the counter, held it as hard as I could with my throbbing right hand, and twisted with the left. *Snik!* The cap came off. I slopped some marmalade on the toast, which was now like rough plywood, ate half, and limped back to bed. Is this what it's like when you're eighty? Every household article a potential adversary?"

"This motorcycle, then," said Robert, interrupting my rant, "will you ride again in the spring? Or are you finished?"

Good question.

WHILE I HAD BEEN CRASHING Hsing's motorcycle, my own bike had been resting at the Ducati shop, receiving its meticulous and expensive annual tune-up. Now, a year since the crash, I still had not collected it. Calgary was a 300-kilometer ride. In the past, I had never minded having to take the bike in; it gave me a wonderful excuse for a ride down the old highway, along the rivers and through the small towns the freeway ignored. Yet this summer had passed and somehow I always had something to do that made it impossible to go get the bike. Finally Brian phoned. His shop was full; the bike was gathering dust; what did I want to do?

I phoned Dave and we borrowed Pasquale's van in case I decided it was best not to ride. "Of course," he said. At the last minute I grabbed my spare helmet and gloves from the basement and took a leather jacket from the hook. I should at least look like I was prepared to ride. The closer we got the more reasons I had for not getting back on. My wrist was still weak. I did not yet have full movement in my neck and could not shoulder-check easily. My back, I was sure, would not tolerate the hard seat and stiff suspension. I was feeling slightly sick to my stomach. Clearly I was coming down with the flu.

Then we reached Calgary and turned the corner in front of the shop. *Bam!* My heart leaped like a salmon on a spawning ladder. For there it was. My Ducati, leaning on the sidestand, ready to roll.

They call it *il Mostro*—the Monster—but it is nothing monstrous. Lithe and lovely, the arc from the rear swingarm up through the trellis frame and down to the front forks is the line of a panther in mid-leap. Always in motion.

Inside the shop they showed me the new catalogue of Ducati goodies. I wanted everything. A tachometer, new boots, a Ducati helmet, a Ducati jacket. My budget evaporated faster than dawn mist on a Texas highway. "How quick can you get it in?" was all I asked.

I had wanted my first time back on the bike to take place in a parking lot, then on a quiet country road, in the warm sun, with no one else around so that I could ease back into (or right out of) motorcycling. It didn't happen. "I can drive," I said confidently, but I wound up facing all my demons at once.

IT'S SATURDAY AFTERNOON and the traffic is moving at a frenzied clip—Calgarians in their pickup trucks auditioning for the pod-racer scene in *Star Wars*. I swing onto the freeway, moving fast in third gear, but the trucks are blowing by me, braiding the freeway with constant lane changes. I hunch down and crack the throttle and the bike lunges forward. But we are still only going 70.

I can't figure it out. The engine is running well. Anyway, I have no time to look at the speedo. A tandem semi is coming at me from an overpass off-ramp. The bike will be fine, but will I? I don't feel panic but I really don't want to be next to those shoulder-high wheels. I do a quick check, move over a lane, and hit fifth gear. Still only 80. Weird. It sure feels faster.

I'm wearing street shoes and a loose jacket and I can feel the wind whipping round my ankles, driving up my sleeves and ballooning the back of the jacket. I watch another pickup truck enter from my left up ahead; he cuts without looking across four lanes of traffic. That would be me you're driving through, buddy.

It's a shooting gallery out here. I'm level with this cowboy now, and the wind is starting to lift my helmet. How fast are we going? No time to look. The cowboy runs up on the bumper of a Ford Escort, snaps over one lane closer to me. I'm getting myself some space. I lean over the tank, twist the throttle and the Ducati roars. I grin inside my helmet. Such sweet thunder. I drop it into sixth. Now we're beyond the last overpass, and at last the traffic is dropping behind me. I've got five empty lanes in front of me as the road curves gently east and then north.

I look at the speedometer again. 105. And then it hits me—my Ducati came with a U.S. speedometer. When they fixed the speedo cable and did the tune-up they must have changed the gearing back. I'm going 105 *miles* an hour—close to 170 kilometers an hour. No wonder I have some space. I ease back to 60 miles/100 kilometers an hour. Well, so much for practicing in a parking lot. I guess I can still do this. But I forget that I'm traveling with Dave. Dave is the rain-maker. If you were crossing the Gobi Desert with Dave and it hadn't seen a drop of precipitation in forty years you would still want to take your Gore-Tex suit. I have left my rain suit at home because it hasn't rained in weeks, but 80 kilometers out of Calgary, sure enough, the rain comes slashing out of the west. The crosswinds snap at the bike and the ruts in the worn pavement fill instantly with water and you have to ride the crest between them so you don't aquaplane.

Dave and I take turns on the bike and driving the van. When I'm in the van, watching him slice through the rain, it looks terrifying. Yet when it's my turn, somehow it's all right. As always, weather looks worse from inside.

Eighty kilometers out of Edmonton the gas warning light comes on. I pull into a gas station and strip off my sodden gloves. The dye has turned my hands a purplish black. I fill up and buy a hot chocolate, wrapping my stiff fingers round the cardboard cup. My soaked leather jacket weighs about 20 kilos.

"Want me to take over?" Dave asks.

"No, I'm good," I say. "I want to take it in."

When we walk back out to the tarmac the sun has come out and is blazing off the puddles.

"This is what I love about prairie storms," I say. "They drench you and move right on."

ACKNOWLEDGMENTS

I know much has filtered into the book from my reading over the years on modernism and about motorcycles, and from discussions with colleagues in both areas. My debts are too numerous to list, but I thank you, and the errors are all mine.

There are specific works I am pleased to acknowledge. For Virginia Woolf I always go back to Hermione Lee's brilliant *Virginia Woolf* (Chatto & Windus, 1996), as well as the *Diary,* scrupulously edited by Anne Olivier Bell and Andrew McNeillie (Hogarth Press, 1977–84), and *Letters,* edited by Nigel Nicolson and Joanne Trautmann (Hogarth Press, 1975–80). The passages on Woolf's driving attempts and motorbike aspirations are from *Vita and Harold: The Letters of Vita Sackville-West and Harold Nicolson,* edited by Nigel Nicolson (Weidenfeld & Nicolson, 1992) and Frances Partridge, *Memories* (Gollancz, 1981).

For information on D. H. Lawrence I used Brenda Maddox's engaging *D. H. Lawrence: The Story of a Marriage* (Simon & Schuster, 1994), along with David Ellis, *Dying Game 1922–1930* (Cambridge University Press, 1998); Sean Hignett, *Brett: From Bloomsbury to*

New Mexico (F. Watts, 1985); and Dorothy Brett, *Lawrence and Brett, a Friendship* (Martin Secker, 1933).

For James Joyce and Sylvia Beach the indispensable sources are Richard Ellmann, *James Joyce* (Oxford University Press, 1972) and Noel Fitch, *Sylvia Beach and the Lost Generation: A History of Literary Paris in the Twenties and Thirties* (Norton, 1983).

The story of *Ulysses* at New York customs comes from Bennett Cerf, *At Random: The Reminiscences of Bennett Cerf* (Random House, 1977); information on Joyce's contract with Random House is from the fascinating *United States of America v. One Book Entitled Ulysses by James Joyce,* edited by Michael Moscato and Leslie LeBlanc (University Publications of America, 1984).

On paratext see Gerard Genette's perceptive and irreverent *Paratexts: Thresholds of Interpretation* (Cambridge University Press, 1997); thanks to Will Goodwin for suggesting this long ago. The porno edition of *Ulysses* is *Ulysses* (Collectors Publications, n.d.); my thanks to Brad Bucknell for supplying his copy for examination.

On the archive, uncited in the book but present in homeopathic proportions, are Jacques Derrida, *Archive Fever* (University of Chicago, 1998) and the chapter on the archive in Michel Foucault's *Archaeology of Knowledge* (Pantheon, 1972); see also Caroline Steedman's terrific *Dust* (Rutgers University Press, 2002). For Seshat there are numerous websites, but the early writers are invaluable: E. A. Wallis Budge, *The Gods of the Egyptians* (Methuen, 1904) and Max Müller, *The Mythology of All Races* (Marshall Jones, 1918).

For information on T. E. Lawrence I have relied primarily on Jeremy Wilson, *Lawrence: The Authorized Biography of T. E. Lawrence* (Atheneum, 1990) and *The Letters of T. E. Lawrence,* edited by David Garnett (Jonathan Cape, 1938), along with Vyvyan Richards, *T. E.*

Lawrence, Book Designer (Simon Lawrence, 1985) and V. M. Thompson, *"Not a Suitable Hobby for an Airman": T. E. Lawrence as Publisher* (Orchard Books, 1986).

The comment on silence by Alfred Brendel is from A. Alvarez, "The Playful Pianist," *The New Yorker,* April 1, 1996. Fintan O'Toole's "The Many Stories of Billy the Kid" is from *The New Yorker,* December 28/January 4, 1999.

The Rilke passage is from Rainer Maria Rilke, *Duino Elegies,* with English translations by C. F. MacIntyre (University of California Press, 1961).

The quotations from Pound's poetry are from *The Cantos of Ezra Pound* (New Directions, 1970). For permission to quote from the letter from Ezra Pound to James Joyce I wish to thank Laura Weldon.

The quotation from Tom Cochrane is from "Life Is a Highway"; my thanks to Tom and Kathleene Cochrane for granting permission and for giving me the proper rendering of "Gimme Gimme Gimme Yeah."

Portions of this work have appeared previously in *Alberta Views, Cycle Canada, English Studies in Canada, enRoute, Joyce Studies Annual, Rider, Woolf Studies Annual,* and *Word Carving: Literary Journalism* from the Banff Center, edited by Ian Pearson and Moira Farr (Banff Center Press, 2003), and *Editing and Interpreting Virginia Woolf,* edited by James Haule (Palgrave/Macmillan, 2002).

I wish to thank the Social Sciences and Humanities Research Council for grants that enabled me to visit archives and afforded me time to write. I also wish to thank the Alberta Federation for the Arts and the Banff Center for the Arts for grants that allowed me to participate in the Banff Center writing programs.

Many individuals contributed and I first want to thank all the people named in the text: you made the story.

I am grateful for the encouragement of Bruce Reeve, editor of *Cycle Canada,* who published my first narrative non-fiction essay, and Jo-Ann Wallace, former chair of the English Department at the University of Alberta, who invited me to give a lecture on motorcycling and reading that became the germ of this project.

I want to thank Carol Holmes and the Banff Center support staff who help create such a productive writing community. I am indebted to the fine editors I worked with at Banff: Curtis Gillespie, Ian Pearson, Alberto Ruy-Sanchez, and guest editor Lawrence Weschler.

My thanks to friends Moira Farr, Maria Coffey, and Myrna Kostash, who gave encouragement and advice on the trade, and to those who read and commented on the work in progress in its various incarnations, from early roadside faxes to complete type-script: Steven Alford, Katherine Ashenburg, Katherine Binhammer, Shannon Black, Robin Bradford, Dave Cockle, Chris Koentges, Jim Haule, Brooke Kroeger, Caterina Loverso, Matt Hart, Suzanne Ferris, Pat Foy, Remy Quinter, Daphne Read, Velcrow Ripper, Lahoucine Ouzgane, Betsy Sargent, Gary Watson, and Glen Worley. I must thank in particular Shani Mootoo, whose buoyant enthusiasm and unsparing critiques over espresso have enriched my writing life.

You would not be holding this book were it not for the efforts of my splendid editor at Penguin, Maria Scala, who understood the project from the start and kept bringing my textual detours back to the main track. Working with the always-affable Brendan Curry at Norton has been a pleasure.

My thanks to my children, James and Erin, whose determination in their own lives constantly inspires me. And thanks above all to Hsing Jou, who made the writing possible.

The text of this book is set in Bembo, a typeface produced
by Stanley Morison of Monotype in 1929,
based on a roman typeface cut by Francesco Griffo in 1495.